The Past, Present, and Future of Early Modern Digital Studies

NEW TECHNOLOGIES IN MEDIEVAL AND RENAISSANCE STUDIES 11

SERIES EDITOR Raymond G. Siemens

The Past, Present, and Future of Early Modern Digital Studies: Iter at 25

Edited by
Laura Estill and Ray Siemens

Iter Press
NEW YORK | TORONTO
2025

Printed in the United States of America

978-1-64959-063-3 (paper)
978-1-64959-064-0 (pdf)
978-1-64959-065-7 (epub)

Library of Congress Cataloging-in-Publication Data

Names: Estill, Laura, editor. | Siemens, Raymond George, 1966- editor.

Title: The past, present, and future of early modern digital studies : Iter at 25 / edited by Laura Estill and Ray Siemens.

Description: New York : Iter Press, 2025. | Series: New technologies in medieval and Renaissance studies ; 11 | Includes bibliographical references. | Summary: "The Past, Present, and Future of Early Modern Digital Studies: Iter at 25 asserts that early modern digital studies is a thriving field that draws in strands from publishing, textual studies, digital humanities, and more. Early modern digital studies is also a rapidly-changing field that needs to be (re-)considered from different perspectives as new projects and tools emerge, change, or disappear, and as we make advances into better understanding the past. The chapters in this volume explore how and what we publish (digitally and otherwise), how we value, evaluate, and sustain those publications and digital projects, and how these projects enable us to ask new research questions about early modern literature and culture. This collection does not seek to be a definitive or final state-of-the-field, but rather, a celebration of existing scholarship and an invitation to even more scholarship about our ever-evolving practices-and, in this, a snapshot in time, at an important moment for the field"-- Provided by publisher.

Identifiers: LCCN 2022016375 (print) | LCCN 2022016376 (ebook) | ISBN 9781649590633 (paperback) | ISBN 9781649590640 (pdf) | ISBN 9781649590657 (epub)

Subjects: LCSH: Digital humanities--History. | Electronic publishing--History. | Iter (Toronto, Ont.)

Classification: LCC AZ195 .P37 2025 (print) | LCC AZ195 (ebook) | DDC 025.060013--dc23/eng/20220711

LC record available at https://lccn.loc.gov/2022016375

LC ebook record available at https://lccn.loc.gov/2022016376

Cover Illustration

Compass illustration from John Davis, *The Seamans Secrets* (London: Thomas Dawson, 1595). Digital image <Davis_John-The_seamans_secrets-STC-63684-1750_04-p7.tif>, British Library <https://www.bl.uk> (2011).

Cover Design

Maureen Morin, Library Communications, University of Toronto Libraries.

Contents

Acknowledgments

The editors of this collection would like to thank Kate Beers for her assistance preparing this volume as well as the Social Sciences and Humanities Research Council of Canada (SSHRC) Connection Grant program that funded the gathering that was the impetus for this volume. We are grateful to and for the team at Iter: Gateway to the Middle Ages and Renaissance, notably Bill Bowen, Margaret English-Haskin, and Marian Cosic. Thanks also to this volume's anonymous readers for their feedback.

List of Figures and Tables

Introduction[1]

Laura Estill
St. Francis Xavier University

Ray Siemens
University of Victoria

The "past, present, and future of early modern digital studies" are a lot to cover in one book, or, indeed, in an entire bookcase of volumes or terabytes of data. The same holds true in any consideration of computational approaches as they have been applied to early modern studies, a practice that has been going on for decades, expanding and extending the ways we can understand our past. It is beyond the scope of any introduction to rehearse the history of digital humanities or early modern studies, let alone their interconnected growth: the boom in digital projects about the early modern period and the concomitant rise in publications about how digital tools and projects can help us better understand our history, literature, and culture. The genre of edited collections such as this one, however, has a particularly important role to play in this field by providing evidence about and reflections on digital early modern studies. Edited collections move beyond single voices and single projects while also offering insights into individual projects at different stages of completion. When it comes to reflecting on how digital practices change our teaching and scholarship of the early modern period, these collections, including this one, are valuable because they gather a breadth of scholarship at a given moment, offering a snapshot in time of part of the larger field, perspectives on its own understanding of its past as well as glimpses of its potential futures. In this tradition, this book draws on and stands alongside other collections that reflect on evolving practices at the intersection of digital humanities and early modern studies, including those in the New Technologies in Medieval and Renaissance Studies series and its initial roots in the partnership between Iter: Gateway to the Middle Ages and Renaissance and the Renaissance Society of America (RSA) in the "New Technologies in Renaissance Studies" panels sponsored at RSA's annual conference. The essays gathered in this volume reflect on past tradition, speak

[1] We would like to thank Kate Beers, who worked as a research assistant on this book, the volume's peer reviewers, and our wonderful collaborators at Iter Press. Thanks also to Aaron Mauro and Kailin Wright for their thoughtful feedback on this introduction. We are grateful for the Social Sciences and Humanities Research Council of Canada's Connection Grant program and the Canada Research Chairs program.

ISBN 978-1-64959-063-3 (paper) ISBN 978-1-64959-064-0 (pdf) ISBN 978-1-64959-065-7 (epub)
New Technologies in Medieval and Renaissance Studies 11 (2025) 5–12

to our present moment in time, and imagine future research practices when it comes to applying digital methodologies to early modern studies.

As many of the essays here outline, Iter: Gateway to the Middle Ages and Renaissance has had an instrumental role in supporting digital scholarship about the early modern period, both by creating a space for professional discussion and consideration but also in seeing some of those discussions through to publications. As William R. Bowen's first chapter details, Iter's far-ranging contributions to digital early modern studies include organizing and supporting conference panels, publishing digital projects such as the important Iter Bibliography, and publishing journals (such as *Early Modern Digital Review,* discussed by Randa El Khatib in this volume) and books in this field. In fact, this volume is the eleventh in Iter Press' New Technologies in Medieval and Renaissance Studies (NTMRS) series, whose past volumes have covered important work on digitization, social knowledge creation, and digital publishing, among other topics. To date,[2] NTMRS volumes have featured contributions by over a hundred scholars, including newcomers, non-traditional academics and practitioners, and well-established faculty; they have been positively reviewed in many languages, and continue to be read and cited around the world today. The books in this series showcase how digital technologies can facilitate a range of different approaches to early modern studies, and this collection is no exception.

Rhetorical positioning or otherwise, it is commonplace for introductions of books about digital scholarship to point to the innovative nature of the works therein; this volume is no exception to that rule—and reasonably so. It is also important to highlight how this volume and its chapters are also traditional, informing methodological innovation while making valuable contributions to the field of early modern studies. Digital scholarship about the early modern period is becoming increasingly common, drawing on both early modern studies and digital humanities. This scholarship has appeared in journal special issues and edited collections; symposia and public talks; and reviews and state-of-the-field review essays. Altogether, such state-of-the-field talks (Basu 2016), reviews (Lamb 2018), and articles (Pangallo 2020) point to the important fact that there is, indeed, a field of digital early modern studies. The new directions in digital early modern studies, such as the turn to pedagogy (Bell and Borsuk 2020; Henderson and Vitale 2021; Silva and Schofield forthcoming), draw on existing scholarly traditions while also

[2] At the time this introduction was written, in 2021, there were seven already-published volumes in the series, with two more in final stages of production.

pointing to new directions. The chapters in this book, with their emphasis on practice and possibility, likewise exist in a thriving field, which was made possible in part by the contributions of Iter.

Work in digital early modern studies is often project-based, ranging from small scale to large—which is also reflected in the literature that stems from these projects. Chapters in this volume are no exception, providing a glimpse into the often-too-obscured behind-the-scenes pragmatics associated with creating digital projects: How are decisions made? What goals do projects have? How are they reached (or not)? What obstacles stand in their way? Furthermore, it is important to publish about digital projects often and at different stages of their development, as they are always being re-worked, updated, or, in too many cases, abandoned. Publications that emerge from different stages of project development offer both important history, otherwise too easily lost, and valuable lessons-by-example for those embarking on their own digital projects. These reflections, furthermore, help people better understand the strengths and limitations of such resources; in short, learning about new digital projects and the decisions that have shaped them helps us become better researchers and teachers. By bringing together project-based analyses and conclusions from those researching and teaching at the intersection of digital humanities and early modern studies, this volume shows some of the through-lines across the field: from thinking about long-term project planning (see chapters by Meneses and Hendriksen, for instance) and collaboration (see chapters by Siemens, Crompton, Powell, Arbuckle, and Shirley and by James and Shami), to creating inclusive resources that support scholars and users from a variety of backgrounds and in different career stages (see, for example, chapters by Grumbach and El Khatib, and a leitmotif in Bowen's chapter).

Our group reflected on these issues, and more, at a 2019 gathering, "Iter and the Present and Future of Digital Studies," aligned with the RSA conference in Toronto, and most of the essays in this collection stem from this gathering.[3] Many of the authors whose work is gathered here have also presented in the "New Technologies for Renaissance Studies" series of panels at the RSA at points over its long history. In 2019 those panels included "Open, Cooperative Early Modern Scholarship," "@JohnDonne," "Collaborations and Communities in Early Modern Scholarship," "Digital Textual Studies," and

[3] We would like to thank the Social Sciences and Humanities Research Council of Canada (SSHRC) Connection Grant program for funding this event and making it possible to bring together participants from around the globe.

"Issues in Digital Publication." Also in 2019, most of the authors in this volume, and others besides, joined in our blue-sky thinking sessions wherein we collaboratively envisioned new directions for academic research, with a focus on the interdisciplinary research that characterizes the study of the early modern period. Some of these discussions have culminated in the publications here and are ongoing in the projects described in these chapters; yet other ideas (such as further digitization, new projects, and increased interoperability between existing projects) are ongoing or yet to come. The chapters in this volume are the outcome of some of these presentations and discussions and will themselves surely elicit more discussion in turn.

Opening with Bowen's description of Iter's history and its contributions, this volume celebrates Bowen as the founder of Iter as much as it showcases the scholarship that has been made possible on so many levels by Iter, from presenting primary sources digitally with Iter's digital projects, to making research findable through the Iter Bibliography, to publishing scholarship itself in books and journals. Many early modernists across disparate disciplines that inform their work will have used Iter-supported and Iter-published scholarship, even if they did not know the entire constellation of Iter's contributions. Other essays in this volume highlight how Iter has contributed to the ways we undertake scholarship about the early modern period. Randa El Khatib outlines the exigence for one of Iter's more recent and also ongoing contributions, the journal *Early Modern Digital Review* (emdr.itercommunity.org). As El Khatib's essay explores, *Early Modern Digital Review* demonstrates the importance of critically reflecting on digital projects from a user's perspective, an important professional function with roots in the first electronic journal in the field, *Early Modern Literary Studies*, but nowhere given clearer focus than in this initiative. The reviews in *Early Modern Digital Review*, then, function as an important counterpoint to many of the creator-driven essays in this collection.

While El Khatib's essay demonstrates how reviews can benefit those creating, reviewing, and using digital projects, Elizabeth Grumbach broadens the question to ask about how we can consider making early modern digital studies more welcoming as a field. As Grumbach asks, "What does intentional community building and care look like within an online scholarly community [. . .] and how can collaboration and intentional community-building be fostered simultaneously (and ethically) in the context of producing humanities research?"(79). Grumbach's chapter offers possible models for those considering creating digital humanities resources about the pre-modern era;

her chapter will also be of interest to those joining existing project teams or inheriting already-created projects.

In their co-authored chapter, Ray Siemens, Constance Crompton, Daniel Powell, Alyssa Arbuckle, Maggie Shirley, and the Devonshire Manuscript Editorial Group model collaborative research practices that reflect on open social knowledge production. This reprinted chapter outlines the creation of a new kind of digital edition, the social edition, and thinks about gatekeeping and editorial theory, applying it to an important Tudor text, the Devonshire manuscript, the first sustained example in the English tradition of men and women writing together in a community. Likewise, Anne James and Jeanne Shami reflect on collaborative practice when it comes to online databases and bibliographies, focusing on making English sermons in manuscripts findable. As James and Shami put it, their essay "outlines the challenges and opportunities of creating a community of both occasional and committed contributors from a multi-disciplinary group of users including early modern social, political, and religious historians; literary scholars; theologians; book historians; church historians; and genealogists" (125). As these two chapters and others in the volume demonstrate, the accessibility of digital resources to a wide-ranging audience is both a challenge and benefit.

Kyle Dase's chapter moves us from networks of contributors and users to networks of information about the early modern period, and, like the two previous chapters, considers how digital media can affect how we think of textual studies and metadata, and highlights the vibrant ongoing scholarship on early modern prose and poetry that is facilitated by digital editions and finding aids. Dase envisions a future where editions include network analysis that is linked across texts, merging textual studies and tools for textual analysis. Luis Meneses, in the next chapter, similarly looks to the future of digital projects on the early modern period by grappling with one of the looming challenges in the field: longevity when faced with changing technologies and standards. Drawing on his background in computer and information/data science, Meneses considers some of the technical challenges of keeping digital projects viable, with a focus on DEx: A Database of Dramatic Extracts. Meneses's assertion that "online digital humanities projects have a limited useful life" (171) can be challenging for humanists steeped in traditional research built on centuries of dialogue.

With her chapter on Iter Press's Other Voice series, Margaret King demonstrates how publishing and editorial studies continue to recuperate and echo voices from these centuries of humanist dialogue. King's essay illustrates how the vibrant Other Voice series highlights a range of genres, written in different European languages, by authors active in different areas of fourteenth- to nineteenth-century Europe. This series, which began at the University of Chicago Press, has been published in print and electronic form by Iter since 2017. Laura Estill's reprinted chapter, likewise, reflects on issues of canonicity and availability, with a focus on the Shakespeare-centric nature of many digital humanities projects. The problem, as Estill outlines, is not with digital humanities methodologies, but rather with funding models and cultural capital that affect how and what we research (digitally or otherwise).

Marieke Hendriksen's chapter, like Estill's, points to the challenges of digital infrastructure when researching the digital period, in this case, specifically with regards to project longevity and sustainability. Drawing on case studies about ARTECHNE and Art DATIS, Hendriksen challenges readers to consider "the institutional, pedagogical, and infrastructural changes that we will need to make in order to create data that last as long as books—if that is possible at all" (246). By explaining and critiquing the existing European support mechanisms, Hendriksen's chapter reminds us that no project is an island, and that successful digital humanities project management will necessarily require collaboration, rethinking our institutional and pedagogical priorities, and a commitment to data stewardship.

The concluding chapter by Michael Ullyot considers how we undertake research in the digital age. Ullyot demonstrates that literary criticism, like much humanities criticism, is often driven by examples that are then used for extrapolations and conclusions. Ullyot looks to large-scale data sets, such as the Early English Books Online-Text Creation Partnership (EEBO-TCP), as a starting point for computer-augmented criticism that can begin to move us into new models for undertaking criticism. This chapter offers a fitting conclusion to this collection because it outlines how we are moving from a past and present model of literary criticism into a future that will not ignore our critical heritage but could take radically new approaches.

This volume enacts some of the principles outlined by the chapters herein: it is a collaboration that showcases voices from different fields taking different critical approaches toward common ends and in the frame of commonly-held values about the importance of this type of work. It considers the challenges we face in the present as we undertake and use digital projects, publish in print and digitally, and contribute to the ongoing scholarly conversation. Individually, these chapters are (and deploy) exemplary criticism (to use Ullyot's term); yet taken together they demonstrate how our research questions and data are connected and could be linked or networked. They offer us opportunities to learn from each other's successes and . . . not successes. While some of the projects discussed are longstanding and successful, others are imagined, not yet extant, or not designed for the long term. By bringing together collaborators who create projects, who facilitate projects, and who support projects in an important area of shared endeavour, this book serves as a record of the careful thought that goes into how we research the early modern period and what we can envision for future research practices. Hendriksen concludes, "do not underestimate the power of a book" (255)—to this we add, especially so if it is an edited collection.

The Past, Present, and Future of Early Modern Digital Studies affirms a thriving field that draws in strands from publishing, textual studies, digital humanities, and more. Early modern digital studies is also a rapidly-changing field that needs to be (re-)considered from different perspectives as new projects and tools emerge, change, or disappear, and as we make advances into better understanding the past. This collection does not seek to be a definitive or final state-of-the-field, but rather a celebration of existing scholarship and an invitation to even more scholarship about our ever-evolving practices—and, in this, a snapshot in time, at an important moment for the field.

WORKS CITED

Basu, Anupam. 2016. "*Tools of the Trade: Digital Humanities and Early* Modern Studies." Keynote address, "Tools of the Trade: Digital Humanities and Early Modern Studies" symposium, Rutgers University. dh.rutgers.edu/early-modern-studies-symposium/.

Bell, Henry, and Amy Borsuk, eds. 2020. "Teaching Shakespeare: Digital Processes." Special Issue: *Research in Drama Education: The Journal of Applied Theatre and Performance* 25 (1): doi.org/10.1080/13569783.2019.1704241.

Henderson, Diana, and Kyle Vitale, eds. 2021. *Shakespeare and Digital Pedagogy: Case Studies and Strategies.* London: Arden.

Lamb, Jonathan P. 2018. "Digital Resources for Early Modern Studies." *Studies in English Literature 1500–1900* 58 (2): 445–72. doi.org/10.1353/sel.2018.0019.

Pangallo, Matteo. 2020. "'A Great Deale of Good Stuff': The Cyberspace Renaissance Continues." *English Literary Renaissance* 50 (1): 116–24. doi.org/10.1086/706227.

Silva, Andie, and Scott Schofield, eds. Forthcoming. *Digital Pedagogy in Early Modern Studies.* Toronto: Iter Press.

Discovery, Collaboration, and Publication: Iter's Present and Thoughts for the Future[1]

William R. Bowen
University of Toronto Scarborough

> Iter, meaning a journey or a path in Latin, is a not-for-profit partnership dedicated to the advancement of learning in the study and teaching of the Middle Ages and Renaissance (400–1700) through the development and distribution of online resources. (itergateway.org)

The approach of a major anniversary in the life of an organization brings opportunities to turn regular planning processes into more substantial exercises wherein past assumptions and accomplishments are weighed against projections of future needs and possibilities. It is in this spirit that, as Iter's founding director, I offer the present chapter to be placed alongside the deliberations of colleagues who participated in a consultation on "Iter and the Present and Future of Early Modern Digital Studies," which was embedded in the 2019 Annual Meeting in Toronto of the Renaissance Society of America (RSA).[2] Accordingly, this chapter articulates Iter's present state and offers preliminary reflections on the future as we head toward the celebration of

[1] It is my honour to recognize the many colleagues who created and shaped Iter and to acknowledge that what is presented in this chapter is very much the result of their contributions to ongoing planning and implementation efforts over a period of more than twenty years. For the ensuing assessment of Iter's present and thoughts for the future, I am especially indebted to the leadership of Ray Siemens (director), Laura Estill (associate director), and Margaret English-Haskin (project manager), who join me on Iter's current executive team. This chapter is my synthesis of our work together.

[2] "Iter and the Present and Future of Early Modern Digital Studies" was a two-day series of meetings and presentations (17–18 March 2019) funded by a SSHRC (Social Sciences and Humanities Research Council of Canada) Connection Grant awarded to Laura Estill (primary investigator), William Bowen (co-investigator), and Raymond Siemens (collaborator). Additional support was received from the Electronic Textual Cultures Lab, University of Victoria, the English Department of St. Francis Xavier University, and Iter. Local arrangements were made by Natalie Oeltjen, assistant to the director of the Centre for Renaissance and Reformation Studies (formerly the Centre for Reformation and Renaissance Studies), Victoria University in the University of Toronto.

ISBN 978-1-64959-063-3 (paper) ISBN 978-1-64959-064-0 (pdf) ISBN 978-1-64959-065-7 (epub)
New Technologies in Medieval and Renaissance Studies 11 (2025) 13–54

the twenty-fifth anniversary of Iter's incorporation on 26 September 1997, and the launch of its first project, the Iter Bibliography, on 22 January 1998.

The selection of these milestone events as the reference point for talking about Iter is not meant to diminish the importance of the personal interventions and hard work that preceded them.[3] Indeed, the full history of Iter dates back to preliminary exchanges in 1994–95 between John Monfasani (then incoming director of the RSA), Konrad Eisenbichler (director of the Centre for Renaissance and Reformation Studies, Victoria University in the University of Toronto (CRRS)), and myself (University of Toronto Scarborough (UTSC)). These conversations soon led to formal commitments made by the CRRS Managing Committee (September 1995) and the RSA Executive (October 1995) to collaborate on the project, which at that time was entirely driven by aspirations to create a comprehensive bibliography: September 1995 has long been viewed as the moment when the project was conceived (Bowen 1999 and 2004).[4] Thereafter, crucial pilot projects were located in the Centre for Instructional Technology Development (CITD) at the University of Toronto Scarborough (1995–96) and in the Faculty of Information (FI), University of Toronto (1996–97);[5] the informal partnership grew to include FI, the Arizona Center for Medieval and Renaissance Studies (ACMRS), and the University of Toronto Libraries (UTL);[6] all supported by in-kind contributions and funding from the associated groups, generously supplemented by Heather Munroe-Blum, the University of Toronto's vice-president research and international development (1995), the Andrew W. Mellon Foundation (1996), and the Gladys Krieble Delmas Foundation (1997). In sum, the years

[3] For a list of key events in Iter's history, see itergateway.org/about/our-history.

[4] The formal agreement was prefaced by a meeting on 10 September 1995, when Konrad Eisenbichler, John Monfasani, and I met for four and a half hours to set the essential foundations, which guided the initiative for some years thereafter. The meeting was held at the Olive Garden Restaurant off the NYS Thruway at exit 46, a convenient venue insofar as it was midway between our locations in Toronto and Albany.

[5] Marla Miller, chief librarian of UTSC's Bladen Library, and William Barek, CITD director, were instrumental in the preliminary testing and development of Iter's bibliographical database. Lynne Howarth, dean of FI, supported the second pilot project, which was directed by Clare Beghtol and led to the establishment of the current form of Iter's Bibliography.

[6] The partnership expanded with the strong support of Lynne Howarth, Robert Bjork (director of ACMRS), Carole Moore (chief librarian of UTL). The day-to-day engagement of these partners was led by Beghtol, Bjork, and Peter Clinton (UTL's director of Information Technology Services).

up to incorporation were intense, exciting, and very productive in laying the groundwork for what was to come. Yet, incorporation and the public launch of the Iter Bibliography mark significant moments when early agreements and prototypes moved to the reality of an independent legal entity and its activities.

While this chapter is in no way a history of Iter, I will regularly refer to historical documents and studies in order to contextualize the current state of the project, which in turn will provide a solid point of departure for future considerations. The chapter begins with a review of Iter Inc.: its purposes and priorities, profile, and organizational structure. Such general matters provide the framework for a brief review of Iter's specific programs, which sit on Iter's online platform, known as Iter Gateway[7] (itergateway.org). The programs facilitate the discovery of the academic resources necessary to our work; create an environment for collaboration, sharing, and developing projects; and enable the distribution and publication of our scholarship. They are realized in the Iter Bibliography, Iter Community, and Iter Press, respectively. Throughout the narrative I will interweave basic questions pertaining to how we might adjust or revise Iter's initiatives in order to be better aligned with the needs of our communities. In due course, these deliberations will feed into the conversation to set targets for the twenty-fifth anniversary in 2022–23 and will inevitably provide direction for what follows.

Iter Inc.

Much has changed and continues to change in our fields of study since the formal incorporation of Iter Inc. as a not-for-profit corporation in New York State in the Fall of 1997.[8] Yet, it is striking that the intentions behind the project continue to have relevance, albeit they have been updated and refined over the years.

---

[7] Insofar as "iter" is Latin for the act of traveling as in a journey, or a course or route followed, it seems appropriate to the underlying concept to imagine Iter's online platform as a "gateway," a starting point for the journey.

[8] Iter Inc. is a corporation as defined in subparagraph (a)(5) of Section 102 (Definitions) of the Not-For-Profit Corporation Law in the State of New York. Incorporation in the United States was recommended by the Office of the Vice-President Research, University of Toronto, in light of the offer by John Monfasani to use RSA resources to facilitate the process.

Purposes and Priorities

The initial legal statements impart important information about Iter's scope wrapped in language that in retrospect seems repetitive and awkward:

> The purpose or purposes for which the corporation is formed are as follows: To encourage, promote and foster the study of the Renaissance and Middle Ages by providing a resource for research and the exchange of information utilizing a World Wide Web based Internet bibliography.
>
> To establish, create and maintain an electronic database for a World Wide Web based bibliography containing all relevant material published from approximately 1700 to the present, encompassing the years 1300–1700 A.D. as the Renaissance and the years 400–1500 A.D. as the Middle Ages.
>
> To provide the scholarly community and other interested parties with a resource for the study of the Renaissance and Middle Ages by utilizing personal computers to interface with the World Wide Web Internet database for sophisticated searches in related areas.[9]

Over the years, the stilted language, tentative references to new technologies, and limited range of activity were smoothed out, leaving a more straightforward and open-ended statement on our website:

> *Iter*, meaning a journey or a path in Latin, is a not-for-profit partnership dedicated to the advancement of learning in the study and teaching of the Middle Ages and Renaissance (400–1700) through the development and distribution of online resources.[10]

I will defer writing about matters pertaining to the community, organizational structure, and activities referenced in the 1997 and 2019 texts to subsequent sections of this chapter in order to focus here on the central statements of purpose. What endures over the two decades between these texts is a commitment to supporting a scholarly community in its activities, though the more recent statement unintentionally masks the active language, "To encourage, promote and foster," in the formality of the "advancement of learning." Similarly, the important notion of "scholarly community and other interested parties" is implicit in the more recent statement of purpose, though explicit elsewhere with regard to Iter's programs. While the brevity

[9] Certificate of Incorporation of Iter, Inc., New York State Department of State, 1997. For the purposes of this chapter, I am using "Iter Inc.," which reflects a change in the Certificate of Incorporation that took effect in June 2020.

[10] itergateway.org/about/about-iter, accessed 22 January 2021.

of the 2019 text brings some loss of richness and depth in expression, it is noteworthy that the shift from "study" to "advancement of learning in the study and teaching" parallels a welcome change in the academy's perception of the role of teaching.

The consistent use in these foundational texts of the terms "Middle Ages" and "Renaissance" within the chronological span of 400 to 1700 will bear thoughtful consideration as we develop our plans for the twenty-fifth anniversary and beyond. There is a slight danger here of the project losing touch with the changes in its communities—"slight," because Iter's programs themselves respond to the research and teaching interests of its communities and partners. Nonetheless, for example, fully engaging with "early modern studies" brings opportunities in broadening both Iter's historical span and its cultural and geographic reach, all of which should be reflected in its statements of purpose and implemented consistently through its programs. Put another way, such deliberations could lead to a simple realignment of the statement of purpose or to a fundamental re-thinking of our fields of study as global, something that is being explored throughout the academy.

Adjacent to the stated purposes of Iter lie certain preferences and priorities that were instilled in the project in the years before Iter's incorporation in 1997 and were articulated thereafter in various conference presentations and publications. They draw in large part on what we imagined were the affordances of online delivery:

> As its primary enterprise, Iter is creating a sophisticated gateway to all relevant resources which employs a network of bibliographies and databases, and which connects as closely as possible to the objects themselves. This gateway for Medieval and Renaissance studies is to be comprehensive in scope, timely in its delivery of new information, and accessible to the academic community both with regard to cost and the use of technology. (Bowen 2008, 102)[11]

These sentences capture the central importance of the Iter Bibliography (our first project) and other finding tools as vehicles to connect those who visit Iter Gateway to the gamut of resources. From the beginning, we were looking to a future when the materials needed by our communities would be available online. Accordingly, to serve our communities, the Iter Bibliography had to be comprehensive—it was never intended to be selective or specialized—current, and actively connected to the described resources, leveraging strengths

---

[11] The ideas appear in print as early as Bowen 1999, paragraphs 1–3.

of the Web that could not be replicated through print publication.[12] Further, this early vision of the "gateway" includes a prominent concern about accessibility, specifically linked to "cost and the use of technology." To these priorities, I add training and early career development. From the beginning, the partners recognized that Iter had a valuable role to play as a training ground for students and as a location to encourage emerging scholars to realize their goals (Bowen 1999, paragraph 3).

Together, these preferences and priorities are fundamental to Iter and will accordingly reappear quite naturally in the ensuing sections of the chapter. Yet there is more to be said. Building a platform, leveraging the possibilities of the Web, making Iter's projects accessible, and serving our communities with particular attention to students and early career scholars—all lie at the heart of important conversations that will contribute to the development of concrete plans for the future in celebration of Iter's twenty-fifth anniversary.

Organizational Structure and Profile

The formation of Iter Inc. as a not-for-profit partnership in 1997 was driven by an early recognition that the aspirations for the enterprise could only be met, not through service relationships, but through a deeply rooted collaboration between experts in the different fields necessary to realize the proposed programs. What emerged is a marriage of expertise offered by the leadership and individual members of the original partner organizations: medieval and Renaissance studies through the Arizona Center for Medieval and Renaissance Studies (Arizona State University), the Centre for Reformation and Renaissance Studies (Victoria University in the University of Toronto), and the Renaissance Society of America (New York); information studies through the Faculty of Information Studies (University of Toronto), and the use of new technologies through the Information Technology Services team at the University of Toronto Libraries.[13] In the ensuing years, the

[12] The initial motivation for Iter Bibliography was to address the substantial time lag before the relevant information was available through print publications. This challenge was exemplified at the time in reference to the *Bibliographie Internationale de l'Humanisme et de la Renaissance* (*BIHR*) where, for example, volume 29 lists 1994 publications but was itself published in 1998. That Droz, the publisher of *BIHR*, announced forthcoming CD-ROM and online versions in 1999 reflected a growing industry-wide recognition of the advantage of online publication with regard to timeliness for standalone bibliographies. Iter's commitment to connecting metadata to data was and continues to be a distinctive feature.

[13] From the perspective of Clare Beghtol, the collaboration was distinctive and an

engagement with organizations devoted to medieval and Renaissance studies grew through the addition of a sixth partner, the Sixteenth Century Society and Conference (SCSC).[14]

It is important to celebrate the commitment of the six partners, who together form Iter's Executive Board, and the durability and success of their partnership. However, for the purposes of this chapter, it is also important to recognize the changing trajectory of the partnership from its conception to its current state. In the early years, there was an essential commitment to pooling substantial resources in order to develop programs and to attain a sustainable business model. For some partners, this commitment was reasonably and necessarily time limited—for example, the RSA increased its membership fees in order to provide several years of financial support—and was also affected over time by new realities facing their own organizations. As a result, the current levels of engagement of the partners with Iter in addition to an important advisory role vary widely from organization to organization: Iter continues to be heavily dependent on the University of Toronto as a home for its staff and offices,[15] and for the human and physical infrastructure provided by UTL's Information Technology Services; ACMRS and CRRS collaborate with Iter on projects of mutual interest; Iter benefits from being recognized as an associate organization by both the RSA and SCSC. At the same time, Iter has established very strong relationships with other organizations, especially the University of Victoria's Electronic Textual Cultures Lab (ETCL). Thus, there is good reason to revisit Iter's organizational structure, if only to clarify the current roles and responsibilities of the executive and the six partner organizations on the executive board, and to define Iter's relationships with other organizations. A preliminary step toward rethinking Iter's structure was taken in 2019 with the incorporation of the affiliated not-for-profit Iter Canada, which recognized the strong Canadian base for Iter and opened up opportunities for Canadian funding.[16]

---

important example for information specialists (Beghtol 2004).

[14] The SCSC converted from associate (2001–04) to full partnership in 2004. This period also saw two other associate partnerships, the Medieval Academy of America (MAA, 2002–10) and the International Society of Anglo-Saxonists (ISAS, 2003–06; the name changed in September 2019 to the International Society for the Study of Early Medieval England), which were fostered by Robert Bjork.

[15] Margaret English-Haskin, Marian Cosic, and Anabela Piersol are employees of the University of Toronto. Their office space is located in Robarts Library (UTL) and financial oversight is provided by UTSC's Department of Arts, Culture and Media.

[16] The Certificate of Incorporation for Iter Canada, 1158302–6, was registered 21 Au-

Yet there is a more profound motivation for revisiting Iter's organizational structure in the need to better align it with an ongoing programmatic response to changing modes of academic interaction. This programmatic response warrants a brief explanation. Excited by the emerging possibilities afforded by the Web, we soon imagined how they might be leveraged in Iter's future, referring, for example, to then current ideas about knowledge bases and collaboratories (Bowen 2008, 108–09).[17] Such musings gave way to a formal, two-year consultative process led by Ray Siemens and reflected in numerous iterations of a white paper that was initially entitled *Iter Vision Document: A Knowledge-Domain Community-Oriented Resource* (8 October 2008), and then renamed in its final versions, *Initial Steps, Following a Larger Vision: A Feature-Oriented Pilot Proposal* (1 April 2010).

The critical framework for the consultation was set in the preamble:

> Iter sits at the centre of the community working with medieval and renaissance culture and its artefacts, facilitating that community's documented work via its framework of bibliographic records and other resources and by providing key services. As such, Iter reflects much more than any other individual entity (or even several entities combined) the "knowledge management" of the community it serves.
>
> The community is changing, as is the way in which it measures, documents, and carries out its work. This change is tied to the level (and the degree of acceptance) within the community of its computational facilitation. Further change is not only possible; it is inevitable. The key indicators of the direction of change are those tied to levels of ubiquitous computing in society, and key among pertinent issues are those of access and "social" interaction.[18]

---

gust 2019. The directors and officers of Iter Canada are the members of the Iter executive. See itercanada.ca.

[17] The exploration of these concepts was largely shared in conference papers, such as Bowen and Siemens 2003; and Bowen 2007. Siemens was involved in a number of initiatives and projects before and during the consultative process that are relevant to Iter's development and were also associated with ETCL and Implementing New Knowledge Environments (INKE): for example, see the presentations and publications related to the Renaissance English Knowledgebase (REKn, the precursor to the Renaissance Knowledge Network, ReKN) and the Professional Reading Environment (PReE) at mcri.inke.ca/projects/publications/.

[18] Siemens 2010, 1.

Given this broad understanding of Iter as an integral part of a community adjusting to the digital turn, the white paper posed questions in an effort to articulate what Iter contributed (e.g., metadata on community's research, publishing, and other services) and what else lies at the center (e.g., individuals, full texts, websites, and electronic resources). What emerged in the exercise was a challenge to "imagine a 10-year plan in which Iter were to expand its role to facilitate, more fully, the professional interaction of the community it serves" possibly through visible and invisible mechanisms to enrich the core data of the bibliography and "a shift in Iter's activity orientation from records production and service provision (though this lies at the core of Iter), to facilitation of a community's 'scholarly primitives,' its basic needs from the perspective of professional/user interactions."[19]

The impact of this planning process is evident in a number of initiatives, all tied to Iter's goal of "the advancement of learning [. . .] through the development and distribution of online resources" but now with a clearer sense of Iter's location and role within the communities it serves and with a direction for further action.

In particular, the white paper provoked experimentation with a space for collaboration launched in 2011, a year later, under the name of "Iter Community," and, inspired by the reference to John Unsworth's "scholarly primitives" (2000), offered a way to frame Iter's programs in terms of different but interrelated facets of our community's professional interactions. This was often expressed through the language of discovery of resources (Iter Bibliography); the facilitation of scholarly communication, information sharing, and collaboration (Iter Community); and publication and distribution of high-quality scholarship (Iter Press): the three program areas are described in more detail in the ensuing sections of this chapter. At the same time, this exercise accelerated the pace of building collaborative relationships with a number of scholarly societies and other academic organizations.[20] And it led

[19] Siemens 2010, 1.

[20] Formal relationships, often starting with project-based commitments, were made with the Medieval Academy of America (2002–10), medievalacademy.org; the Digital Humanities Summer Institute (DHSI, 2004–), dhsi.org; ETCL (2006–), etcl.uvic.ca; MOISA: The International Society for the Study of Greek and Roman Music and Its Cultural Heritage (2007–12), moisasociety.org; The Institute for Research in Classical Philosophy and Science (IRCPS, 2010–), ircps.org; the Canadian Society for Renaissance Studies / Société canadienne d'études de la Renaissance (CSRS-SCER, 2011–), csrs-scer.com; INKE (2012–), inke.ca; the Toronto Renaissance and Reformation Col-

to a concerted effort to increase opportunities for engagement of individuals and self-identified groups, most notably through committees attached to Iter Community.

With the close in early 2020 of the vision document's ten-year window, we may claim many accomplishments, which are reported in the following sections of this chapter alongside observations regarding possibilities for inclusion in the next planning document. In the context of Iter's structure, the current model of a partnership of organizations might well expand to more directly involve its communities by learning from models of shared governance. This would entail a shift in thinking about Iter's governance, that is, in terms of institutional partners delivering resources, to reimagining Iter as the shared enterprise of its engaged communities.

Iter Bibliography

In future planning documents, the Iter Bibliography might reasonably be placed among the finding aids published and/or distributed by Iter Press. Yet, because of the sheer size of the project and its significance in the history of Iter, the bibliography warrants separate consideration here prior to reporting on the community and press. Indeed, it would be hard to underestimate the impact of the bibliography on the genesis of the partnership, and, more importantly for this chapter, on how the partnership's activities were conceptualized and named. In 1997, the partners looked to Paul Oskar Kristeller's *Iter italicum: A Finding List of Uncatalogued or Incompletely Catalogued Humanistic Manuscripts of the Renaissance in Italian and Other Libraries* for inspiration (1963–97).[21] This massive finding aid served as a model of scholarship and exemplified a response to the fundamental need for the tools to discover research materials. Further, Kristeller's use of the Latin word "iter," which means "a going" as in a "journey," or a "way" or "path," was adopted and used to characterize the enterprise. As a consequence, it informed the selection of Iter Gateway as the name for the online platform and influenced the choice of visual imagery, beginning on the very first website with a woodcut of a ship preparing for a voyage and thereafter with images of early compasses. With this background in mind, it is useful to return to the 2008 statement quoted earlier and unpack the various elements relevant to the bibliography.

---

loquium (TRRC, 2012–), trrc.itergateway.org; REKn/ReKN (2013–), rekn.org; and the Advanced Research Consortium (ARC, 2014–19), arc.dh.tamu.edu.

[21] Kristeller had a strong connection to the RSA, having served as its second president from 1957 to 1958.

Scope

During the testing and prototyping period that preceded the official launch of the Iter Bibliography in January 1998, we agreed to create a comprehensive online finding tool for medieval and Renaissance studies.[22] To that end, the chronological period is roughly defined as 400 to 1700, with the understanding that the date range is a flexible guideline in order to enable the bibliography to adjust to changes in the fields of study. Thus, for example, scholarship spilling over into the eighteenth century is included. To accomplish our goals in a way that addresses the most pressing needs of our communities, we developed a set of simple priorities. Our focus has been on the contents of journals (first indexing articles and then review articles, reviews, and other materials, such as abstracts, bibliographies, catalogs, and discographies) and, similarly, on the contents of essay collections and entries in encyclopedias and exhibition catalogs, because these secondary resources are not represented in sufficient detail in publicly available finding tools, such as library catalogs. The order for indexing journal titles follows the advice of subject experts, who at the beginning of the project compiled a master list of journal titles and identified a set of "core" journals to be indexed first. Finally, to make the most efficient use of our time, we do a retrospective bibliography for the full run of the journal when we take it up and commit to regular updates to keep it current.

A quantitative report on our progress is provided in detail on the Iter Bibliography site at itergateway.org/resources/iter-bibliography. Based on the August 2019 update, the record and title count are summarized in Table 1.1:[23]

---

[22] The details of Iter's formative period are beyond the scope of this chapter. In brief, at the time there was no comprehensive online bibliography for Renaissance studies. In 1995 we started a conversation with the Fédération Internationale des Sociétés et Instituts pour l'Étude de la Renaissance and Droz, the publisher of *BIHR*, about opportunities for collaboration. The negotiations wound down in 1999 without an agreement and Droz proceeded to publish a CD-ROM of the bibliography. Medieval studies were well served by the *International Medieval Bibliography* (*IMB*), which was available in both print and CD-ROM versions in 1995, moving online thereafter. Efforts to develop a comprehensive database for both periods through a partnership between Iter, Brepols (the *IMB* publisher), and the University of Leeds Institute for Medieval Studies (the home for the creation of the *IMB*) began in 1995. Negotiations were undertaken in earnest in 1999–2000 and ended without an agreement.

[23] For a complete list of journal titles with details of what has been indexed thus far, see itergateway.org/indexed-journals. For a complete list of essay collections, see

Record Count	
Journal contents	987,587
Essays and entries	335,412
Monographs	114,084
Other (e.g., dissertation abstracts)	19,723
TOTAL RECORDS	**1,456,806**
Title Count	
Journal titles	2,173 publ. since 1784[24]
Essay collections	14,634 publ. since 1874[25]

Table 1.1. Iter Bibliography record and title count.

To put these numbers in perspective, the bibliography has grown in excess of sixty thousand records per year since its launch in 1998 and the contributors are actively indexing 87 percent of the 2,500 journal titles on the master list. At this rate, in the short term we will come close to indexing all of the 2,500 journal titles on the current list and will surpass 1,650,000 records during the year of the twenty-fifth anniversary.

There are important longer-term considerations in building a plan for the future with respect to types of materials and methods of ingesting the metadata. An early interest to enter the field of primary sources by developing an authority list of manuscripts proved too daunting with our resources. However, it would be exciting to explore collaborative or cooperative relationships with publishers of major finding tools for manuscripts and early books. For example, in collaboration with Brill, in 2002 Iter launched the online edition of Kristeller's *Iter italicum* and in 2008 digitized the entire F. E. Cranz's *A Microfilm Corpus of the Indexes to Printed Catalogues of Latin Manuscripts before 1600 A.D.*[26] It is not hard to imagine partnerships leading to an online interface

itergateway.org/indexed-essays.

[24] For a complete list of journal titles with details of what has been indexed thus far, see itergateway.org/indexed-journals.

[25] For a complete list of essay collections, see itergateway.org/indexed-essays.

[26] Both projects were generously supported by The Gladys Krieble Delmas Foundation

where the user could engage in a federated search with filters for primary or secondary sources and their various subcategories. In the same vein, though more easily configured within Iter, we might gradually adjust the allocation of our own resources to improve the coverage of monographs and to extend our reach to other formats and media, such as audio-visual publications (e.g., CDs and DVDs) and digital-born online projects. There are serious challenges in such endeavors, in large part because there is no obvious way to implement a systematic approach as we have with the journals. Alternatives, such as using computational methods with robust tools for harvesting metadata, deduplication of records, and engaging in some form of social knowledge sharing may prove effective. Certainly, early research undertaken in 2006 by ETCL on behalf of Iter showed significant benefits.[27] However, it also raised daunting questions pertaining to quality control regarding data entry and the eligibility of resources for inclusion the further we move from traditional publication modes, as in podcasts, personal websites, and more ephemeral kinds of communication.

Stepping back from the granular consideration of the types of materials to be indexed to more general issues of scope, it is worth revisiting the potential shifts suggested in the earlier reference to early modern studies in order to clarify the implications for long-term plans for the Iter Bibliography. Given the early assumption of a bibliography detailing European history and culture, there is way forward through embracing the full chronological span of the study of early modern Europe. The change would entail extending our current coverage beyond 1700 to the end of the eighteenth century and would represent a straightforward update of the original vision and practices for the bibliography that could be implemented over the course of the next planning period.

This approach also has an advantage in bringing no theoretical disruption to the current program of covering European interactions with other cultures. A crude illustration of the timing and scale of a shift in looking beyond Europe to European engagement in the Americas, Asia, and Africa can be seen in the data for *Renaissance and Reformation / Renaissance et Réforme* (*R&R*), one of the core journals published by Iter Press (Figure 1.1).

---

with grants in 1999 (Kristeller) and 2008 (Cranz).

[27] Siemens and Bowen, et al. 2006. For a summary regarding metadata standards, cataloging processes, and the assessment of Web resources, see the report funded by the Mellon Foundation in 2014–15 (Siemens and Bowen, et al. 2017, rev. 2020, 21–22).

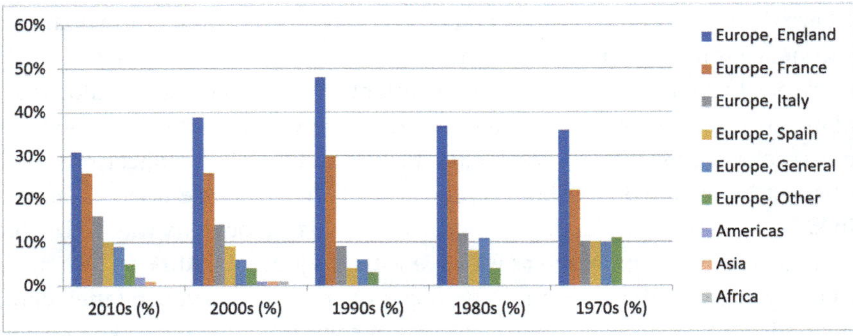

Figure 1.1. Main location of area of focus by journal articles published in *Renaissance and Reformation / Renaissance et Réforme.*

Not surprisingly for a bilingual (English/French) journal, the chart for geographic locations of the subject matter in published articles shows that England and France dominate.[28] The data for the decades from 2000 to 2019 is suggestive of an ongoing trend of rebalancing across the European countries and, more importantly for our purposes, hints at a move beyond Europe-based studies to those located in the Americas, Asia, and Africa.[29] This modest shift toward a more global approach to European history and culture is easily accommodated within the Iter Bibliography without a change in the current guidelines. Nonetheless, it does raise significant practical questions, not the least of which is the extent to which the bibliography team would be expected to scan publications in non-European languages.

What remains to be considered is the even more exciting prospect of creating a bibliography for the medieval and early modern worlds that does not take Europe as its starting point. Contemplating the immense benefits to communities of thinking both regionally and globally brings me back to the early days of Iter when a daunting challenge was met by looking at opportunities for collaboration and partnership.

---

[28] The chart is used with permission and is taken from the journal's unpublished annual report for 2019. For further information, contact iter.renref@utoronto.ca.

[29] It is worth noting in this context that the number of articles published has grown by 50 percent since 2009, so that the bars represent significantly more articles than in previous decades.

Industry-Wide Standards

In addition to matters of scope, the 2008 statement speaks to other aspirations that can be loosely bundled together under the use of well-established library standards to facilitate access to and sharing of data, and the connection of the metadata to full texts and other objects of study. To begin, it was decided during the pilot project at the University of Toronto's Faculty of Information to employ internationally recognized systems for the metadata. Accordingly, for example, the records are structured in MARC format for bibliographic data with minor adaptations for creating individual records for the contents of journals, collections of essays, and encyclopedias; and subject information in selected records uses Library of Congress Subject Headings, Dewey Decimal Classification notations, and added keywords (see Beghtol 1998, 2001, and 2003).

There is a strategic advantage in committing to this approach over developing an idiosyncratic system in so far as the bibliography is likely to be interoperable with other major bibliographies and delivery systems. To illustrate the point, the protocols underlying the data in the Iter Bibliography work well with OpenUrl and Zotero so that institutions can dynamically establish connections between our records and their digital holdings, which is a step toward "connect[ing] as closely as possible to the objects themselves" (Bowen 2008, 102). Individuals can download records in a format of their choice. Standardized systems can also bring disadvantages, however. Large-scale subject classification systems lack the nuance and subtleties of more focused, dedicated systems, such as has been developed for the International Medieval Bibliography (Izbicki 2003, 12). We opted for interoperability in anticipation that it will continue to pay dividends in the future as the landscape for online bibliographies evolves.[30]

One of the further benefits of using well-known library standards in the formation of the metadata is the relative ease in mounting the Iter Bibliography on major delivery platforms. Through our partnership with the University of Toronto Libraries, we have been able to take advantage of generations of such platforms, currently Sirsi Dynix with Endeca for faceted searches. The result is a robust interface with extensive features for finding relevant citations, and, through the implementation of OpenUrl, connecting to full texts

[30] The efforts by organizations such as the Dublin Core Metadata Initiative (dublincore.org) and, on a smaller scale, ARC to create less cumbersome yet still comprehensive metadata are promising.

when they are available at the local institution. Figures 2, 3, and 4 show the three components of a single search and results screen, and give a good idea of the capacity for sophisticated searches and filters.[31]

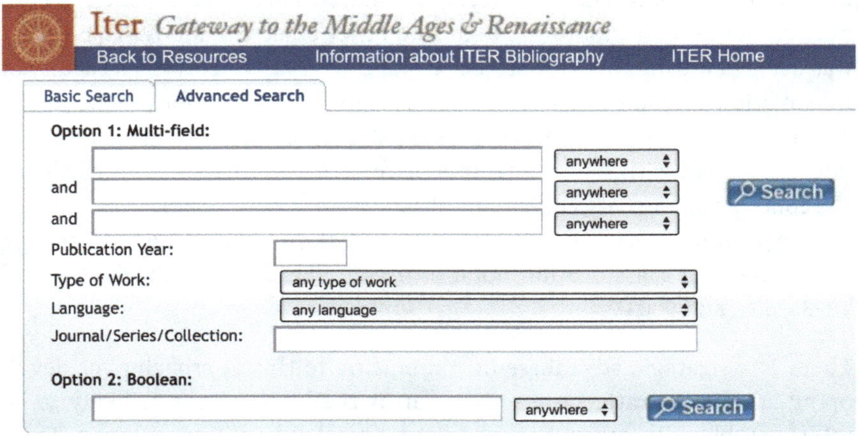

Figure 1.2. Iter Bibliography Advanced Search options.

The advanced search function allows the user to specify multiple terms to be applied to five different fields in the bibliographic records and/or to limit a search according to the year of publication; the type of work (ten types are tracked); language (a large number of languages are included, though non-Latin-based text is transliterated); and journal or book series. There is also an option to use Boolean search operators.

A search of "Milton" anywhere in the bibliography finds 9,757 items (see Figures 1.3 and 1.4). The faceted search sidebar, "Refine Results," breaks down the search results by type of work, publication year, language, author, and a number of subject filters. The active links allow the user to limit the search results to the top layer categories, which are visible in Figure 1.3, or to subcategories (e.g., each selection in the year of publication is further resolved into decades).

---

[31] The screen shots were taken from the Iter Bibliography, search.itergateway.org/Iter/search.jsp, accessed 28 June 2022.

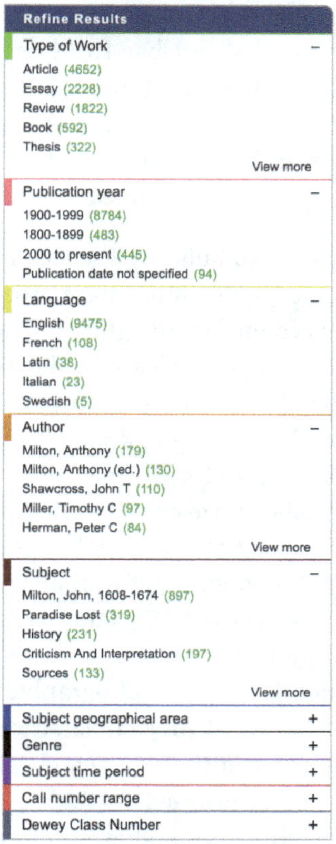

Figure 1.3. Iter Bibliography's faceted search ("Refine Results").

Figure 1.4. Sample Iter Bibliography search results for "Milton."

It is possible to sort the results by relevance, title, author, and publication date. Using the "Refine Results" sidebar to filter the 9,757 items by type (Review Article) and publication year (post 2000) brings four titles, which are seen in Figure 1.4. From this screen it is possible to view the full record and the MARC version, to search individual authors, and to select or mark records to be copied, emailed, printed, or sent to RefWorks.

While the standards adopted in building the Iter Bibliography with regard to metadata formation and presentation have stood us in good stead over the past decades, there is room for thoughtful review and consideration of how best this finding tool might evolve in order to serve its communities in the future.[32] The potential of supplementing current processes by adding records through Web harvesting and adding or annotating records by means of social networking has already been mentioned. To this potential, which would increase the sheer size of the bibliography itself, we might add the enhancement of the experience of the bibliography by leveraging other resources: for example, by connecting to other databases and by offering different, personalized interfaces to the data. But to do this and to ensure the most effective use of time and resources, we need a more precise understanding of how colleagues use online bibliographies and catalogs. We might find, for example, that traditional subject classification systems, which are extraordinarily labor intensive at the article and essay level, are less helpful in practice than what would be accrued through expanding a search of citations to related metadata, abstracts, and even full texts. Working in concert with others, this model could allow the user to be more efficient in narrowing down the list of resources to be pursued. Such a direction might complement adding value to the records themselves through community-based input—embracing the challenge of facilitating helpful, useful interaction among members of a community connected by a corpus of bibliographic records.[33]

---

[32] For reviews of the bibliography, see Izbicki 2003, Newton and Tellman 2010, and Sandstrom 2017. Following a methodical assessment, Newton and Tellman conclude, "In sum, our analysis shows that researchers should use both Iter and the *IMB* [International Medieval Bibliography] to find the greatest number of citations relevant to medieval history" (2010, 272).

[33] Ideas about personalized interfaces and the bibliography as part of an integrated network of databases and full texts have been part of a longstanding conversation, which was given a more definitive shape in the consultative process led by Siemens (see Bowen 2008, 107–09). They will undoubtedly be a prominent part of the plan for the future.

Iter Community

Encapsulating the current state and future possibilities for Iter's bibliography and press is quite straightforward, in large part because of their derivation from well-known models in the academic world. Perhaps it is not surprising that the story of Iter Community is very different and requires a slightly more historical narrative in order to delineate the prominent threads of a work in progress adapting to a changing environment.

To begin, a strong impetus to facilitate the interactions of communities brought together by Iter's partner and associate societies long pre-dates the formal launch of the first iteration of Iter Community in April 2011. Indeed, the initiatives date back to Iter's formative years before and shortly after incorporation and the launch of the bibliography. They include the following:

a. Website development and hosting, 1996–present
In conjunction with the first pilot project for the Iter Bibliography, we launched the original websites for the CRRS and RSA on the CITD servers at the University of Toronto Scarborough in October 1996. After incorporation, Iter took official responsibility for developing and hosting the RSA website, which was re-located to UTL servers from January 2001 to August 2004. Later activities are exemplified by consultation with the Medici Archive Project on its website and database (2000–06, medici.org); The Newberry on the Mellon funded project, French Renaissance Paleography (2014–16, paleography.library.utoronto.ca); and the development and hosting of websites belonging to associate organizations, e.g., MOISA and the IRCPS, both starting in 2007.

b. Listserv communications support, 1996–present
In partnership with the University of Toronto's Information Technology Services and Information Commons, from 1996 to 2005 we provided an email list for the RSA Executive Board. This same service was employed for the membership of certain associate organizations, e.g., MOISA, 2007–present.

c. Conference tools, 2000–12
In response to requests from the partners, in 2000 Iter started to develop modules for the online management of conferences, beginning with the submission and evaluation of conference papers. This first module was launched for RSA 2001 (Chicago) and was followed thereafter with membership and conference registration tools.

Modified versions of the system were used for the next decade or so by the ACMRS, CRRS, ISAS, RSA, and SCSC.[34]

d. Community directories, 2001–09
In partnership with the CRRS and SCSC, we offered online distribution of two directories: the CRRS's *International Directory of Renaissance and Reformation Associations and Institutes* converted into an online database (2001–05) and the 2000 edition of the SCSC's *Scholars of Early Modern Studies* (*SEMS*). The latter was soon superseded by *The International Directory of Scholars* (*IDS*, 2001–10), which was quite remarkable for its time: "The *IDS* is a comprehensive resource which accommodates not only the usual directory contact information, but also detailed information on the research and teaching careers of scholars around the world. Since scholars might update their own entries, new information is collected and displayed in a timely fashion."[35] The *IDS* interacted with the Iter Bibliography by enabling the automated insertion of relevant bibliography into individual records. Access was limited to RSA and SCSC members.

e. Conference panels, 2001–present
This activity pertains to an ongoing series of conference panels sponsored by Iter and its partners. The panels focus on the use of digital methods, offering a venue for sharing of exemplary projects and for discussion of both theoretical and practical issues of the digital humanities in relation to our areas of research and teaching. The initiative began in 2001 when, as the RSA's director of electronic media, I organized two panels for the 2001 RSA annual conference in Chicago and then, for RSA 2002 in Scottsdale, adopted the current RSA title, "New Technologies in Renaissance Studies." The RSA series grew quickly thereafter with Ray Siemens joining as co-organizer in 2003.[36]

f. News and announcements, 2002–2008
Research into the development of a sophisticated community-styled calendar and announcements service led to the launch of Iter News

---

[34] The system was also adopted by groups outside the Medieval and Renaissance communities: The Association for Jewish Studies used the module from 2003 to 2006, and UTSC for Buddhist studies conferences in 2007, 2010, and 2012.

[35] itergateway.org/iter/iter1a3 from 30 October 2001, accessed on the Wayback Machine (archive.org). IDS was updated until May 2010 and taken down in 2017.

[36] The record of the panels is located at itergateway.org/sites/default/files/NTMRS%20panel%20history_April%2030%202019.pdf.

and Announcements in early 2004 (see Figure 1.5).[37] The platform, using the content management system phpWebSite, allowed individuals to submit announcements and categorize them according to type (see Figure 1.5). The site enabled RSS feeds to facilitate the timely sharing of information. The site was decommissioned in 2008, in large part because of the drain on resources to maintain such a complex system.

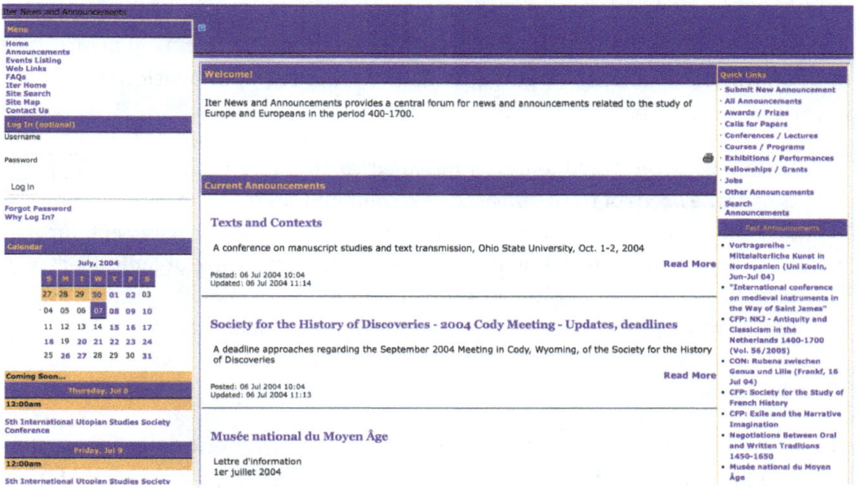

Figure 1.5. Iter News and Announcements from 2004.[38]

While individual projects worked well in isolation, what we lacked, especially with the game changing opportunities afforded by Web 2.0, was a theoretical framework to make sense of our strong inclination to do more than the bibliography and publications, that is, to facilitate collaboration and engagement.

Placed in this light, the consultation led by Ray Siemens from 2008 to 2010 was crucial to jump-starting a repositioning of Iter Gateway and inspired further theorizing about the platform as a whole, thereby bringing Iter into the extensive conversation within the academy. Such deliberations led to the creation of experimental spaces brought together under the name of Iter Community. The first pilot project was made public in Spring 2011, and

[37] Dylan Reid, one of the team involved in the early development of Iter, was responsible for the research and, in 2004, worked with Alex Laney, our developer.

[38] community.itergateway.org/index.php from 7 July 2004, accessed on the Wayback Machine (archive.org).

was built around an installation of Drupal Commons, hosted by the Information and Instructional Technologies Services at the University of Toronto Scarborough, and developed in collaboration with the ETCL.[39] While there is much to be admired in Drupal Commons, the paradigm of social business communities ultimately proved not to be a good fit for the goals we had in mind, bringing the team to begin development of a second iteration of Iter Community in 2014, now based in the lab at ETCL (see Bowen, Crompton, Hiebert 2014, 3–5).

The theoretical framework that emerged in tandem with creating prototypes at ETCL was comprehensive and ambitious.[40] In a 2014 publication, Iter Community was described as follows:

> Put simply, [Iter Community] is intended to change and grow, to adapt itself to the needs of the members of the communities that it serves. Indeed, it is the underlying vision of IC to provide a flexible environment for communication, exchange, and collaboration that will evolve organically as its participants work out their particular priorities and challenges. In this way, IC will play an important role in realizing Iter's mandate in a manner that resonates with the possibilities of Web 2.0. (Bowen, Crompton, and Hiebert 2014, 8).

This sweeping statement comprehended commons functionality and more in a dynamic, public-facing, social knowledge creation environment that was fully integrated with the other facets of Iter Gateway. Ensuing papers and publications engaged further with current debates, exploring the possibilities of Iter Community in terms of social knowledge creation and as a "community of practice," thereby updating and bringing clarity and depth

[39] Iter's longstanding partnership with ETCL in the development of Iter Community continues. Luis Meneses (assistant director, technical development) is funded by Iter and is embedded within the lab's team, which is coordinated by Jannaya Friggstad Jensen (assistant director, coordination and operations) and supervised by Alyssa Arbuckle (associate director) and Raymond Siemens (director).

[40] Some of the research for this phase in the life of Iter Community was undertaken by Matthew Hiebert in 2013 during a MITACS Accelerate Postdoctoral Fellowship co-directed by Bowen (Iter) and Siemens (ETCL). The project was entitled, "Building Social Community Integrations." The research specific to Iter Community was supported by Iter and ETCL, and benefitted from the backdrop of Iter's participation in two funded projects: from 2012 to 2016, I was a member of the Modelling and Prototyping research group within INKE, directed by Siemens and funded by the SSHRC Major Collaborative Research Initiatives program; in 2014, Mellon awarded Bowen and Siemens a planning grant for ReKN.

to ideas that have surrounded the initiative since its inception (Hiebert, Bowen, and Siemens 2015). Accordingly, in this theoretical framework, Iter Community could aspire to be a "community of practice" for the facilitation of scholarly communication and information sharing, including the social formation around Iter record sets, aggregation of information (e.g., scholar profiles, shared calendar, social media), and the capacity for incubator or sandbox development, website hosting, and a digital repository.

Fortunately, learning from our practical experience in grappling with the complexity of identifying, engaging, and sustaining a community's scholarly activities, we eventually settled on a more modest program toward rebuilding Iter Community and reimaging Iter Gateway as an integrated platform.[41] Recognizing the huge benefits of leveraging what has been developed elsewhere, especially in light of the launch of Modern Language Association's Humanities Commons (2016), we deferred further work on commons functionality.[42] This left us with the more straightforward task of consolidating and building on some of our longstanding initiatives, wherein we made a concerted effort to establish a well-defined environment for partnership and collaboration.

Accordingly, we focused on conference activities and project development under the umbrella of a simple statement of the purpose of Iter Community, which "facilitates and supports communication, collaboration, and digital project creation for research communities of the Middle Ages and the Renaissance."[43] The organization of RSA conference panels devoted to the use of digital methods was expanded to include other partners and associates.[44] And a related program of travel grants and conference support, started in 2010, was codified in order to be clear about eligibility, funding, and application processes, and also extended beyond the RSA.[45]

---

[41] The ideas generated by the participants in ReKN are particularly relevant here with regard to how they imagined Iter's role and, more generally, to thinking deeply about knowledge creation ecosystems (Powell et al. 2015; Siemens and Bowen et al. 2017).

[42] One of the interim production versions of the Iter Community site included an implementation of Commons in a Box (Hiebert, Bowen, and Siemens 2015, 5).

[43] itercommunity.org, accessed 22 January 2021.

[44] The concept of Iter-sponsored panels devoted to digital methods was taken to SCSC (2012, 2014–15), TRRC (2014, 2018), CSRS-SCER (2016–17), and ACMRS (2020; ReKN sponsored the panels from 2016–19). See itergateway.org/sites/default/files/NTMRS%20panel%20history_April%2030%202019.pdf.

[45] Iter's program of travel grants has supported New Technologies sessions at the RSA since 2010. Travel grants and conference funding have also been awarded to SCSC

Further, the early collaboration with Iter's partners in online projects and websites was given a thorough overhaul and reimagined in terms of matching funding, currently under the program heading of Iter Community Partnership Project Development Awards:

> Iter Community is pleased to be able to partner in the development of resources that advance learning in the study and teaching of the Middle Ages and Renaissance. Its Partnership Project Development Award supports collaborative partnership in the development and distribution of online resources, including by providing incubator/sandbox space for digital projects and offering website hosting and repository services.[46]

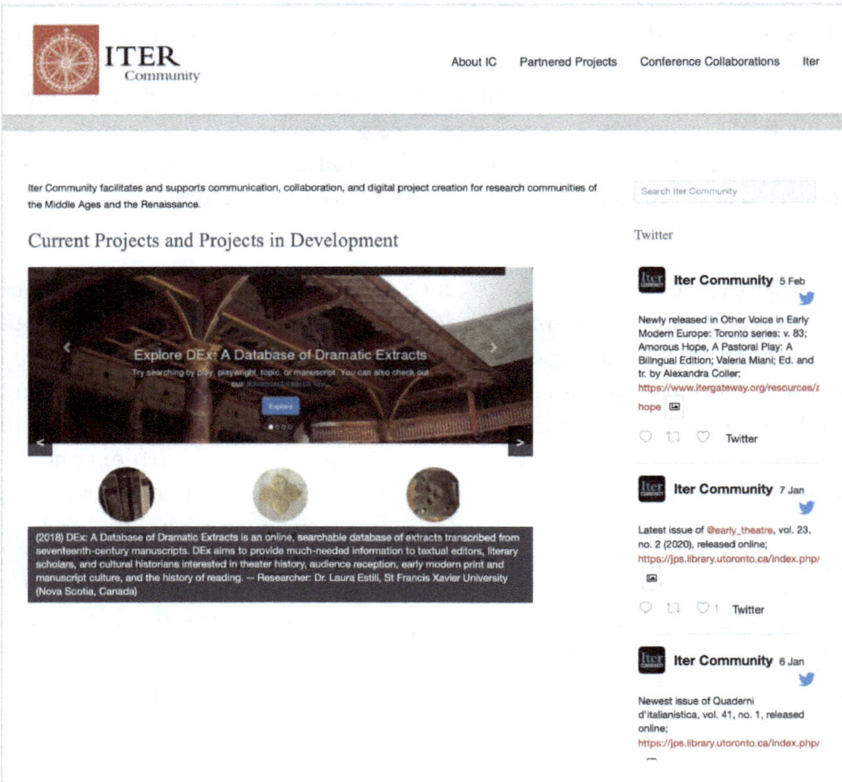

Figure 1.6. Iter Community landing page.

(2012, 2014, 2019), TRRC (2014, 2018), CSRS-SCER (2016–17), and the Society for the History of Authorship, Reading and Publishing (2017). See itergateway.org/NTRS%20 panels_subventions.

[46] itercommunity.org/partnered-projects/, accessed 22 January 2021.

Through an online application process accompanied by clear statements about collaboration, individuals and groups are able to enter a partnership with Iter toward the development and distribution of online projects, almost exclusively open access.[47] In order to address the challenge of determining manageable and affordable technical requirements, the preliminary phase of the collaboration focuses on such practical issues as software and platform standards, expectations regarding shared costs, and long-term maintenance and future development.

As a result of this process of consolidation, we are able to present Iter Community through a simply designed website with a modest number of subpages (see Figure 1.6).[48] Reflecting on the history of Iter Community, I am struck by the significant steps taken to adjust to a quickly changing environment, to clarify relationships and expectations, and to bring greater definition to our programs so that we make the best use of our finite resources. Reviewing the many individual projects undertaken thus far and the potential for so many more, I am mindful that the Iter Community projects that contribute the most to Iter Gateway as a whole are the ones that have organic connections across the platform. It is worth offering a few examples in order to characterize possibilities that have been tested thus far:

a. From conference panel to publication
   The New Technologies panels have fostered a growing community by providing opportunities for regular meetings since 2001. With the inception in 2008 of the Iter Press series, New Technologies in Medieval and Renaissance Studies (NTMRS), edited by Bowen and Siemens, this initiative was taken to another level through the publication of volumes of selected papers from Iter-sponsored panels. The travel grants offered in support of conferences and conference panels add another dimension in so far as this complementary program helps emerging scholars, who then have the opportunity to submit their work for publication.

b. Pre-publication development
   There are various possibilities here for digital-born work where development leads to formal publication. Iter's interactions with the

[47] The application is at docs.google.com/forms/d/1OMfKf6-bMR0A0QW4IYr8N8GbBxt-OF56RPda24lsfM8/viewform?edit_requested=true.

[48] A review of Iter Gateway that predates the simplified landing page for Iter Community raised a concern about the difficult of understanding the site, which has now been addressed (see Sandstrom 2017).

ground-breaking project, *A Social Edition of the Devonshire Manuscript MS (BL Add. MS 17492)*, as partner, host of one manifestation in Iter Community, and publisher in the NTMRS book series exemplify a rich set of possibilities.[49] A more recent partnership is with Laura Estill and Beatrice Montedoro in hosting and developing DEx: A Database of Dramatic Extracts, with contributions from an Iter Community Partnership Project Development Award.[50]

c. Post-publication public engagement
Iter Community serves as the location for websites that complement Iter Press book publications by mounting open-access supplementary information (e.g., The Other Voice in Early Modern Europe: The Toronto Series (OVIEME) website outlines the history of the project and lists published and future titles; see Margaret King's essay in this volume about that series).[51] Some websites also facilitate public engagement in the form of commentary and annotation, such as the websites for the aforementioned *Social Edition of the Devonshire Manuscript* (Siemens, Armstrong, and Crompton 2015) and later volumes in the NTMRS series, including *Early Modern Studies after the Digital Turn* (Estill, Jakacki, and Ullyot 2016) and *Social Knowledge Creation in the Humanities* (Arbuckle, Mauro, and Powell 2017).[52]

d. Website hosting
Hosting websites can enhance active, ongoing relationships. For example, Iter Community and Iter Press have provided support for the websites of the CSRS-SCER and TRRC, two of the organizations

---

[49] On Iter as partner, see en.wikipedia.org/wiki/User:DMSEG, accessed on 21 January 2021; for the Iter Community site, dms.itercommunity.org; and for the published volume, Siemens, Armstrong, and Crompton 2015, itergateway.org/resources/social-edition-of-the-devonshire-manuscript. For more on the social edition and its development, see Siemens et al. reprinted in this volume.

[50] The beta version of *DEx* is available at dex.itercommunity.org. For more on DEx's technical implementations, see Meneses in this volume.

[51] With the passing of Albert Rabil, Jr., on 8 January 2021, we agreed to recognize his legacy as founding editor of The Other Voice in Early Modern Europe: The Toronto Series by publishing all of the 2021 volumes of the series in his honour. The work continues under the leadership of Margaret L. King (founding editor) and Elizabeth H. Hageman (English texts, 2011–). The website is othervoiceineme.com/index.html.

[52] The complementary websites for *Early Modern Studies after the Digital Turn* and *Social Knowledge Creation in the Humanities* are ems.itercommunity.org and ntmrs-skc.itercommunity.org respectively.

> that co-own the journal *Renaissance and Reformation / Renaissance et Réforme* (*R&R*), which is published by Iter Press.[53] These associate organizations also collaborate with Iter in the presentation of panels devoted to digital methods at their conferences. Similarly, the open access journal, *Early Modern Digital Review* (*EMDR*), discussed by Randa El Khatib in this volume, was recently established in partnership with ETCL and is published by Iter Press.[54] There is a further interconnection in that *EMDR* is available both through an Iter Community website and as part of *R&R*. Finally, Iter's longstanding relationship with the Renaissance Knowledge Network (ReKN) most recently involved a Mellon-funded research project from 2014 to 2016, which produced a substantial report (Siemens and Bowen 2017) that gave detailed attention to the Iter Bibliography in the context of discussing an online environment for Early Modern studies, contributed to the development of Iter Community, and led to the creation of *EMDR*.

That the examples almost exclusively connect activities of Iter Community with the publications of Iter Press reflect the current state of play. Yet, it brings to mind a few questions for future consideration in the context of prioritizing coherence and integration of Iter Gateway. How might we draw Iter Community and Iter Bibliography closer together? It is incumbent on Iter to find ways to leverage the affordances of Web 2.0 in building and adding value to its bibliography and other finding tools.

While we have theorized and experimented with "commons" functionality since Iter's early days, would the platform benefit from something along the lines of the Humanities Commons or INKE's Canadian Humanities and Social Sciences (HSS) Commons? A resoundingly positive response is appropriate, taking us far beyond our tentative use of social media. But it might help to have a more precise understanding of the different modes of scholarly communications and interactions that are best aligned with the expectations of the individuals brought together through the Iter Gateway platform, many of whom are likely committed to several organizations with similar aspirations. Accordingly, our ongoing partnership with INKE makes huge strategic sense as a way to participate in important conversations across the

---

[53] The websites for CSRS-SCER, TRRC, and *R&R* are found at csrs-scer.com, trrc.itergateway.org, and rr.itergateway.org.

[54] The founding editors of this open-access journal are William R. Bowen, Laura Estill, and Ray Siemens, with managing editor Randa El Khatib: emdr.itercommunity.org/index.php/emdr.

humanities and to contribute to the development of a platform in a not-for-profit environment.[55]

To these two questions, I might explicitly raise a more fundamental query about the profiles of the members of our community. We recognize and celebrate the contributions of Iter's leadership team and staff, the representatives of partner and associate organizations, advisory committee members, the hundreds of colleagues who presented papers or attended Iter-sponsored panels, the recipients of close to five hundred graduate research assistants, the many individuals who contribute to Iter Community projects and Iter Press publications, and even our extended family through collaboration with other organizations, such as ETCL and INKE. Unlike an academic society with a defined membership, Iter is an open community with many named contributors and a much larger set of unnamed participants. Finding mechanisms to better understand the interests of the entire community (e.g., using Google analytics on Iter Gateway) is important to guiding next steps in the planning process, particularly with the goals of empowering individuals to engage on an integrated platform.

Iter Press[56]

The roots of Iter Press are very nearly as deep as those for the bibliography and community and are driven by much the same motivation to leverage the possibilities of the Web on behalf of the partners and their communities. How this motivation was realized, thereby laying the foundations for Iter Press, can be illustrated through a brief review of early projects in chronological order of their initial development:

a. Finding tools, 1997–present
Conversations started in 1997 with Julian Deahl (senior acquisitions editor, Brill) about extending access to Kristeller's *Iter Italicum* (6 vols., 1963–92) by replacing the CD-ROM version of 1995 with an online edition.[57] This led quickly to proof of concept in the same

[55] INKE's impressive network of partners (including Iter) contributing to the development of the Canadian HSS Commons and their link to the Humanities Commons is outlined at inke.ca/canadian-hss-commons/.

[56] The imprint has changed over time, beginning with Iter Inc. (2008–14), then Iter Academic Press (2014–16), and now Iter Press (2016–). For the purposes of this chapter, Iter Press is used throughout.

[57] The publication history of *Iter Italicum*, including print and CD-ROM versions, is found at italicum.itergateway.org/about. John Monfasani was instrumental in bring-

year. Years of development work to migrate the massive dataset to an online database, funded in part by the Delmas Foundation, preceded the launch of the new edition in 2002. There are significant parallels in the paths taken for subsequent projects, including, for example, John Shawcross's *Milton: A Bibliography for the Years 1624–1700 (Revised) and for the Years 1701–1799*, released in September 2006, which is a revised and much expanded version of a 1984 print publication.[58] The bibliography began as a Claris Works file—a program that was no longer supported in 2001 when the project was brought to Iter. The conversion to an online bibliography via Microsoft Word required substantial hands-on intervention to correct errors created by the automated processes.[59]

b. Journals, 2001–present
The initiative to encourage online distribution of journals began with the RSA's journal, *Renaissance Quarterly*. From 2002 to 2005, Iter mounted the first full-text, online version of current issues of the journal and made them available to individual members of the society and to institutional subscribers. Iter expanded this initiative in 2005 with the addition of *Early Theatre* and *R&R*, and thereafter with *Quaderni d'Italianistica* (2010), *Confraternitas* (2010), *Early Modern Women: An Interdisciplinary Journal* (2011), *Aestimatio* (2016), *Early Modern Digital Review* (2018), and *Italian Canadiana* (2021).[60] Iter offers the complete journal runs in collaboration with the University of Toronto Libraries' Information Technology Services and their Journal Production Services, using the Public Knowledge Project's Open Journal Systems software.

c. Books, 2007–present
Our entry into book publication brought the first explicit recognition of Iter in the role of publisher. In close alignment with Iter's purpose, the first series, New Technologies in Medieval and Renaissance

ing this project to Iter.

[58] See itergateway.org/resources/milton-bibliography.

[59] A third project, Betty Travitsky's Bibliography of English Women Writers 1500–1640, had a similarly long trajectory. With the support of the Delmas Foundation in 2003, the initial version was migrated to an online platform and thereafter revised and expanded before it was released in January 2010. itergateway.org/resources/beww.

[60] See itergateway.org/iter-press/Journal and jps.library.utoronto.ca for information and access to the journals.

> Studies, publishes collections of essays on the use of digital methods. The series launched in 2008 as a co-publication with ACMRS and opened with *New Technologies and Renaissance Studies* (Bowen and Siemens 2008), which was awarded a book subsidy by the RSA. The second project, The Other Voice in Early Modern Europe: The Toronto Series, started as a co-publication with the CRRS and later with the ACMRS. The series publishes writings by women and their male advocates, beginning in 2009 with *Journey of Five Capuchin Nuns* (Owens 2009); for more on this, see King's chapter in this volume. The Delmas Foundation has supported the series with publication grants from 2008 onward.[61]

The summary suggests a number of foundational elements that instruct Iter's ongoing approach to publication. The strategic underpinnings lie in collaboration, in terms not only of the scholarly enterprise but also of the requisite technical support and infrastructure. Further, external funding in the form of publication subsidies has proven to be essential. Yet, while such general observations are helpful in confirming the shared realities of academic publishing, it is also important to remark the lengthy development time for the publication of data sets. Our experiences here were hard-learned lessons in the challenges of converting or migrating data sets from one platform to another, the benefits of collaboration with the creative team from the beginning, and the huge demands on human and financial resources. It is fair to connect these lessons to Iter Community's experiments with partnership in sandbox development. Finally, there is the progression from initial work on finding tools (1997–) to journals (2001–) and books (2007–).[62] To a certain extent, this can be equated with the growth of a small organization. But the critical factor was the change in online reading environments. Although online publication of books was considered by the partners as early as 1997, the consensus was that sustained reading of online text was not feasible at that time.

More than twenty years later, the goals and aspirations of Iter Press have remained the same, centering on the online publication of high-quality

---

[61] In addition to the 2008 grant, the Delmas Foundation awarded book subventions in support of OVIEME in 2016, 2017, and 2018.

[62] I am passing over our brief engagement with the scanning of printed books in 2004–05. At the invitation of UTL's chief librarian, Carole Moore, we took part in identifying books relevant to Renaissance studies at the University of Toronto, specifically in the CRRS Library and the John M. Kelly Library, that were out of copyright. The books were scanned for local distribution and the Internet Archive.

scholarship, facilitating the shift from print to digital-born publication, and exploring new approaches to knowledge creation and mobilization. To these ends, the reliance on collaboration and partnership continues, but now in an environment wherein major players provide a wide range of services in support of online publication. Accordingly, while Iter Press continues to offer production (e.g., copyediting and typesetting) and online distribution services to the ACMRS and CRRS for their publications, we have begun to avail ourselves of robust marketing and subscription services for Iter Press publications as a supplement to what we are able to do in-house.[63] To be specific, beginning with *R&R* in 2019, we are signing agreements with Érudit (apropos.erudit.org/en/) for the dissemination of our Canadian journals as part of a larger strategy to have many points of access for each journal.[64] Similarly, for our books we have entered into an agreement with the University of Chicago Press effective July 2020, taking advantage of their extensive world-wide marketing and distribution services, notably through their Marketing, Chicago Distribution Center, and BiblioVault divisions.

Such adjustments reflect an online publication environment still heavily dependent on print-based models. This has affected Iter Press in at least two ways. In facilitating a shift to online publication, almost all of our publications have both print and online versions. It is curious to me that the adoption of publication solely online is not happening as quickly as I anticipated more than two decades ago. Even with journals, where there is a considerable history and proven business models for online distribution, a significant percentage of individuals and institutions rely on print copy. For example, roughly 25 percent of *R&R* institutional subscribers require print subscriptions—admittedly, the percentage is rapidly declining. In any case, hanging on to print editions has led us to explore cost-effective strategies, such as initial, very short print runs followed by print on demand. The second way is related to the hope of facilitating a shift to digital-born publication beyond finding tools and other databases. While the ability to search, connect, annotate, and share texts is invaluable, Iter Press publications have yet to move

---

[63] This strategy first led Iter to sign an agreement with EBSCO in April 2012 for the distribution of Iter Bibliography. EBSCO did not implement the agreement, but revived the conversation in 2018, thus far without any concrete results.

[64] It seems reasonable to anticipate that the opportunities for distribution of a journal are increased by having multiple points of access. Accordingly, for example, *R&R* is available not only through Iter Press, but also through Érudit, Scholars Portal (Ontario Consortium of University Libraries), and a number of major aggregators (i.e., EBSCO, Gale (Cengage), and JSTOR). It is also widely indexed.

significantly beyond the model of the printed page. Some answers may lie in the role of Iter Community as the connective tissue for Iter as a whole, but also in further collaboration with organizations dedicated to these issues. Accordingly, our relationship to INKE and other networks has a high strategic value for the future.[65]

In sum, Iter Press is moving incrementally in response to opportunities within the world of academic publishing in order to accomplish its goals. Figure 1.7 is a useful reminder of the measured growth from databases to journal to books and, at the same time, highlights a significant contribution to our communities.

A full assessment of whether or to what extent Iter Press has achieved its goal of publishing high quality scholarship is best left to others. Nevertheless, it seems appropriate at this juncture to gesture to the indirect evidence in the acclaimed scholars who have contributed as authors and editors, the collaborations with well-known organizations within and outside the partnership, and the financial support from established foundations (e.g., Mellon, Delmas). More specifically, I note the impressive success of The Other Voice in Early Modern Europe: The Toronto Series in consistently attracting strong reviews and for being recognized with seventeen awards since 2013 from the Society for the Study of Early Modern Women and Gender (SSEMWG).[66] The extraordinary support for The Other Voice by the series editors, volume editors and translators, and the academic community as a whole has enabled the press to publish seventy-six volumes from 2009 to 2020 and to anticipate a similar pace for the second half of the titles on the list. Setting aside such indicators of quality, what the current list shows is an ongoing commitment to leveraging the opportunities afforded by the Web: specifically, in building a variety of online finding tools, in bringing journals and books to an online platform, and in directly advancing the discussion of digital methods in Medieval and Renaissance studies through its NTMRS series.

---

[65] The announcement in Spring 2020 that INKE was successful in its application to SSHRC for a Partnership Grant (2020–27) augurs well for the future. Iter is one of the partner organizations in the project Implementing Open Scholarship: Foundations for Social Engagement at Scale.

[66] Book reviews are listed in the information for each title on the Iter Press site. For the awards from 2012 to 2019, see the SSEMWG websites ssemwg.org/2019-awards/ and ssemwg.org/awards/previous-award-recipients/.

Figure 1.7. Excerpt from the Iter Press landing page.

I have saved for last a return to Iter's commitment to accessibility, thereby building on considerations offered earlier in the review of the bibliography. However, rather than look again at matters that impinge on technologies and communication standards, I will introduce elements that come into play in making our publications (especially the bibliography) accessible in terms of costs. This requires a brief outline of practical matters pertaining to the self-sustaining partnership and the costs arising from research, production, and marketing, all leading to the resulting subscription costs and book prices, and to opportunities for open access:

a. Self-sustaining partnership
Our shared understanding of long-term sustainability assumes significant in-kind contributions and matching funding. Accordingly, for example, those organizations participating in our programs provide in-kind support through local supervision and financial oversight, plus workspace and equipment. In return, Iter offers funding for research assistants, which, in the case of the University of Toronto, has been matched by the Faculty of Arts and Science since 2001.[67] Similarly, the Toronto office benefits from the generosity of UTL with respect to office space, server space, and technical support, and of UTSC for financial oversight. As a result, Iter's major expenses are salaries (staff and developers), research, and production costs.

b. Research
In accord with standard practices, most authors and editors who contribute to Iter Press publications are funded by their employers. Where Iter departs from this model is in the work on the Iter Bibliography. For this project, Iter funds many research assistants and fellows, who are locally supervised by faculty and staff and are further coordinated and supervised by an Iter staff member, Marian Cosic, a graduate of the Faculty of Information Studies.[68] With this level of oversight, we are able to ensure the requisite quality and to invest in the training and support of the next generations of scholars.

---

[67] The 2001 agreement signed by Pekka Sinervo, dean of the Faculty of Arts and Science, was championed by John Magee, director of the Centre for Medieval Studies. This agreement has funded more than a hundred research fellowships, which are coordinated by the CRRS assistant to the director.

[68] Tracy Castell, Iter's first project manager (1996–98), published a preliminary study of information management issues including detailed descriptions of workflows, which illustrates the care and attention to the details of creating high-quality bibliographic records (Castell 1997). While the workflow has changed over time, the culture of attending to detail and the commitment to quality remain. See also Beghtol 2004.

c. Production
The costs associated with copyediting, typesetting, and printing and/or hosting online are formidable. To ameliorate production costs, presses commonly turn to article processing charges or to book subventions, both of which are problematic mechanisms to download costs to the authors or their employers, thereby privileging those who can afford to pay. Iter Press does not engage at all in the former and carefully uses the latter by encouraging modest subventions but not requiring them. To decrease the strain of production costs, Iter has had considerable success in seeking funds from granting agencies such as Delmas, Mellon, the National Endowment for the Humanities, and the Social Sciences and Humanities Research Council of Canada.

d. Marketing
The advantages of online distribution over print are well known and do not need to be rehearsed here. But what is less well understood is the investment necessary to get the word out, to market the publications. Iter Bibliography's current subscribers are outlined in Figures 1.8 and 1.9.

Based on information regarding the Iter Bibliography, Figures 1.8 and 1.9 show that the vast majority of the institutional subscribers are located in North America, with more than 70 percent in the USA, and that smaller institutions are under-represented. A slightly more granular study shows that we are doing well world-wide in reaching top-tier and large public research institutions, but not the many, many smaller universities and colleges. At this level of analysis, it seems reasonable to postulate that the bibliography's English interface and subscription fees are contributing factors alongside institutional commitments to medieval and Renaissance studies. However, more work needs to be done to better understand our communities, to align our publications with their needs, and to put remedies in place to address the barriers to access. This kind of strategic planning requires an ongoing investment in marketing, which we innocently figured was unnecessary in Iter's formative years because of our close alignment with individual membership of the academic societies.

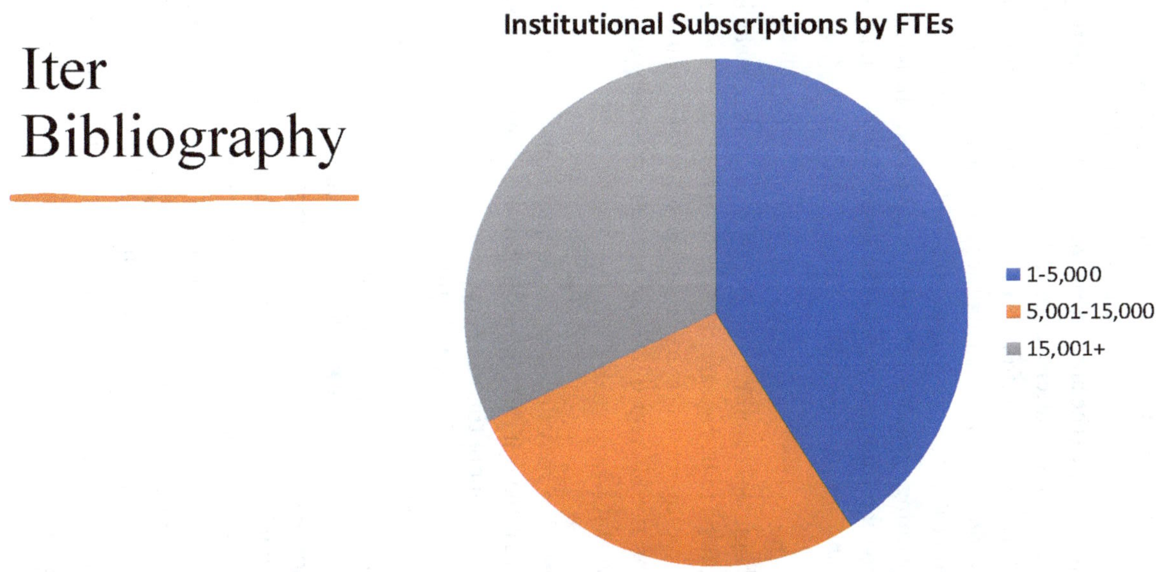

Figure 1.8. Institutional subscriptions to the Iter Bibliography by size of institution (measured in full-time equivalency students, FTEs). Created by Marian Cosic.

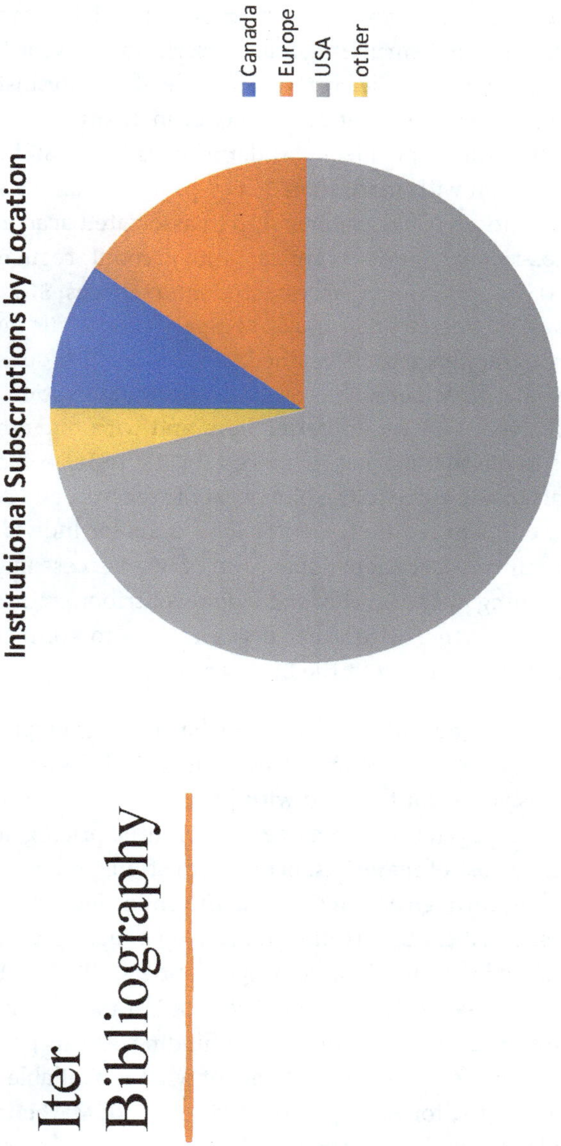

Figure 1.9. Institutional subscriptions to the Iter Bibliography by location. Created by Marian Cosic.

This brief overview of funding and costs will help to contextualize what we have managed thus far in terms of subscriptions and book pricing, and to consider opportunities for open access.

Given the significant support of the partners, much of which is targeted at the Iter Bibliography, it is not surprising that subscription fees for the bibliography are deeply discounted. The current schedule of fees for institutions is based on student population so that, for example, an institution with up to 1,500 FTE students (full time equivalency students) pays $305 USD for unlimited access; an institution with more than 35,000 pays $1,232. The schedule for individual subscriptions takes membership in associated academic societies and status (i.e., regular, student/ retiree) into account: regular society members pay $25 USD for unlimited access, students/retirees, $18; for non-affiliated individuals, the fees are $30 and $23 respectively. While publishers of other online bibliographies are not inclined to publicize their subscription schedules, from what I have been able to glean, Iter subscription fees are more than competitive.[69] Can we do better here and with our other finding tools? It seems to me that marketing more robustly to raise our profile, enabling individuals to add value to the bibliographic records, and revisiting the fee schedule in order to reduce the entry level costs for individuals and institutions are worth consideration. Some form of open access might even work, perhaps beginning at the level of individual contributors. A different approach would be to partner with other organizations to see if there are economies of scale that could benefit the Bibliography.

The opportunities for our journals and books can be briefly exemplified with reference to *Renaissance and Reformation / Renaissance et Réforme* and our book series. While *R&R* has yet to cut the cord with print publication, the shift to online delivery is encouraged through modest differential pricing, in part to account for the heavy cost of materials, print production, and mailing. The good news here is that, through a SSHRC award, the online journal has a one-year embargo for subscribers and is immediately open access to members of the groups associated with the four copyright holders: CRRS, CSRS-SCER, Pacific Northwest Renaissance Society, and the TRRC. A move to gold open access awaits more substantial and more secure funding. At this point, there are no funding programs for books at the scale of what is available to Canadian journals. Accordingly, for example, NTMRS and OVIEME benefit from institutional, foundation, and government subsidies but are not yet able to

[69] It is suggestive that Brepols charges individual members of the Medieval Academy of America $70 USD for online access to the International Medieval Bibliography.

move decisively to open access. In the short term, there are options to be explored, such as digital-born publications (especially attractive in the case of NTMRS) and hybrid publications with print and online components. However, the most promising in terms of cost-free access is some form of brief embargo, which, as in the case of journals, might eventually disappear when new funding models are tested and established.

Closing Reflections

Iter and its platform, Iter Gateway, are works in progress even though we approach the twenty-fifth anniversary of incorporation and the launch of the bibliography. This is as it should be given the context of a fast-changing environment for teaching and learning. Yet it is daunting to imagine how much more could and must be done. The course remains clear if we hold to an iterative process of identifying a unique position that builds on the original purposes of Iter and the community around it. Here Iter has certain advantages. By its nature and brief history, Iter has a greater agility and openness than many more traditional structures, thereby bringing opportunities to navigate issues related to electronic and print media in the context of changing patterns of production and consumption of academic scholarly products. Further, with its longstanding commitment to collaboration and partnership, to the empowerment of individuals and communities in facilitating a response to a digital world, it is ideally aligned to thrive. The tough part will be not so much to build on our past in a way that remains flexible and effective, but to set realistic priorities for the next several years from the myriad opportunities being explored today.

WORKS CITED

Arbuckle, Alyssa, Aaron Mauro, and Daniel Powell, eds. 2017. *Social Knowledge Creation in the Humanities.* Toronto: Iter Press. itergateway.org/resources/social-knowledge-creation-in-the-humanities.

Beghtol, Clare. 1998. "Knowledge Domains: Multidisciplinarity and Bibliographic Classification Systems." *Knowledge Organization* 25 (1/2): 1–12. nomos-elibrary.de/10.5771/0943-7444-1998-1-2-1/knowledge-domains-multidisciplinarity-and-bibliographic-classification-systems-volume-25-1998-issue-1-2.

———. 2001. "Knowledge Representation and Organization in the Iter Project: A Web-Based Digital Library for Scholars of the Middle Ages and Renaissance." *Knowledge Organization* 28 (4): 170–79. ergon-verlag.de/isko_ko/downloads/ko2820014c.pdf.

———. 2003. "The Iter Bibliography: International Standard Subject Access to Medieval and Renaissance Materials (400–1700)." In *Subject Retrieval in a Networked Environment: Proceedings of the IFLA Satellite Meeting held in Dublin, OH, 14–16 August 2001*, edited by I. C. McIlwaine, 74–80. Munich: K.G. Saur, 2003. doi.org/10.1515/9783110964912.

———. 2004. "The Iter Gateway to the Middle Ages and Renaissance: Collaboration between Information Specialists and Subject Specialists in the Arts and Humanities." *Journal of Digital Information Management* 2 (1): 4–8. citeseerx.ist.psu.edu/viewdoc/download?doi=10.1.1.474.454&rep=rep1&type=pdf.

Bowen, William R. 1999. "Iter. Where Does the Path Lead?" *TEXT Technology* 9 (2) (Summer): 5–28. Reissued as Bowen 2000, "*Iter*: Where Does the Path Lead?" *Early Modern Literary Studies* 5 (3): 1–10. purl.oclc.org/emls/05-3/bowiter.html.

———. 2004. "The Evolution of Iter: Gateway to the Middle Ages and Renaissance." *Canadian Association of Music Libraries Review* 32 (1): 25–27. caml.journals.yorku.ca/index.php/caml/article/view/1328/654.

———. 2007. "Iter as a Knowledgebase." Paper presented at the Annual Meeting of the RSA, Miami, March.

———. 2008. "Iter: Building an Effective Knowledge Base." In *New Technologies and Renaissance Studies*. Edited by William R. Bowen and Raymond Siemens, 101–09. Toronto: Iter and Tempe: ACMRS. itergateway.org/resources/new-technologies-and-renaissance-studies.

Bowen, William R., Constance Crompton, and Matthew Hiebert. 2014. "Iter Community: Prototyping an Environment for Social Knowledge Creation and Communication." *Scholarly and Research Communication* 5 (4): 9 pp. doi.org/10.22230/src.2014v5n4a193.

Bowen, William R., and Raymond Siemens. 2003. "The Role of Text Analysis in the Creation of a Knowledgebase: Preliminary Thoughts on the Future of Iter: Gateway to the Middle Ages and Renaissance." Paper presented at the Canadian Symposium for Text Analysis, University of Victoria, November.

———, eds. 2008. *New Technologies and Renaissance Studies*. Toronto: Iter and Tempe: ACMRS. itergateway.org/resources/new-technologies-and-renaissance-studies.

Castell, Tracy. 1997. "Maintaining Web-Based Bibliographies: A Case Study of Iter, the Bibliography of Renaissance Europe." *Proceedings of the ASIS Annual Meeting* 34: 174–82.

Cranz, F. Edward. 1982. *A Microfilm Corpus of the Indexes to Printed Catalogues of Latin Manuscripts before 1600 A.D.* New London, Conn.: s.n.

Estill, Laura, Diane K. Jakacki, and Michael Ullyot, eds. 2016. *Early Modern Studies after the Digital Turn*. Toronto: Iter. itergateway.org/resources/early-modern-studies-after-the-digital-turn.

Hiebert, Matthew, William R. Bowen, and Raymond Siemens. 2015. "Implementing a Social Knowledge Creation Environment." *Scholarly and Research Communication* 6 (3): 9 pp. doi.org/10.22230/src.2015v6n3a223.

Izbicki, Thomas. 2003. "Iter Bibliography of Medieval and Renaissance Europe." *The Charleston Advisor* 4 (4): 11–13.

Kristeller, Paul Oskar, compiler. 1963–97. *Iter Italicum: A Finding list of Uncatalogued or Incompletely Catalogued Humanistic Manuscripts of the Renaissance in Italian and Other Libraries*. 6 volumes and 3 indexes. London: The Warburg Institute and Leiden: E.J. Brill. Itergateway.org/resources/iter-italicum.

Newton, Daniel, and Jennalyn Tellman. 2010. "A Comparison of the Iter Bibliography and the International Medieval Bibliography: Tools for Researching the History of the European Middle Ages." *Reference & User Services Quarterly* 49 (3): 265–77. jstor.org/stable/20865262.

Owens, Sarah E., ed. and trans. 2009. *Journey of Five Capuchin Nuns*. Toronto: Iter. itergateway.org/resources/five-nuns.

Powell, Daniel, Raymond Siemens, William R. Bowen, Matthew Hiebert, and Lindsey Seatter. 2015. "Transformation through Integration: The Renaissance Knowledge Network (ReKN) and a Next Wave of Scholarly Publication." *Scholarly and Research Communication* 6 (2): 17 pp. doi.org/10.22230/src.2015v6n2a199.

Sandstrom, John. 2017. "Iter: Gateway to the Middle Ages & Renaissance." *The Charleston Advisor* 19 (1): 31. doi.org/10.5260/chara.19.1.30.

Shawcross, John. 2006 (revised from 1984). *Milton: A Bibliography for the Years 1624–1700 (Revised) and for the Years 1701–1799.* itergateway.org/resources/milton-bibliography.

Siemens, Raymond. 2010. *Initial Steps, Following a Larger Vision: A Feature-Oriented Pilot Proposal.* Unpublished document, 1 April.

Siemens, Raymond, Karin Armstrong, and Constance Crompton, eds. 2015. *A Social Edition of the Devonshire Manuscript (BL MS Add 17,492).* Toronto: Iter. itergateway.org/resources/social-edition-of-the-devonshire-manuscript.

Siemens, Raymond, William R. Bowen, Jessica Natale, Karin Armstrong, Alastair McColl, and Greg Newton. 2006. "Iter Database: Research Report on the Inclusion of Electronic Resources." Unpublished whitepaper, ETCL, University of Victoria.

Siemens, Raymond, and William R. Bowen, eds., with Daniel Powell, Lindsey Seatter, Alyssa Arbuckle, and the ReKN Research Group. 2017, revised 2020. *Towards an Integrated Digital Environment for Early Modern Studies: A Report of the Renaissance Knowledge Network (ReKN) Group.* Toronto: Iter and Victoria: Electronic Textual Cultures Lab, (revised 2020). rekn.org.

Unsworth, John. 2000. "Scholarly Primitives: What Methods Do Humanities Researchers Have in Common, and How Might Our Tools Reflect This?" Presentation at "Humanities Computing: Formal Methods, Experimental Practice," King's College, London. 13 May 2000. johnunsworth.name/Kings.5-00/primitives.html.

Drawing Digital Scholarship into the Academic Conversation: The Exigency of *Early Modern Digital Review*

Randa El Khatib
University of Toronto Scarborough

Review articles are common in the humanities, including in the field of early modern studies. To date, they have primarily focused on more traditional scholarly outputs such as books, volumes, and articles, despite the increasing reliance on digital resources and tools for carrying out research. At the time of writing this chapter, the Renaissance Society of America's website (rsa.org/page/onlineresources) alone lists over one hundred digital projects relevant to early modern studies—many of which are large, grant-funded projects carried out by entire teams, spanning resources such as editions, databases, archives, 3D models, digital reconstructions, and other types. Nor is it an exhaustive list. Digital tools created specifically for the study of early modern works, or that can be applied to such, have facilitated many creative and insightful research applications and findings. Together, building and using digital resources for early modern studies is becoming increasingly common, although this has yet to be more formally acknowledged in the field through the systematic publication of reviews that demarcate academic trends, or within the university structure by counting toward tenure and promotion—despite the meticulous labor that digital projects require in terms of time, skills, and funding. This scarcity of formal reviews and evaluations of digital projects does not reflect the current scholarly landscape, which has prompted the launch of *Early Modern Digital Review* (jps.library.utoronto.ca/index.php/emdr; hereinafter *EMDR*), a refereed journal that is dedicated entirely to reviewing digital resources that study the early modern world.

This chapter constitutes three parts: a closer look at the place of digital resources in the humanities today and existing efforts to review them; an overview of *EMDR*, including journal structure, purpose, and publication details of regular and special issues; and a discussion of some of the challenges inherent in reviewing digital resources.

ISBN 978-1-64959-063-3 (paper) ISBN 978-1-64959-064-0 (pdf) ISBN 978-1-64959-065-7 (epub)
New Technologies in Medieval and Renaissance Studies 11 (2025) 55–73

Digital Resources in the Contemporary Scholarly Landscape

Reviews play an important part in the humanities, including literary studies; they reflect evolving scholarly trends, and highlight what scholarly circles value and how academic discourse changes over time. Casey Brienza reminds us of the importance of writing reviews as a public service to the field; in Brienza's own words, "They [reviews] are, rather, for the collective good; they are important voluntary inputs into the wider system of academic book publishing upon which the contemporary academic profession is symbiotically dependent" (2014, n.p.). Reviews not only benefit those scholars whose work is being reviewed, but as Brienza points out, they benefit publishers, readers, and reviewers as well—by making certain scholarship, those supporting it, and those reviewing it more visible. Laura Estill drew on Brienza's work in her Toronto Renaissance and Reformation Colloquium presentation, where she argued that reviews offer the opportunity to showcase recent publications in an emerging field, are part of the service we do for the profession, and are important because we are invested in our fields and want to be involved in a conversation about where they are and where they should go. To date, reviews have primarily focused on established scholarly outputs that are valued in the field: books, editions, collections of works, special editions, and sometimes even scholarly articles. As Estill points out, digital projects do not fit neatly into our models of publication; although they are appearing more frequently, they are still not the norm. As early as 2013, Michael Ullyot raised the question of the weight of digital resources with respect to other, more traditional scholarly outputs in his review essay of digital humanities projects in *Renaissance Quarterly*. He writes:

> With digital resources now firmly established as an essential scholarly research tool, the question remains: what status do we afford databases relative to other forms of publication, like editions or monographs? The question is pertinent not just to tenure and promotion decisions, as the MLA Committee on Information Technology recently advocated, but more fundamentally to the circulation and provocation of ideas. (937)

Jere Odell and Caitlin Pollock (2016) also highlight this issue by pointing out that the recurring problem in digital humanities is that projects do not readily align with the standards for tenure and promotion, especially since digital humanities projects come in so many forms and formats. Even today, the valid "scholarly" output for a digital project is publishing it alongside peer reviewed publications that discuss the project rather than reviewing the project itself, adding labor to an already arduous trajectory (2016, 1).

With digital resources ever more firmly moving toward the centre stage in scholarly research, surely we must give them this attention through refereed engagements, not only to point to their existence but also to demonstrate how they function and what type of research is possible through their means.

Several scholarly societies in the humanities have also been advocating for digital projects to be regarded as contributions to knowledge in themselves, to count toward tenure and promotion, and to be peer reviewed in their own right. The Modern Language Association published "Guidelines for Evaluating Work in Digital Humanities and Digital Media" in 2012 (MLA 2012) to encourage and guide the review of digital resources directly, rather than as supplementary materials. Numerous scholarly societies have published something similar, including the Renaissance Society of America (RSA 2020), the American Historical Association (AHA 2015), the Medieval Electronic Scholarly Alliance (MESA n.d.), and others. Taking it a step further, the Society for Classical Studies (SCS 2019)—the primary North American learned society for studying ancient Roman and Greek civilizations, languages, and literatures—motivated by the lack of post-publication peer review for digital resources and projects, has started reviewing digital resources and projects directly on their website. This initiative, led by the board's chair Chris Francese, was launched in 2019 and produces about one review per month.

Some existing journals have addressed the gap by dedicating sections to reviewing digital resources—such as *Manuscript Studies*, *Borrowers and Lenders: The Journal of Shakespeare and Appropriation*, *The Public Historian*, *Renaissance Quarterly*, *American Quarterly*, and others.

Similar trends can be seen with academic subject-specific websites. For example, the Digital History Project, led by Douglas Seefeldt and William G. Thomas (University of Nebraska-Lincoln), has a section titled "Project Reviews" (Seefeldt and Thomas 2006) wherein scholars can submit their project to be reviewed by graduate students. Overall, the website has about fifty reviews of digital history projects, as well as several "Tool Reviews" of digital tools that can be or have been applied to topics in digital history.

In addition, there have been several review journals dedicated entirely to reviewing digital projects and resources. An example is *RIDE* (ride.i-d-e.de), the *Review Journal of the Institute for Documentology and Scholarly Editing* (IDE), a digital editing and resources review journal that has published eight issues on digital editions, three on text collections, and one on tools and environments. The motivation for this review journal is the lack of formal reviews of digital editions, which marginalizes them from the scholarly conversation, and in effect prioritizes print editions. *RIDE*'s editors argue that many digital editions provide high quality texts, are often freely accessible, and make significant contributions to their fields, which is why they launched the open-access journal in 2014 ("Editorial"). *Reviews in Digital Humanities* (Guiliano and Risam 2019, reviewsindh.pubpub.org) is another peer reviewed journal of digital humanities scholarship and its outputs launched in 2019 by Jennifer Guiliano (Indiana University / Purdue University) and Roopika Risam (Salem State University). The journal features projects with a short description from project leads, alongside reviews by members of the digital humanities community. Additionally, the editors are compiling a registry of digital scholarship comprising projects that have been or are being reviewed. Both review journals were inspired by the lack of recognition of digital projects and their formal contributions to knowledge. *RIDE* focuses on digital editions and digital projects, in general; *Reviews in Digital Humanities* reviews all types of digital projects; whereas *EMDR* focuses specifically on digital projects at the intersection of digital humanities and early modern studies, or on digital tools that can be applied to early modern scholarship.

The last decade has seen attempts to more formally recognize and evaluate digital projects, both in terms of producing sound evaluations of resources to guide those in the field toward new avenues for research, and to more formally acknowledge the labor and intellectual contribution of digital resources in a format that could count toward tenure and promotion. To the knowledge of the editorial team, *EMDR* is the only current and ongoing systematic resource for evaluating digital resources in the field of early modern studies. In what follows, *EMDR* is explained in more detail.

Early Modern Digital Review

Released quarterly, *EMDR* is an online, open-access journal that publishes reviews of digital projects related to early modern society and culture. The journal is committed to productive evaluation of established digital resources, as well as recent digital tools and projects. Its publications are distributed online by the journal (jps.library.utoronto.ca/index.php/emdr, see Figure 2.1) under a Creative Commons 4.0 BY license, permitting reuse and reprint with authorial attribution. *EMDR* is also published by *Renaissance and Reformation / Renaissance et Réforme.* The journal released its first issue in the last quarter of 2018, appearing in *Renaissance and Reformation / Renaissance et Réforme*'s 41.4 issue. *EMDR* was co-founded by William R. Bowen (University of Toronto at Scarborough), Laura Estill (St. Francis Xavier University), and Ray Siemens (University of Victoria), and is currently edited by myself. For volumes 1–4, I served as *EMDR*'s managing editor.

Early Modern Digital Review (EMDR) is an online, open-access, and refereed journal publishing high-quality reviews of digital projects related to early modern society and culture. It is committed to productive evaluation of both established digital resources and recent tools and projects. Its publications are distributed online by the journal and its partners, and in print by *Renaissance and Reformation / Renaissance et Réforme*.

EMDR is supported by *Iter: Gateway to the Middle Ages and Renaissance*, *Renaissance and Reformation / Renaissance et Réforme*, and the Electronic Textual Cultures Laboratory (ETCL). It was founded by the Renaissance Knowledge Network (ReKN), which has received support from the Mellon Foundation, the Advanced Research Consortium, Iter, and ETCL.

Figure 2.1. ***Early Modern Digital Review*** **home page, jps.library.utoronto.ca/index.php/emdr.**

The journal came into fruition as a result of discussions held by the Mellon-funded Renaissance Knowledge Network (ReKN) research group based in the Electronic Textual Cultures Lab (ETCL), in partnership with Iter: Gateway to the Middle Ages and Renaissance. ReKN is concerned with augmenting digital scholarship in early modern studies through an integrative approach. Their primary work involves amalgamating digital projects that study the early modern world—projects that are often dispersed and siloed—and bringing them to the attention of the scholarly community. ReKN's mission also involves qualitative assurance and appropriate recognition and discovery of digital projects. The idea for *EMDR* was formed in this context, and the first few issues of the journal were dedicated to reviewing the projects that are listed on the ReKN website's (rekn.org/legacy) environmental scan of resources.

Since the parameters for reviewing a digital resource differ from those for a book or article, the editorial team has put together author guidelines specifically for reviewing digital resources (*EMDR* 2018). While many of our reviewers are engaged with digital scholarship, many also do not actively participate in digital humanities and instead bring their content expertise to the review. Whether reviews are written by digital humanities experts or not, all contributors are asked to comment on the content of the project, as well as on the technical elements, for a non-digital humanities audience. While early modernists and digital humanists are our target audiences, the journal is primarily interested in exposing new avenues for research and bringing to light digital projects for a non-expert audience so that they may engage with new scholarship and resources. Reviewers must take into account the project's scope and intended audience, as well as the quality of the content and academic rigour. They comment on the project's usefulness in scholarly work and the potential avenues for research that it makes possible, as well as the interface and overall usability of the project (*EMDR* 2018). Reviewers are also encouraged to comment on the use of standardized technologies, such as the platform or coding language that was used to build the project, as well as interoperability, metadata standards, and licensing information (*EMDR* 2018). Many reviews to date have also focused on the ease of locating information on the interface and on how intuitive the navigation is between different parts of the project.

The first two volumes of *EMDR* contained five to six reviews per issue, and since 2020 this number was increased to ten or more reviews per issue. The types of reviewed projects so far include databases, editions, archives, bibliographies, repositories for images, tools, digital reconstructions, and more. As a general rule, *EMDR* does not exclude any formats or types of projects as long as they intersect with early modern studies. Here are listed the regular issues published by *EMDR* so far:

EMDR 1.1:

- The Unabridged Acts and Monuments Online by Joseph Black
- Juxta by Matthew Evans Davis
- DigitalDonne: The Online Variorum, vol. 6 by John Lavagnino
- Bpi:1700: British Printed Images to 1700 by Meaghan Brown
- WordHoard by Michael Ullyot
- The Lost Plays Database by Paul Brown

EMDR 2.1:

- World Shakespeare Bibliography by Louise Geddes
- SIMILE Widgets: Timeline by Elizabeth Grumbach
- Database of Early English Playbooks by Joshua J. McEvilla
- Netlytic by Luis Meneses
- REED Online by Jesús Tronch Pérez

EMDR 2.2:

- Incunabula Short Title Catalogue: The International Database of 15th-century European Printing by Robert E. Bjork
- Lexicons of Early Modern English by Heather Froehlich
- Union First Line Index of English Verse, 13th – 19th Century by Beatrice Montedoro

- The Casebooks of Simon Forman and Richard Napier, 1596–1634: A Digital Edition by Barbara H. Traister
- brat Rapid Annotation Tool by Jon Saklofske
- Virtual Paul's Cross Project: A Digital Recreation of John Donne's Gunpowder Day Sermon by Brent Nelson

EMDR 3.1:

- Digital Cavendish: A Scholarly Collaborative by Megan Peiser
- Early Americas Digital Archive by Amy E. Earhart
- Richard Brome Online by Colm MacCrossan
- The Diplomatic Correspondence of Thomas Bodley, 1585–1597 by Gabriella Mazzon
- Reconstructing the Rose: 3D Computer Modelling Philip Henslowe's Playhouse by Joanne Tompkins (see Figure 2.2)
- Women's Early Modern Letters Online by Amy Bowles
- Fleuron: A Database of Eighteenth-Century Printers' Ornaments by Andie Silva
- Verse Miscellanies Online: Printed Poetry Collections of the Sixteenth and Seventeenth Centuries by Joshua M. Eckhardt
- The Recipes Project—Food, Magic, Art, Science, and Medicine by Jessica Marie Otis
- Shakespeare Census by Andrew Griffin

EMDR 3.3:

- Bess of Hardwick's Letters: The Complete Correspondence, c.1550–1608 by Leah Knight
- Henslowe-Alleyn Digitisation Project by Kara J. Northway
- Shakespeare and the Players by Michael John Goodman
- Records of Early English Drama: Patrons & Performances by Michael Poston and Stacey Redick
- The UK Reading Experience Database by Rebecca Munson
- Renaissance Cultural Crossroads Catalogue by Joshua Reid
- The Hartlib Papers by Evan Bourke
- Short Title Catalogue Flanders by Alexandra Hill
- Italian Paleography by Crystal Hall
- Arkyves by Rachel M. Carlisle

EMDR 4.1

- The Rulers of Venice, 1332–1524 by Giorgos Plakotos

- World of Dante by Brenda Deen Schildgen
- Records of London's Livery Companies Online: Apprentices and Freemen 1400–1900 (ROLLCO) by José Miguel Alcolado Carnicero
- Who Were the Nuns? A Prosopographical Study of the English Convents in Exile 1600–1800 by Jaime Goodrich
- The Poly-Olbion Project / The Children's Poly-Olbion by Sandra Logan
- Early Modern Female Book Ownership by Brenda M. Hosington
- Orlando: Women's Writing in the British Isles from the Beginnings to the Present by Baylee Staufenbiel
- Early Modern London Theatres (EMLoT) by Dibyajyoti Ghosh
- The London Stage Database by Renae Satterley
- AntConc (Version 3.5.8) / WordSmith Tools (Version 8) by Emily Louisa Smith

Figure 2.2. Reconstructing the Rose: 3D Computer Modelling Philip Henslowe's Playhouse, reviewed by Joanne Tompkins in *EMDR* 3.1.

EMDR aims to published two to three special issues per year, with ongoing regular issues that draw on a wide range of resources that study the early modern world. The first special issue, *EMDR* 2.3 (December 2019), was guest edited by Estill who foregrounds her introduction with the question "what online Shakespeare texts are the best?" (167), pointing to how the "best" texts will change depending on the audience and purpose, such as whether it is needed for easy access, editorial apparatus, a plain text to perform textual analysis with, and so on. To that end, the digital Shakespeare texts that appear in this issue identify the most useful texts for a variety of audiences and purposes within and without academia, such as texts for performance and performance studies, teaching Shakespeare in schools, and more. The special issue includes reviews of:

- Shakespeare Quartos Archive by Matteo Pangallo
- Internet Shakespeare Editions by Elizabeth Zeman Kolkovich
- Shakespeare's Words by Amanda Henrichs
- Open Source Shakespeare by Rachel Aanstad and Laura Estill (an interview-style review)
- MIT Shakespeare by Danielle Rosvally
- Folger Digital Texts by Molly Barger

The issue was motivated by the following questions about Shakespeare's editions: What benefits do certain editions have in comparison to others? What digital editions are best suited for what purposes: rehearsal? pedagogy? research?

The second special issue addresses the topic of "Women's Authorial Agency and Print Culture," and is guest edited by Marie-France Guénette (Université Laval); reviews in this special issue "address the impact of women's writing, authorial agency, and broader issues pertaining to print culture in early modern England and beyond" (Guénette 2019; 159). In particular, Guénette draws together reviews of digital resources that identify the various factors that can contribute to our understanding of women's authorial agency and print culture, many of which were previously inaccessible. Resources reviewed in this special issue are:

- Women Writers Online by Erin McCarthy (see Figure 2.3)
- Margaret Cavendish's Poems & Fancies: A Digital Critical Edition by Lara Dodds
- The Reception and Circulation of Early Modern Women's Writing by Guénette
- PLRE.Folger: Private Libraries in Renaissance England by Olga Stepanova
- Mapping the Republic of Letters by Catherine Medici
- The Recusant Print Network Project (Beta) by Eilish Gregory

The projects reviewed in this issue encompass a transnational network of interactions of early modern intellectuals by investigating literary reception, book ownership, and the circulation of ideas.

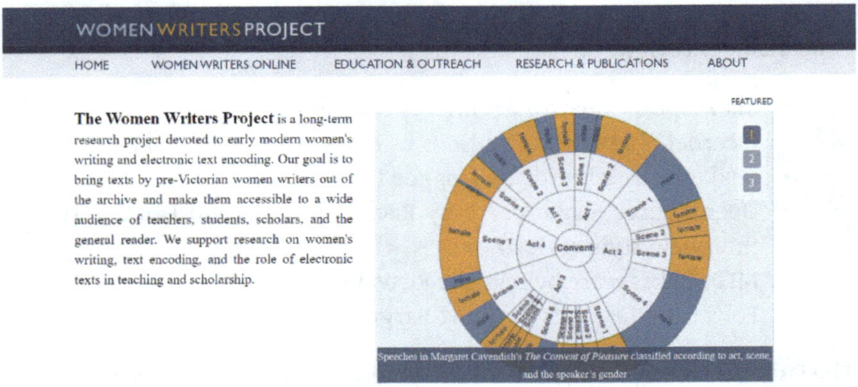

Figure 2.3. The Women Writers Project, reviewed by Erin McCarthy in *EMDR* 2.4.

In the special issue on Digital Paleography (*EMDR* 3.2), guest editor Isabella Magni (Rutgers University) argues that the field of paleography has flourished since the digital turn because of the improved methods for paleographic training that tools offer due to their interactive and visual nature, as well as the increased ease and access to interpreting scripts that they provide (Magni 2020). Magni defines paleography as the study of handwritten text and scripts, taking the text as a cultural product of its time and place. From this perspective, paleography then involves examining each document "in its original historical and cultural contexts by studying the relationship between the containers, their scripts, and their contents" (293). This issue includes a representative collection of digital paleography resources, including tools for understanding texts, increased access to newly digitized materials, pedagogical tools for paleographic training, crowdsourced transcription initiatives, new research paths, and others. These are:

- Thematic Pathways on the Web by Alberto Campagnolo
- Scribes of the Cairo Geniza by Gary A. Rendsburg
- Early Modern Manuscripts Online by Whitney Sperrazza
- Digital Analysis of Syriac Handwriting by David Calabro
- Spanish Paleography Tool by Susanna Allés-Torrent
- French Renaissance Paleography by Elizabeth K. Hebbard
- vHMML School by Christopher D. Fletcher
- DigiPal by Isabella Magni
- Thélème by Laura K. Morreale
- Scripto by Anthony E. Guidone

Hilaire Kallendorf's (Texas A&M University) special issue on early modern Spain (*EMDR* 3.4, 2021) brings together various resources studying the Spanish Renaissance, taking into account Spain's position as a world superpower at a time when, to various extents, Spain controlled many regions in Europe, Asia (the Philippines), and a large part of the Americas. Therefore, Kallendorf argues (2021), the study of the Spanish Renaissance ought to encompass Hispanic voices and cultures as well, recognizing these far-reaching, transnational networks. This special issue brings together a representative variety of digital resources that study the early modern Hispanic world, including databases, archives, websites, libraries, and other resources whose focus encompasses everything from artifacts to theatre. The reviews in this issue are:

- ASODAT: Bases de Datos Integradas del Teatro Clásico Espanol by Alex Samson
- Out of the Wings by Jesús Tronch
- Association for Hispanic Classical Theater by Edward Friedman
- Teatro Clásico Español (part of Biblioteca Virtual Miguel de Cervantes) by David Amelang
- TeatrEsco: Antiguo Teatro Escolar Hispánico by Branden Grayson
- Calderón en Red by Minni Sawney
- Pan-Hispanic Ballad Project by Jennifer Wollock
- CORDE: Corpus Diacrónico del Español by Dale Shuger
- BIDISO: Symbola in Biblioteca Digital Siglo de Oro by Amaranta Saguar Garcia
- The Baroque Art Project: A Data Collection of Hispanic Baroque Painters and Paintings from 1550 to 1850 by Elena Monzón
- Edición digital y estudio de la polémica gongorina by Marsha Collins
- The World of Don Quixote: Digital Collections for the Classroom by Damián Robles
- Bibliography of Cervantes Titles and Materials at the Folger by Kathryn Vomero Santos
- PARES: Portal de Archivos Españoles by Ted Bergman
- An ARTery of EMPIRE: Conquest, Commerce, Crisis, Culture and the Panamian Junction by Evan Haefeli
- DialNet by John Ardila
- IBIS: Base de datos del patrimonio bibliográfico de Patrimonio Nacional by Enrique Fernández
- Biblioteca Digital de Emblemática Hispánica by Pedro Germano Leal

In her special issue, Beatrice Bi-Qi Lei points to the upsurge of theatrical productions in digital environments since COVID-19 has shut the doors to in-person viewings in many parts of the world. This shift has resulted in unprecedented access to theatrical performances, where Lei notes that in just six weeks, the productions posted on the National Theatre's free YouTube channel in 2020 reached fifteen million views worldwide. The focus of the special issue is on digital projects that host contemporary Shakespeare performances and accompanying materials, categorized by geographical distribution. The first category reviews projects that host Shakespeare performances across national and linguistic borders, and has a truly global focus. The second category predominantly focuses on productions of Shakespeare in North America and Europe. The final category looks at national archives for performing and adapting Shakespeare in Canada, Spain, Taiwan, and the Philippines. Lei's issue highlights how the digital revolution in theatre has helped tear down some boundaries to access, bringing Shakespeare to more people across the world. The reviews in this issue are:

- MIT Global Shakespeares Video and Performance Archive by Zoltán Márkus
- Asian Shakespeare Intercultural Archive (A|S|I|A) by Mark Thornton Burnett
- Performance Shakespeare 2016 by Ricardo Rocha
- Reviewing Shakespeare by Marcus Cheng Chye Tan
- Canadian Adaptations of Shakespeare Project (CASP) by Kathryn Prince
- Shakrep: Shakespearean Performance in Spain by Isabel Guerrero
- Taiwan Shakespeare Database by Lia Wen-Ching Liang
- Shakespeare in the Philippines: A Digital Archive of Research and Performance by Michaela Atienza
- Globe Player by Ronan Paterson
- Stratfest@Home by Christie Carson
- Drama Online by Sheila T. Cavanagh

The spatial humanities special issue, guest edited by myself, points to how our contemporary world and the early modern period have both witnessed substantial leaps in the advancement of cartographic technology with the creation of Geographical Information Systems (GIS) in the former and modern cartography in the latter, as well as increased public access through the internet and the advancement in printing technologies that led to the proliferation of atlases and maps respectively, highlighting this intersection as a fruitful area of study encapsulated in the field of spatial humanities.

The ten reviews in this special issue look at projects that challenge top-down historical narratives of oppression communicated through maps; expand our knowledge of the past through rich, dynamic maps and by overlaying urban spaces with guided tours; and move beyond the confines of GIS to visualize imaginary cartography. Reviews also point to global cartographic advancements in the early modern period; approaches to making archival information more accessible through geographic visualisations; and technologies for social annotation of texts and images to continue expanding our knowledge of the early modern period. Projects reviewed are:

- The Down Survey of Ireland by Brendan Kane
- Selden Map of China by Annie Hongping Nie
- Hidden Florence by Clément Godbarge
- The Atlas of Early Printing by Katherine H. Hart
- Digging into Early Colonial Mexico: A Large-scale Computational Analysis of Historical Sources by Ernesto Priani Saiso
- Amerasia by Lauren Beck
- The Map of Early Modern London by David Joseph Wrisley
- The Grub Street Project by Marta Kvande
- Recogito by Ian Gregory

In his special issue on computational approaches to examining early modern texts, Darren Freebury-Jones highlights how current computational technologies for studying texts have led to research findings beyond the scope of what was possible in the pre-digital age. According to Freebury-Jones, computers' ability to count words and trace verbal repetition allows to determine patterns in texts that can objectively verify authorial self-repetition, similarities between several texts, and language patterns in entire corpora of works. The special issue consists of thirteen reviews of digital tools and computational approaches to manipulating textual data, as well as tutorials on how to use them, meant to demonstrate the usefulness of these techniques for research and to encourage early modernists to apply them to their own work. Resources reviewed in this special issue are:

- WCopyfind by Dennis McCarthy
- InfoRapid Search & Replace by Brian Vickers
- Literature Online (LION) by Mark Hulse
- Collocations and N-grams by Darren Freebury-Jones
- Sketch Engine by Mel Evans
- R. Stylo by Thomas Merriam
- Craig's Zeta by Ros Barber

- DocuScope by Marcus Dahl
- Editing Aphra Behn in the Digital Age by Joseph Rudman
- George Thomason's English Newsbooks by Yann Ryan
- Southwark Parishioners by Heloise Senechal
- Ancestry by Laurie Johnson
- The Programming Historian by Rachel White

Some forthcoming issues in *EMDR*'s fifth volume are on early modern Italy by Amanda Madden and on emblem studies by Mara R. Wade and Pedro Germano Leal.

EMDR, as mentioned earlier, is an open-access online journal that is also published with *Renaissance and Reformation / Renaissance et Réforme*. This is not unlike the way that review journal *Neo-Latin News* appears as a sub-section of the review journal *Seventeenth-Century News*, while being under separate editorial leadership. The driving motivation behind this arrangement is the need to shed a critical light on digital resources that contribute to scholarship and teaching in a way that will be recognized by the academic community and establishment. Much is accomplished simply by emulating the model of academic reviews by authors who can speak with authority. However, this publication model also takes into consideration intersecting strategies for publication and discoverability. Being published online leads to access through online distributors such as JSTOR (jstor.org) and Érudit (erudit.org/en/), and discoverability through well-formulated, well-circulated metadata. In addition, while *EMDR* open access publications extend the reach of the audience, publishing reviews with *R&R* helps put sites and tools on the radar for early modern scholars who might not be tuned into social media or other venues where they would typically hear about digital resources. By leveraging traditional and open-access pathways, *EMDR* is navigating issues of visibility and access while creating an output that is aligned with norms recognized by the academy, such as tenure committees.

Challenges Associated with Reviewing Digital Resources

Selecting works to review can be tricky for any journal. The editorial team needs to balance established works, trending ones, and emerging scholarship, while also taking into account numerous other details. Additional factors add complexity to selecting digital resources. Patrick Sahle highlights the source of these challenges by pointing to the difference between digital and print resources. According to Sahle, digital resources are usually published iteratively than finally; the moment of publication is often uncertain, since resources are released in several versions and are ever changing. Print publications, on the other hand, are final in their form and content. In this way, then, digital resources can often be conceived of as being under actual or potential expansion or change. At the same time, it is hard to tell when a project is being updated, so knowing whether the resource might change or cease to exist after the review is written can pose a challenge.

Another factor is that the lifespan of an online project, unlike print material, depends on continuous maintenance and funding, and often requires an active team to ensure its functionality. With larger, well-known, and well-funded resources, we can expect some permanence, although even then there is no guarantee of long-term stability. This applies even more to smaller or independent projects and tools. Since *EMDR*'s conception, we have run into a few issues related to the unstable nature of digital objects. For example, when Jon Saklofske was reviewing brat Rapid Annotation Tool, a key functionality of the tool stopped working in the middle of the revision process and was no longer customizable for an early modern example—which is a key criterion for the journal. What editorial guidelines can help address situations that are likely to arise when dealing with digital resources? At that time, we decided to move forward with the review and include an explanation for readers. Interestingly, in the later stages of the revision process, Saklofske noticed that the tool was functional again, like nothing had happened over those several months. This is not to single out a specific tool—anyone who has worked on developing a tool or who uses them often has probably encountered a similar situation. Rather, this is an example that can be widely generalized: digital resources are always in a sort of transitional state and need continuous and careful maintenance to continue functioning.

One challenge emerged when the editorial team considered commissioning a review of Scriptorium: Medieval and Early Modern Manuscripts Online, a resource that produced a digital archive of some twenty medieval and early modern manuscripts, focusing on digitized versions of commonplace books and miscellanies dating from 1400 to 1720. Scriptorium was built for researchers interested in the genres of the commonplace book and miscellany, and the digital objects contained within. At the time that we scoped it for review, it had been offline since 2016, and a target date for the restoration of the site had not been set. More recently, Scriptorium was integrated into the Cambridge Digital Library (cudl.lib.cam.ac.uk/collections/scriptorium) through which it now offers access to the project's manuscripts. While the project was restored, it prompted the editorial team to think specifically of the value that defunct digital projects hold for scholarly communities, and to consider dedicating a special issue for scholarly resources that now exist only in the Wayback Machine (web.archive.org). Maintenance and access could be elements of the discussion here, across reviews of such resources.

These considerations of a digital project's "life cycle" and quick turnover point to a dynamic and rapidly evolving field; for editors working in the digital medium, they also raise questions about how to set our guidelines (for more information on project longevity, see Hendriksen in this volume). At what stage do we review resources: in development? Completed, like the print model? Versioned, across several releases? Post-current, defunct as some can become? And how might we handle interim-state or in-development reviews, given that most online resources are always in some sort of in-development state? These questions are especially important, since the journal is not trying to unjustly evaluate any resources but rather to point to their potential for scholarship and contributions to knowledge when they are ready to be assessed in that way. With this understanding, we try to steer away from assigning resources that are visibly in-progress, outdated, or waiting for new funding, although, as mentioned earlier, it can often be difficult to assess the state of a project from its public-facing content. The non-final nature of digital projects also opens the door for a change in culture around scholarly communication. Willard McCarty (2008) alludes to this in reference to computing's trajectory "away from the monumental toward the conversational" (255). If digital objects are ever-changing, then the way we review them might be different from the way we review "final" works like print books and volumes: taking into account not the finality and totality of a work but rather its digital iterative development and change over time.

Conclusion

Reviewing digital resources challenges us to think more critically about digital objects and how they contribute to research carried out in early modern studies. As we continue to adjust our guidelines to improve strategies for selecting and evaluating digital resources, we must also build a deeper understanding of the "lifecycle" of a digital object and its various stages, not unlike the work carried out in book history and manuscript studies that addresses the production and materiality of our objects of study and corresponding scholarly outputs. However, despite the many unresolved challenges that digital resources pose, it is clear that even today they make up a central part of the scholarly landscape and enrich our knowledge of the early modern world. This role is becoming recognized with the increasing efforts to formally evaluate digital resources for scholars to integrate them in their research, while at the same time recognizing digital scholarship as valid intellectual work that can count toward tenure and promotion. *Early Modern Digital Review* demonstrates the importance of evaluating digital scholarship, a practice that will surely keep gaining momentum.

WORKS CITED

AHA (American Historical Association). 2015. "Guidelines for the Professional Evaluation of Digital Scholarship by Historians." historians.org/teaching-and-learning/digital-history-resources/evaluation-of-digital-scholarship-in-history/guidelines-for-the-professional-evaluation-of-digital-scholarship-by-historians.

American Quarterly. n.d. Accessed 6 June 2021. americanquarterly.org/submit/digital_projects.html.

Borrowers and Lenders: The Journal of Shakespeare and Appropriation. n.d. Accessed 6 June 2021. openjournals.libs.uga.edu/borrowers/index.

Brienza, Casey. 2014. "Why You (Yes, You!) Should Write Book Reviews." *Inside Higher Ed.* 5 December 2014. insidehighered.com/advice/2014/12/05/essay-argues-young-academics-should-write-book-reviews.

Davis, Matthew Evans. 2018. "Juxta." *Early Modern Digital Review* 1 (1): 181–85. doi.org/10.25547/emdr.v1i1.36.

Early Modern Digital Review. 2018. "Author Guidelines." emdr.itercommunity.org/index.php/emdr/about/submissions.

Estill, Laura. 2018. "Valuing Digital Scholarship: The Exigence of *Early Modern Digital Review.*" Conference presentation, "Toronto Renaissance and Reformation Colloquium," Toronto, ON, 26 October 2018.

———. 2019. "Introduction: Special Issue, Digital Shakespeare Texts." *Early Modern Digital Review* 2 (3): 167–70. doi.org/10.25547/emdr.v2i3.67.

Grumbach, Elizabeth. 2019. "SIMILE Widgets: Timeline." *Early Modern Digital Review* 2 (1): 333–36. doi.org/10.25547/emdr.v2i1.56.

Guénette, Marie-France. 2019. "Introduction: Special Issue, Women's Authorial Agency and Print Culture." *Early Modern Digital Review* 2 (4): 159–62. doi.org/10.25547/emdr.v2i4.78.

Guiliano, Jennifer, and Roopika Risam. 2019. *Reviews in Digital Humanities.* reviewsindh.pubpub.org/.

Kallendorf, Hilaire. 2021. "Introduction: Special Issue, Digital Resources for Studying the Spanish Renaissance." *Early Modern Digital Review* 3 (4): 219–23. doi.org/10.33137/rr.v43i4.36389.

Magni, Isabella. 2020. "Introduction: Special Issue, Digital Paleography." *Early Modern Digital Review* 3 (2): 293–97. doi.org/10.33137/rr.v43i2.34800.

Manuscript Studies. 2016. "Digital Project Review Information." mss.pennpress.org/author-and-reviewer-guidelines/digital-project-review-information.

———. n.d. "Manuscript Studies Digital Project Review Information." Accessed 6 June 2021. mss.pennpress.org/author-and-reviewer-guidelines/digital-project-review-information.

McCarty, Willard. 2008. "What's Going On?" *Literary and Linguistic Computing* 23 (3): 253–61. doi.org/10.1093/llc/fqn014.

Medieval Electronic Scholarly Alliance. 2013. "Peer Review." mesa-medieval.org/.

MESA (Medieval Electronic Scholarly Alliance). n.d. Accessed 6 June 2021. mesa-medieval.org/about/peer-review.

MLA (Modern Language Association). 2012. "Guidelines for Evaluating Work in Digital Humanities and Digital Media." mla.org/About-Us/Governance/Committees/Committee-Listings/Professional-Issues/Committee-on-Information-Technology/Guidelines-for-Evaluating-Work-in-Digital-Humanities-and-Digital-Media.

Neo-Latin News. n.d. oaktrust.library.tamu.edu/handle/1969.1/158483.

Odell, Jere, and Caitlin Pollock. 2016. "Open Peer Review for Digital Humanities Projects: A Modest Proposal." Conference Presentation, THATCamp Indiana 2016. doi.org/10.7912/C2NC7S.

The Public Historian. n.d. Accessed 6 June 2021. online.ucpress.edu/tph.

Renaissance and Reformation / Renaissance et Réforme. n.d. Accessed 6 June 2021. jps.library.utoronto.ca/index.php/renref.

Renaissance Quarterly. n.d. Accessed 6 June 2021. cambridge.org/core/journals/renaissance-quarterly.

RIDE. Review Journal of the Institute for Documentology and Scholarly Editing. 2008. Institute for Documentology and Editing. ride.i-d-e.de/.

RSA (Renaissance Society of America). 2020. "RSA Best Practices for Digital Scholarship 2020." rsa.org/page/bestpracticesdigitalscholarship.

Sahle, Partick. 2016. "What Is a Scholarly Digital Edition." In *Digital Scholarly Editing: Theories and Practices*, edited by Matthew James Driscoll and Elena Pierazzo, 19–40. Cambridge, UK: Open Book Publishers. doi.org/10.11647/OBP.0095.

Saklofske, Jon. 2019. "brat Rapid Annotation Tool." *Early Modern Digital Review* 2(2): 180–89. doi.org/10.25547/emdr.v2i2.64.

Scriptorium: Medieval and Early Modern Manuscripts Online. 2006. Cambridge University Library. cudl.lib.cam.ac.uk/collections/scriptorium.

Seefeldt, Douglas, and William G. Thomas. 2006. "Project Reviews." Digital History Project. digitalhistory.unl.edu/p-reviews.php.

Seventeenth-Century News. n.d. oaktrust.library.tamu.edu/handle/1969.1/94990.

SCS (Society for Classical Studies). 2019. "SCS Digital Project Review Guidelines." classicalstudies.org/publications-and-research/scs-digital-project-review-guidelines.

Ullyot, Michael. 2013. "Review Essay: Digital Humanities Projects." *Renaissance Quarterly* 66 (3): 937–47.

———. 2018. "WordHoard." *Early Modern Digital Review* 1 (1): 169–74. doi.org/10.25547/emdr.v1i1.40.

Considering Place, Publics, and the Present: Creating Digital Spaces for Medieval and Early Modern Scholars

Elizabeth Grumbach
Arizona State University

In January 2019, the now former president of the United States renewed his demand for a border wall between the US and Mexico in an address from the Oval Office. While I will not repeat any of his speech (or tweets) here, I will quote the words of medieval and early modern scholars who responded. These scholars took to online platforms and Twitter because journalists, Democrats, and the current administration were using the medieval city as a metaphor for this demand. First used by Democrats and journalists as an insult, and then embraced by the president as a metaphor for military strength and intelligence, public writing by scholars immediately revealed the mischaracterization of medieval borders (Milbank 2019). Matthew Gabriele pointed out that not only were medieval walls "poor tools of defense," but they "had more to do with reassuring those who lived inside them than with dividing self from other" (2019). Jacqueline Jung clarified on Twitter that "medieval city walls were not built to separate people of diff[erent] ethnic or national identities. Gates were open during the day and closed at night" (2019). David M. Perry firmly stated that the medieval period was "not simple, isolated, pure[,] or homogenous," and this mischaracterization of the historical facts of medieval cities, territories, and walls proves how "desperately we need more historical literacy" (2019). There are many reasons why writing for a public audience, and the work of public humanities, seem urgent in this current historical moment, but no call to this work is stronger than the desire to reach an audience that "desperately" needs the humanities to understand our current moment. Illuminating the realities of medieval cities, borders, and walls throws into productive contrast the premodern world, revealing to publics (in this case, Twitter followers and the audiences reached by the *Washington Post* and CNN online) a detailed sketch of the past that can help us comprehend our present moment to then imagine alternative and more humane futures.[1]

[1] It is vital to note that in the years since the first draft of this essay was presented, in April 2019, the world has experienced the resurgence of the movement for Black lives

ISBN 978-1-64959-063-3 (paper) ISBN 978-1-64959-064-0 (pdf) ISBN 978-1-64959-065-7 (epub)
New Technologies in Medieval and Renaissance Studies 11 (2025) 75–98

This contribution is an exercise in imagining a future for premodern studies as an intentionally feminist, anti-racist, and radically inclusive space built on the principles of public humanities. For, as Lauren F. Klein and Matthew K. Gold express in the introduction to *Debates in the Digital Humanities 2019*, digital humanities is/are/can be united in working towards a more just future:

> By enabling communication across communities and networks, by creating platforms that amplify the voices of those most in need of being heard, by pursuing projects that perform the work of recovery and resistance, and by undertaking research that intervenes in the areas of data surveillance and privacy, the "artist-theorists, programming humanists, activist-scholars, theoretical archivists, [and] critical race coders" whom Tara McPherson, writing in the first volume of *Debates in the Digital Humanities,* called into being, have now been united with their task. (Klein and Gold 2019)

My intention is to journey through models, methods, and examples from digital public humanities, existing collaborative collectives and digital communities, and foundational critical race scholarship in order to propose ways of structuring ethical principles and values for a medieval and early modern community online that builds on the knowledge and social infrastructure of Iter.

This conversation, this future-building exercise, would not be possible without the foundations that Iter has constructed over the past twenty-five years. As Michael Ullyot said in his presentation at RSA 2019, "[t]he story of Iter is a story of striving: striving to describe and catalogue the state of knowledge about the middle ages and the Renaissance, that era and those places that compel our attention" (2019). Founded in 1995 and incorporated in 1997, Iter has been a cornerstone of premodern research, and the continued development of Iter Community (formerly Iter Commons) directly addresses the need for a digital space to explore and experiment with new forms of knowledge production online.[2] As we look toward the twenty-fifth anniversary of Iter, this contribution focuses on how we may be able to build inclusive digital communities within the existing structure of Iter Community. The below will

and Black Lives Matter and undergone a pandemic that has rocked the foundation of academia. As the world heads into the final months of 2020, mutual aid networks, bailout funds, and activist organization structures have given us new ways to think about structuring anti-racist and feminist work, and the exercise outlined in this essay fits in parallel to that work.

[2] For a chronological history of Iter, see "Our History," itergateway.org/our-history/.

not, however, be full of technical recommendations, but instead explorations of social and outward-facing methodologies.

The below would also not be possible without my experiences working for the Nexus Digital Research Co-op at Arizona State University as a project manager from 2017 to 2018, during which I had the opportunity to think through the challenges of cooperative work structures in a capitalistic and academic setting with former Nexus director Jacqueline Wernimont and graduate student researcher Nikki Stevens. In addition, and integral to my understanding of networked collaboration and digital community building, my time spent as the director of digital content and special programs for the Humanities, Arts, Science, and Technology Alliance and Collaboratory (HASTAC)[3] deepened my understanding and appreciation of collaborative structures based on mutual care. Throughout the sections below, I will heavily and intentionally cite colleagues and scholars who have influenced my understanding of community in the digital humanities.

Why Public Humanities?

For the purposes of this experimental exercise in imagining inclusive futures, I will define public humanities as any engagement—digital or otherwise—with a reflection on the importance of histories, literatures, cultures, and all humanities disciplines to our current historical moment. For a history of public humanities as a discipline, Robin Schroeder's "What is Public Humanities?" traces the movement in academia from the 1970s to the present (Schroeder 2017). Schroeder also references the Wikipedia definition, which was written and revised by students and faculty from Brown University's MA program in Public Humanities:

> Public humanities is the work of engaging diverse publics in reflecting on heritage, traditions, and history, and the relevance of the humanities to the current conditions of civic and cultural life. Workers within the public humanities endeavor to create physical and virtual spaces where the public can engage in conversation, learning and reflection about issues and ideas ("Public humanities").

---

[3] The HASTAC team that I had the honor of collaborating with included HASTAC founding director, Cathy Davidson, HASTAC director of programs and administration, Katina Rogers, HASTAC scholars director, Kalle Westerling, HASTAC co-director (ASU) Jacqueline Wernimont, and HASTAC technical assistant and graduate student worker, Dharmin Dholiya.

This purposefully unconstrained definition of public humanities highlights conversation with and co-learning alongside diverse publics as a method of revealing connections between the past and the present. Jesse Stommel similarly defines this field as work that "starts with humans, not technologies or tools" and produces "a conversation, one that engages a broad public while blurring the distinction between research, teaching, service, and outreach" (2015). These two scholars outline two basic tenants of public humanities work, digital or otherwise: 1) an emphasis on conversation and process, and 2) a specific method of engagement that blurs existing distinctions between research, pedagogy, and service.

This blurring of boundaries may sound familiar to digital humanists, as project management, networked collaboration, pedagogy, and mentorship are large parts of a DH workday. However, public humanities intentionally faces outward at the moment of project inception *and* culmination, and therefore reflects inward before it aims outside the academy. This slightly different method of collaboration productively disturbs our hierarchical, neoliberal understandings of labor and expertise in the academy—publics are active collaborators and audiences. Subsequently, digital public humanities projects take many forms: podcasts (*Remixing the Humanities*), participatory digital editions (Siemens et al. in this volume), Wikipedia edit-a-thons (Evans, Mandiberg, Mabey, and Ptak), mobile makerspaces (Martin, Compton, and Hunt 2017), public and crowdsourced resources for scholars,[4] digital projects that explore deep time (Heng and Noakes n.d.), and experimental projects that examine our historical past to reveal a critical issue in our present (Stevens and Wernimont 2018).

---

[4] For examples of public and/or crowdsourced resources, and in the hopes that these inspire expanded efforts in open resource sharing for premodern digital studies, see:

a. ReKN Bibliography, accessed 14 August 2019, rekn.itercommunity.org.
b. Uprooting Whiteness [Supremacy and Domination] – Resources, accessed 14 August 2019, docs.google.com/document/d/1F8v8BQOcN3kODBxntkPS7snNjIuV1Cz5QDLEeq5XPa8/edit.
c. The Black Panther Syllabus, accessed 5 June 2021, https://msinc.medium.com/the-black-panther-syllabus-the-cultural-film-and-moment-from-yesterdays-today-s-and-tomorrow-s-25845314a6db.
d. US Latinx and Southwestern Digital Humanities Projects, accessed 14 August 2019, docs.google.com/spreadsheets/d/1wtOeETfLvCv4ZYKxj0xiB6mqh3GfFqvRv8U9LVr_OkM/htmlview.
e. Black Digital Humanities Projects & Resources, accessed 14 August 2019, docs.google.com/document/d/1rZwucjyAAR7QiEZl238_hhRPXo5-UKXt2_KCrwPZkiQ/edit?usp=sharing.

As I turn to imagining an inclusive vision for premodern studies, it seems apt to use Wendy F. Hsu's definition of public humanities as "a process, not a product" that "include[s] the public at earlier phases of our work" as an integral focal point of our potential new digital space (2016). The realignment of our sightlines outward enables us to better engage with the publics that our humanities discipline can, or should, encounter. Most importantly for the future-building exercise below, if we construct digital communities on the principles of public humanities work, this privileges the human, the conversation, and the process over the individual, the archive as abstract entity, or the end product. Any digital community that follows the principles of public humanities in effect values collective goals and healthy communication.

Collaboration, Commons, Communities

In the context of humanities research and collaboration online, where digital spaces like Humanities Commons exist as opportunities for networking and sharing work, where do possibility, play, and inclusion fit into the mission statement? Examining spaces where collaboration was either necessary for the success of a project or purposefully placed as a central tenet of a community may reveal foundational principles for this exercise in imagining communities.

As a project manager for the Early Modern OCR Project (EMOP, 2012–15), I consider one of our major successes to have been creating a collaborative communication network of scholars working on the early modern optical character recognition (OCR) problem. Funded by the Andrew W. Mellon Foundation, EMOP has as its goal to provide open source workflow solutions to the problem of inaccurate machine-generated text from early modern printed documents. In a write-up of our Digital Humanities 2014 conference presentation, the project team observed that agile development strategies and sustained communication were necessary to create effective large project teams (Mandell et al. 2015). Therefore, community-building and attention to the labor inherent in that work were necessary for the success of the project. What does intentional community building and care look like within an online scholarly community, however, and how can collaboration and intentional community-building be fostered simultaneously (and ethically) in the context of producing humanities research?

One possible model is the Humanities, Arts, Science, and Technology Alliance and Collaboratory (HASTAC). HASTAC provides an open digital platform for a community of interdisciplinary scholars interested in "changing the way we teach and learn" and is also founded on the principles of public scholarship, interdisciplinary collaboration, and a commitment to engage with users and user data ethically.[5] These principles, and the labor, time, and funding commitments of HASTAC staff and leadership, foster a community in which scholars of all ranks can contribute public scholarship individually or in collaborative groups. Importantly, the HASTAC community also holds an annual conference that provides scholars with an opportunity to network in-person and share their scholarship. HASTAC grew from a need to share work, collaborate, and connect to others, and the current leadership at CUNY and Dartmouth sustains a digital space where collaboration and organic community engagement and care co-exist and align.

A second possible model for a digital collaborative community is Digital Frontiers, which also grew from a shared mission: to bring together the makers and users of digital resources in order to imagine better futures for the field of digital humanities. Founded as an annual conference in 2012, Digital Frontiers is guided by the principles of interdisciplinarity and inclusivity, and by the explicit intention to foster connections. In the initial years of the conference, attendance was for the most part from the southern United States, but in recent years it has expanded exponentially. Digital Frontiers 2019: Tear Down the Walls included presenters from across North America and from forty-three different institutions.[6] The community generates more than an annual conference, however. Because of the networks formed by the event, and because of the leadership of Spencer Keralis, Digital Frontiers (now a non-profit organization where I serve on the board of directors) supports inclusive satellite events and symposia such as "Realizing Resistance: An Interdisciplinary Conference on Star Wars, Episodes VII, VIII & IX."[7] Digital Frontiers commits to not only providing physical spaces for learning and sharing scholarship, but structuring digital spaces where this work happens, as well. The open access journal *Research and Destroy* is the latest experiment in bringing the collaborative, inclusive, and social justice-oriented mission of Digital Frontiers into an online community space; the board intends to organize online community book launches (mostly through Twitter), and Digital Frontiers online workshops will begin streaming in the next year.

[5] To learn more about the ongoing mission of HASTAC, see "About HASTAC," accessed 30 August, 2019, hastac.org/about-hastac.

[6] An interactive map of institutions participating in Digital Frontiers 2019, along with information about the mission of the annual conference and organization, can be found at digital-frontiers.org/df2019 (accessed 30 August 2019).

[7] For more on Realizing Resistance, see digital-frontiers.org/past-events/resistance (accessed 2 September 2019).

Similar to the structure of HASTAC, Digital Frontiers continues to provide spaces for connection and scholarly work because of the time and labor commitment of its leadership and partner institutions, all of whom are detailed explicitly on the organization's website (Digital Frontiers, "Governance and Organization").

Perhaps most important for this experiment in imagining spaces where public humanities scholarship thrives online is *Eidolon*, an online journal and platform dedicated to public, accessible "writing about the Classics that isn't formal scholarship" (Zuckerberg, "About *EIDOLON*"). Dedicated to promoting a digital space for "classics without fragility," the mission statement articulates that *Eidolon* has as its aim to make the classics "political and personal, feminist and fun" ("*Eidolon*'s Mission Statement"). Like Digital Frontiers and unlike HASTAC, *Eidolon* is supported by an educational non-profit organization, The Paideia Institute. The journal runs on the Medium open publication platform, a platform that also hosts *The Sundial*, a new, open access publication of the Arizona Center for Medieval and Renaissance Studies (ACMRS).[8] Importantly, both *Eidolon* and *The Sundial* are not part of the Medium partner program, and therefore readers can access articles for free without hitting a paywall. *Eidolon*, *The Sundial*, and *Research and Destroy* reflect some of the basic tenets of digital public humanities, among them: 1) scholarship should be accessible to not only scholars, but larger publics, 2) scholarship should be embedded within our current historical moment, 3) the current structure of academic peer review is restrictive and prone to gate-keeping, and, finally, 4) there is a need for explicitly feminist and inclusive spaces for public scholarship.

These online projects, publications, and community platforms have heavily influenced the Digital Humanities Initiative at Arizona State University, which I currently lead. Housed in the Institute for Humanities Research (IHR) at ASU, the DH Initiative runs on the power of collaboration and mutual care by necessity. All initiatives run out of the IHR have a program lead, and like me, these program leads are not dedicated staff; we have other positions within the university. The DH Initiative receives some funding and staff support from the IHR, but relies on the digital humanities community at ASU to create and generate meaningful work. This necessitates a culture of coworking and collaborative thinking, and it also requires that we have a structure for supporting both projects and each other.

---

[8] See "The Sundial (ACMRS)," accessed 31 August 2019, medium.com/the-sundial-acmrs.

The Digital Humanities Initiative at ASU relies on consultations, connections, and creating space for the community to drive thematic project development. As program lead, I designed a tiered consultation structure (consultation, collaboration, staff time buyout) that would allow faculty, staff, and students to talk through project design, development, and challenges.[9] The Initiative also funds and organizes several DH meet-ups every semester, and these meet-ups (not meetings) range from reading groups to working groups to no-agenda coffee hours. Scholars attending regular meet-ups drive the structure and focus of the semester's theme, collaborative project, or reading schedule. This allows the Initiative to reflect, not drive, the goals and professional needs of ASU's digital humanities community. Our Initiative also partners with projects and units at ASU to address emerging humanities concerns; for example, a partnership with Connected Academics and the Graduate College emerged when several graduate students expressed an interest in forming a Digital Humanities and Pedagogy workshop.[10]

With the above said, my goal as program lead for the Initiative is to create a sustainable structure for digital humanities at ASU that does not rely on a dedicated staff member. By using language that differentiates consultation from collaboration, enabling the flexible structure of meet-ups, and building networks of shared interest and need among humanities units at ASU, I intend to foster a community with the tools and connections needed to sustain itself without a lone central figure at the center. Otherwise, this initiative

[9] Consultation structure details are forthcoming on an upcoming redesign of the IHR website, ihr.asu.edu. The first tier is consultation, in which I schedule an hour every two to six months with scholars developing digital projects to talk through challenges or experiment with potential digital platforms; there are currently six active scholars at this tier. The second tier is collaboration, in which I become an active participant on the project by scheduling regular (no more than one per month) working meetings with a project team. The third tier is partnership, in which either I or the Institute for Humanities Research are named in a successful grant proposal and a Memorandum of Understanding is written to ensure credit, scope, and responsibilities of all parties. Since its activation at the IHR, this structured support has necessitated that project leaders or teams think through questions of labor, credit, and project development timelines.

[10] This workshop, which was called the First Institute on Digital Humanities and Pedagogy at ASU, brought in two outside scholars, Danica Savonick and Whitney Sperrazza, to co-lead with ASU staff and graduate students a three-day event that included ASU faculty and staff, community college faculty from the Phoenix area, and graduate students.

replicates the scarcity and power structures that plague collaboration in the digital humanities and that, as Griffin and Hayler state when discussing the neoliberal forces that silence collaborative efforts, "denies the 'co' of collaboration and, due to its competitive underscoring, reinforces pre-existing inequalities between different kinds of collaborators" (2018). The intentional focus on conversation, play, and collective need moves our community away from neoliberal forces that reinforce what would otherwise be transactional, capitalist, and exploitative. Laying similar foundations and utilizing the methods and values of the above existing communities for an inclusive medieval and early modern digital community could possibly overcome the challenges of sustainability and labor exploitation.

Making Space

When I first presented a version of this paper at the 2019 Renaissance Society of America conference, Ray Siemens asked a question that fueled multiple drafts of this work. With apologies to Siemens for paraphrasing, that question was: If everything is influenced by late-stage capitalism, how do we work against or outside of the hierarchies and structures of power that reinforce inequality/inequity?

I still unfortunately have no workable or tested answer to this question, but I propose that experimenting with methods of fostering sustainable inclusivity in addition to making central the principles of public humanities may reveal the answer. By placing the human and the public at the center of academic work, these final sections will imagine guiding principles for and a vision of an inclusive, ethical, feminist, and anti-racist space for premodern studies online.

I say this with a caveat: *these spaces already exist for scholars*. There is a battle over the Middle Ages and the classics raging online, and that work has necessitated not only communities of support and mutual care to arise, but also a new wave of open, critical scholarship that connects our current political moment with the misappropriation of classical and medieval texts and images (Morse 2018; Zuckerberg 2018; Kim 2017; Bond 2017). The need for active and supportive scholarly communities in our discipline has resulted in the formation of the ACMRS RaceB4Race conference series, the professional organization Medievalists of Color,[11] the amazing work of every single scholar involved in the #ShakeRace (Shakespeare and Race) movement, and

[11] See "On Race and Medieval Studies," 2017, accessed 2 September 2019, medievalistsofcolor.com/statements/on-race-and-medieval-studies/.

public writing projects such as *Eidolon*. Since the initial drafting of this chapter, these communities have activated several calls to action and conversations. While the final sections of this chapter will focus on possible guiding principles for a premodern digital humanities environment, I would highly recommend pausing here to engage with the work of these communities, in particular Kimberley Anne Coles, Kim F. Hall, and Ayanna Thompson's "BlacKKKShakespearean: A Call to Action for Medieval and Early Modern Studies" in *Profession* (2019), the Shakespeare Association of America's plenary panel session "Looking Forward: New Directions in Early Modern Race Studies" organized by Peter Erickson and chaired by Ayanna Thompson (2019), and the letter from the RaceB4Race Executive Board: "It's Time to End the Publishing Gatekeeping!" (2020).

This moment, this political and politicized moment we live in, calls upon academics to provide historical literacy, but more importantly calls upon us to boost the voices of our colleagues who have already taken up these issues. This moment also demands that we take action, and that I, as a white woman working in academia, intentionally ensure these existing communities continue to thrive by relentlessly *making space for them.*

In the first volume of *Debates in the Digital Humanities*, Lisa Spiro's "Why We Fight" outlined a list of potential core values for the digital humanities community. Like Spiro, I seek with the below articulation of inclusive methods, values, and resources to begin discussion and foster action. Because "articulating a set of values for a community should be done by the community," I invite and anticipate further discussion (Spiro 2012). Unlike "Why We Fight," which seeks to define values for an expansive digital humanities community, the below will explore how to design medieval and early modern digital communities around methods of making space.

Amplification of Diverse Voices: Decolonization and Black Feminist Thought

An intentionally ethical and inclusive community must address the colonial past and present to actively work towards decolonization.[12] Roopika Risam advises that "when invoking the relationship between decolonization and digital humanities—the central question is not how digital humanities itself could be decolonized but how digital humanities has contributed to the epistemic violence of colonialism and neo-colonialism" (2018). In practice, this

[12] The scholarly efforts and advocacy of Global Outlook—DH (globaloutlookdh.org), #TransformDH (transformdh.org), #DHPoco (dhpoco.org)—are central to this effort.

means ensuring that our exercise in imagining a digital community must attend to difference and must not privilege dominant narratives of history, communication, or knowledge systems. As stated by Babalola Titilola Aiyegbusi, in order to include the voices of those traditionally excluded, "DHers need to be aware of the economic and social milieu of other countries, and second, they need to be sensitive to the differences in orientation and culture" (2018).[13] Perhaps the call here is to expand the work started by the Global Middle Ages project, which aims to "to see the [medieval] world whole in a large swathe of time," by continuing to enrich existing digital materials with the narratives of those too often excluded from our archives and scholarship.

The creation of any actively feminist and anti-racist scholarly space must first fully recognize and internalize the historical silencing of non-white perspectives that pervades academia. In the second edition of *Black Feminist Thought*, Patricia Collins observes that not only has the exclusion of Black women from positions of power in academia "led to the elevation of elite White male ideas and interests" but that white feminist scholars have contributed to the suppression of Black feminist thought by assuming white women's perspective to be universal (1999). Collins also warns that other patterns of suppression pervade academia, specifically the shallow support for diversity that takes no action and the intentional incorporation, transformation, and subsequent depoliticization of Black feminist ideas. Ensuring that inclusion moves beyond lip service and into action means acknowledging the silencing of non-white perspectives in academia *and* actively working against silencing forces.

What does that look like in practice for a digital community? The Cite Black Women movement stands as one example; the movement's Five Guiding Principles acknowledge both material and personal methods of anti-racist academic practice:

> 1) Read Black women's work.
> 2) Integrate Black women into the CORE of your syllabus (in life & in the classroom).
> 3) Acknowledge Black women's intellectual production.
> 4) Make space for Black women to speak.
> 5) Give Black women the space and time to breathe ("Cite Black Women").

---

[13] Aiyegbusi's work here specifically focuses on African digital humanities, but his recommendation seems applicable to a wide-range of potential collaborations and conversations in a global context.

Working towards integrating active anti-racist practice into a community relies on professional and personal engagements. There is no room for lip service to diversity and inclusion in the above guiding principles. The call is to #CiteBlackWomen, but also to read Black women's work, incorporate that work into knowledge products and pedagogy, and, importantly, make space for Black women to thrive in your discipline, in your department, and in your office.

Support the Professional; Support the Personal

The amplification of diverse voices, like any engagement with digital public humanities, requires communication structures that actively build community and structures of support. An inclusive digital community of scholars must pay close attention to project management, labor, and appropriate credit, but also make room for the personal. Similar to the above fifth principle of the Cite Black Women movement, we need methods of prioritizing the personal in our work, and this prioritization only becomes more important in a distributed, virtual, and perhaps global environment.

This may look like slowing down our process of project development to attend to the personal, individual, and professional needs of our colleagues, or it may look like speeding up to address urgent calls for support or activism. We must act responsively not just as agile developers of products, but as colleagues and coworkers. Above all, community building should move at the pace of community members. adrienne maree brown's "Principles of Emergent Strategy," written for community organizers of all human systems, especially social justice movements, may guide us in fusing together a cohesive professional and personal practice in our imagined digital community:

> Small is good, small is all. (Be like water.)
> There is always enough time for the right work.
> There is a conversation in the room that only these people at this moment can have. Find it.
> Never a failure, always a lesson.
> Trust the People. (If you trust the people, they become trustworthy.)
> Move at the speed of trust. Focus on critical connections more than critical mass—build the resilience by building the relationships.
> Less prep, more presence.
> What you pay attention to grows. (brown 2017, p. 41–2)

Emergent strategy, or "the way complex systems and patterns arise out of a multiplicity of relatively simple interactions," and public humanities have similar principles: people, processes, and connections should come first, though the final product remains important (brown 2017, p. 13).

The principles of emergence live in Torn Apart / Separados, a project that began with a six-day intensive collaboration between scholars to document the effect of the 2018 United States "Zero Tolerance Policy" for asylum seekers at all US Ports of Entry.[14] This critical intervention and rapid DH work is reminiscent of the response of scholars to the renewed demand for a US-Mexico border wall in late 2018. Yet, the process that led to the digital product and the production of new knowledge on this humanitarian crisis differ. In the words of emergence, this project was made possible by the "critical connections" formed by networks of scholars working on borderlands and social justice. Even though the scholars that organized, designed, and contributed to this project are at various stages of their career, not co-located in one physical space, and may not have digital humanities work written into their position descriptions, there is, as brown states, "always enough time for the right work" (2017, p. 41).

With that said, the model of rapid prototyping and "process-based scholarship" that Torn Apart / Separados employs does not map onto all collaborative community building goals or needs. At the 2019 Association for Computing in the Humanities (ACH) conference, Kristen Mapes observed that an emergent theme for the conference was "a call for slow DH, for spending time with archives and data and material and the people within them" (2019).[15] If we move at the "speed of trust," then the needs of the community, of our colleagues, and of our current moment in space and time will dictate the pace of development.

If, in our future medieval and early modern digital community, we decide together to value both the professional and the personal, the needs and realities of the individual and the collective, we can build, as Bethany Nowviskie imagines, "platforms that promote an understanding of the temporal vulnerability of the individual person or object; that more beautifully express the relationship of parts; [. . .] and that instill, by cultivating depth of feeling in their users, an ethic of care" that responds to the challenges of an uncertain academic landscape and global future (2019). We have seen this responsiveness in our professional organizations, as conferences such as the ACH and Digital

[14] See "Torn Apart / Separados," accessed 30 August 2019, xpmethod.plaintext.in/torn-apart/credits.html.

[15] For a full sense of what panels and conversations prompted this tweet, see the thread on Twitter: twitter.com/kmapesy/status/1154395656464818176.

Frontiers adopt detailed statements of inclusion and diversity, but the construction of a digital community of scholars that can foster radical inclusiveness depends upon a shared commitment to responsiveness, trust, and care.[16]

Where (and How) Do We Go from Here?

As we look back on the work Iter has done for premodern studies, and as we move into an era of digital humanities that thinks critically about what digital scholarship can and should look like, it now seems an apt time to imagine together a future community that works towards ethical methods of structuring DH work and the cultivation of inclusivity and care.

That future may look like an expansion of the work that Iter community already undertakes; it may look like the open and collaborative community of scholars that HASTAC supports; it may look like an online version of the Digital Humanities Initiative at Arizona State University; or it could look like *Eidolon*, an experiment in public-facing, explicitly feminist scholarship for our field.

Whatever form this nebulous future community takes, I will propose below several first steps that I hope take form in the near future. Below this conclusion is a reading and resource list for a proposed reading group. This list contains work immediately relevant to the building of our inclusive community, including the work of feminist scholars, critical race theorists, and medieval and early modern scholars of color. Structuring a regular reading group that pairs these readings with the extensive bibliography compiled by the Renaissance Knowledge Network will put premodern digital scholarly projects in conversation with explicitly feminist, anti-racist methodologies ("ReKN Bibliography").

My second, and related, proposal is the creation of a digital presence on Iter Community dedicated to exploring what alternative models for digital communities look like for our field. Based on the models of FemTechNet (a network of scholars working at the borders of science, technology, and feminism) and *Eidolon*, this resource should be open and able to organically grow based on the thematic and scholarly goals of involved scholars. Lastly, and taking this cue from the Women and Gender Minorities in Digital Humanities (WoGeM-DH) group,[17] this potential community should consider providing multiple means of communicating and engaging virtually.

---

[16] For a related discussion on how labor, service, and care are not only interrelated but also need to be better integrated into the profession, see Brown 2019.

[17] WoGeM is a network of scholars, but it is also a discussion listserv, a project team

With these suggestions, and with the inspiring forces of countless open and collaborative platforms discussed and not discussed here, I will reiterate that the mission of inclusive, feminist, anti-racist communities is to make room for many voices. Like the Digital Humanities Initiative at ASU, a self-sustaining model for community building cannot be built on either scarcity or inequity. As digital humanities itself has a problem with precarious labor, our community must reflect the realities of the academy and the state of digital humanities work (Boyles et al. 2018). I also acknowledge that community-building work, networking, and even digital scholarship are often invisible labor in the eyes of our academic institutions. Digital humanities projects, and especially public digital humanities projects, can be a risk for scholars on limited-term contracts, finishing their theses or dissertations, going up for tenure, being subtly or aggressively attacked for their activist scholarship, or who are already engaging in service work by mentoring students of color. And so, with these challenges and roadblocks acknowledged, I promise to work towards a future for premodern studies that is socially embedded in our political present and self-reflexive and reactive to the challenges of academia, and that takes seriously the commitment to provide credit for labor especially in an academic culture and climate that traditionally celebrates the individual. As this exercise in imagining future inclusive communities draws to a close, I hope you consider joining me in making it a reality.

An (Incomplete) Reading and Resource List: Critical Race, Premodern Studies, and Digital Public Humanities

Ahmed, Sara. 2014. "The Problem of Perception." feministkilljoys.com/2014/02/17/the-problem-of-perception/.

———. 2016. *Living a Feminist Life.* Durham, NC. Duke University Press.

Albin, Andrew, Mary C. Erler, Thomas O'Donnell, Nicholas L. Paul, and Nina Rowe, eds. 2019. *Whose Middle Ages? - Teachable Moments for an Ill-Used Past.* New York: Fordham University Press.

---

that designed and presented a poster at Digital Humanities 2019, a group of scholars who organize regular virtual "conversations" around specific issues "relevant to being a woman or gender minority in digital humanities," and a voluntary collective of scholars advocating for visibility and change (see "Women and Gender Minorities in Digital Humanities," dhwogem.org/).

Anderson, Jane, and Kimberly Christen. 2019. "Decolonizing Attribution." *Journal of Radical Librarianship* 5 (June): 113–52.

Bailey, Moya. 2015. "#transform(ing)DH Writing and Research: An Autoethnography of Digital Humanities and Feminist Ethics." *Digital Humanities Quarterly* 9 (2): digitalhumanities.org/dhq/vol/9/2/000209/000209.html.

Bailey, Moya Z. 2012. "All the Digital Humanists Are White, All the Nerds Are Men, but Some of Us Are Brave." *Journal of Digital Humanities.* 1 (1): journalofdigitalhumanities.org/1-1/all-the-digital-humanists-are-white-all-the-nerds-are-men-but-some-of-us-are-brave-by-moya-z-bailey/.

Benjamin, Ruha. 2019. *Race After Technology: Abolitionist Tools for the New Jim Code*. Medford, MA: Polity Press.

"Borderlands Archives Cartography." www.bacartography.org.

Brown, Susan, and Laura Mandell. 2018. "The Identity Issue." (Introduction). *Journal of Cultural Analytics.* 3 (2): culturalanalytics.org/article/11036-the-identity-issue.

Casey, Jim. 2019. "Digital Shakespeare Is Neither Good Nor Bad, But Teaching Makes It So." *Humanities* 8 (2): 112. doi.org/10.3390/h8020112.

Coaston, Jane. 2019. "The Intersectionality Wars." vox.com/the-highlight/2019/5/20/18542843/intersectionality-conservatism-law-race-gender-discrimination.

"Collaborators' Bill of Rights." 2011. *Off the Tracks* (blog). 2011. Accessed 2 September 2019. mcpress.media-commons.org/offthetracks/part-one-models-for-collaboration-career-paths-acquiring-institutional-support-and-transformation-in-the-field/a-collaboration/collaborators%e2%80%99-bill-of-rights/.

Crenshaw, Kimberlé. 2019. *On Intersectionality: Essential Writings*. New York: New Press.

"Critical Race & Digital Studies Syllabus." 2019. *Center for Critical Race and Digital Studies*. April 18, 2019. criticalracedigitalstudies.com/syllabus.

Davidson, Cathy N. 2008. "Humanities 2.0: Promise, Perils, Predictions." *PMLA* 123 (3): 707–17.

Di Pressi, Haley, Stephanie Gorman, Miriam Posner, Raphael Sasayama, and Tori Schmitt. 2015. "A Student Collaborators' Bill of Rights." HumTech - UCLA. June 8, 2015. Accessed 2 September 2019. humtech.ucla.edu/news/a-student-collaborators-bill-of-rights.

Ehrenberg, Hannah. n.d. "SAA15 Early Modern Race Bibliography Public." docs.google.com/document/d/1AaMp1al8y715FklUq1x5scqBHYS9QpzvMzgYU_ZyFow/.

Eklund, Hillary, and Wendy Beth Hyman, eds. 2019. *Teaching Social Justice Through Shakespeare: Why Renaissance Literature Matters Now*. Edinburgh: Edinburgh University Press.

Enimil, Sandra. 2019. "Feminist-Centered Collaborative Scholarly Communication Living Toolkit / Caja Viva de Herramientas Para La Comunicación Académica, Colaborativa, y Feminista." trianglesci.org/ 2019/07/30/feminist-centered-collaborative-toolkit/.

Erickson, Peter, and Kim F. Hall. 2016. "'A New Scholarly Song': Rereading Early Modern Race." *Shakespeare Quarterly* 67 (1): 1–13.

Estill, Laura. 2019. "Digital Humanities' Shakespeare Problem." *Humanities* 8 (1): 45. doi.org/10.3390/h8010045.

Fitzpatrick, Kathleen. 2019. *Generous Thinking: A Radical Approach to Saving the University*. Baltimore: Johns Hopkins University Press.

Gaertner, David. 2019. "Decolonial DH?: The Maker Movement Across Indigenous Studies and the Digital Humanities." *Novel Alliances*. novelalliances.com/2019/06/05/decolonial-dh-the-maker-movement-across-indigenous-studies-and-the-digital-humanities/.

Hankivsky, Olena. 2014. "Rethinking Care Ethics: On the Promise and Potential of an Intersectional Analysis." *The American Political Science Review* 108 (2): 252–64.

Harrison, Matthew. 2018. "Where's The On-Ramp: Teaching the Diversity of the Past." www.thrumpledumthrum.com/?p=299.

Hsy, Jonathan, and Julie Orlemanski. 2017. "Race and Medieval Studies: A Partial Bibliography." *Postmedieval* 8 (4): 500–531.

Jones, Lori, and Richard Nevell. 2016. "Plagued by Doubt and Viral Misinformation: The Need for Evidence-Based Use of Historical Disease Images." *The Lancet Infectious Diseases* 16 (10): e235–40.

Kafer, Alison. 2013. *Feminist, Queer, Crip*. Bloomington: Indiana University Press.

Kendi, Ibram X. 2019. *How to Be an Antiracist.* New York: Penguin Random House.

Kimbro, Devori, Michael Noschka, and Geoffrey Way. 2019. "Lend Us Your Earbuds: Shakespeare/Podcasting/Poesis." *Humanities* 8 (2): 67. doi.org/10.3390/h8020067.

Lothian, Alexis, and Amanda Phillips. 2013. "Can Digital Humanities Mean Transformative Critique?" *Journal of E-Media Studies* 3 (1): doi.org/10.1349/PS1.1938-6060.A.425.

"Manifesto – FemTechNet." n.d. Accessed 2 September 2019. femtechnet.org/publications/manifesto.

"Mapping Violence." n.d. mappingviolence.com/.

McGrath, Jim. 2019. "Go Fast / Go Slow: Supporting Digital Public Humanities At Various Speeds." jimmcgrath.us/teaching/go-fast-go-slow-supporting-digital-public-humanities-at-various-speeds/.

McGregor, Hannah. 2021. "Secret Feminist Agenda." secretfeministagenda.com/.

McPherson, Tara. 2012. "Why Are the Digital Humanities So White?: Or Thinking the Histories of Race and Computation." In *Debates in the Digital Humanities*, edited by Matthew K. Gold. Minneapolis: University of Minnesota Press. dhdebates.gc.cuny.edu/read/untitled-88c11800-9446-469b-a3be-3fdb36bfbd1e/section/20df8acd-9ab9-4f35-8a5d-e91aa5f4a0ea.

Mihai, Adriana. 2019. "Romanian Users' YouTube 'Shakespeares': Digital Localities in Global Fields." *Humanities* 8 (2): 84. doi.org/10.3390/h8020084.

Opel, Dawn, and Michael Simeone. 2019. "The Invisible Work of the Digital Humanities Lab: Preparing Graduate Students for Emergent Intellectual and Professional Work." *Digital Humanities Quarterly* 13 (2): http://www.digitalhumanities.org/dhq/vol/13/2/000421/000421.html.

Piepzna-Samarasinha, Leah Lakshmi. 2018. *Care Work: Dreaming Disability Justice*. Vancouver: Arsenal Pulp Press.

"Postdoctoral Laborers Bill of Rights." 2019. doi.org/10.17613/7fz6-ra81.

"Recoding Relations." recodingrelations.org/.

Reid, Alexander. 2012. "Graduate Education and the Ethics of the Digital Humanities." In *Debates in the Digital Humanities*. Minneapolis: University of Minnesota Press. dhdebates.gc.cuny.edu/read/untitled-88c11800-9446-469b-a3be-3fdb36bfbd1e/section/b4f365e7-eefa-4546-9857-dfd35b316183.

Risam, Roopika. 2018. "Diversity Work and Digital Carework in Higher Education." *First Monday* 23 (3): doi.org/10.5210/fm.v23i3.8241.

Thompson, Ayanna. 2011. *Passing Strange: Shakespeare, Race, and Contemporary America*. Oxford and New York: Oxford University Press.

Tripp, Aili Mari. 2016. "Towards an Ethics of Care: Response to 'Power, Intersectionality and the Politics of Belonging.'" In *The Palgrave Handbook of Gender and Development: Critical Engagements in Feminist Theory and Practice*, edited by Wendy Harcourt, 382–94. London: Palgrave Macmillan UK.

Uszkalo, Kirsten C. 2011. "The Witches in Early Modern English Project." witching.org/.

Visconti, Amanda. 2019. "A Management Charter (Part 1)." *Scholars' Lab*. scholarslab.lib.virginia.edu/blog/management-charter-part1/.

Waddell, Brodie. 2017. "A Reading List of Scholarship by People of Colour on Slavery and Colonialism, c.1500–1750." manyheadedmonster.wordpress.com/2017/07/25/a-reading-list-of-scholarship-by-people-of-colour-on-slavery-and-colonialism-c-1500-1750/.

Whitaker, Cord J. 2019. *Black Metaphors: How Modern Racism Emerged from Medieval Race-Thinking*. Philadelphia: University of Pennsylvania Press.

Williams, Nora J. 2019. "@Shakespeare and @TwasFletcher: Performances of Authority." *Humanities* 8 (1): 46. doi.org/10.3390/h8010046.

Windholz, Jordan. 2019. "Not Something, Not Nothing, Not Shakespeare: Digitized Playbooks and the Question of Access in the Undergraduate Literature Classroom." *Humanities* 8 (2): 61. doi.org/10.3390/h8020061.

WORKS CITED

Aiyegbusi, Babalola Titilola. 2018. "Decolonizing Digital Humanities: Africa in Perspective." In *Bodies of Information: Intersectional Feminism and Digital Humanities*, edited by Elizabeth Losh and Jacqueline Wernimont. Minneapolis: University of Minnesota Press. dhdebates.gc.cuny.edu/read/untitled-4e08b137-aec5-49a4-83c0-38258425f145/section/c9862793-ef00-4d6b-a30c-2f3d354e4e94.

Bond, Emily. 2017. "Hold My Mead: A Bibliography for Historians Hitting Back at White Supremacy." *History From Below* (blog). 10 September 2017. sarahemilybond.com/2017/09/10/hold-my-mead-a-bibliography-for-historians-hitting-back-at-white-supremacy/.

Boyles, Christina, Anne Cong-Huyen, Carrie Johnston, Jim McGrath, and Amanda Phillips. 2018. "Precarious Labor and the Digital Humanities." *American Quarterly* 70 (3): 693–700. doi.org/10.1353/aq.2018.0054.

brown, adrienne maree. 2017. *Emergent Strategy: Shaping Change, Changing Worlds*. Reprint edition. Chico, CA: AK Press.

Brown, Susan. 2019. "Delivery Service: Gender and the Political Unconscious of Digital Humanities." In *Bodies of Information: Intersectional Feminism and the Digital Humanities*, edited by Elizabeth Losh and Jacqueline Wernimont, 261–86. Minneapolis, MN: University of Minnesota Press. doi.org/10.5749/j.ctv9hj9r9.18.

"Cite Black Women." Cite Black Women. Accessed 2 September 2019. citeblackwomencollective.org/.

Coles, Kimberly Anne, Kim F. Hall, and Ayanna Thompson. 2019. "BlacKKKShakespearean: A Call to Action for Medieval and Early Modern Studies." *Profession*. Accessed 28 January 2021. profession.mla.org/blackkkshakespearean-a-call-to-action-for-medieval-and-early-modern-studies/.

Collins, Patricia Hill. 1999. *Black Feminist Thought: Knowledge, Consciousness, and the Politics of Empowerment*. 2nd edition. New York: Routledge.

Digital Frontiers. 2018. "Governance and Organization." Digital Frontiers. Last modified 20 October 2018. Accessed 2 September 2019. digital-frontiers.org/committee/.

Eidolon. 2017. "*Eidolon*'s Mission Statement." *Medium*. Accessed 2 September 2019. eidolon.pub/eidolons-mission-statement-d026012023d5.

Evans, Sian, Michael Mandiberg, Jacqueline Mabey, and Laurel Ptak. n.d. "Art+Feminism Wikipedia Edit-a-Thon." Art + Feminism. Accessed 2 September 2019. artandfeminism.org/.

Gabriele, Matthew. 2019. "Perspective | Trump Says Medieval Walls Worked. They Didn't." *Washington Post*, 10 January 2019. washingtonpost.com/outlook/2019/01/10/trump-says-medieval-walls-worked-they-didnt/.

Griffin, Gabriele, and Matt Steven Hayler. 2018. "Collaboration in Digital Humanities Research – Persisting Silences." *Digital Humanities Quarterly* 12 (1). digitalhumanities.org/dhq/vol/12/1/000351/000351.html.

Heng, Geraldine, and Susan Noakes. n.d. "About GMAP | GLOBAL MIDDLE AGES." Accessed 2 September 2019. globalmiddleages.org/about.

———. n.d. "GLOBAL MIDDLE AGES." Accessed 2 September 2019. globalmiddleages.org/.

Hsu, Wendy. 2016. "Lessons on Public Humanities from the Civic Sphere." In *Debates in the Digital Humanities* 2016, edited by Matthew K. Gold and Lauren F. Klein. Minneapolis: University of Minnesota Press. dhdebates.gc.cuny.edu/read/untitled/section/0c337efc-8ed6-4af0-b997-5bdae84ce0d8.

Jung, Jackie. 2019. "A PSA: Apart from the Great Wall of China, Built in an Effort to Protect People from the Justly Feared Mongol Armies, Medieval City Walls Were Not Built to Separate People of Diff Ethnic or National Identities. Gates Were Open during the Day and Closed at Night." Tweet. *@ProfJackie*. 9 January 2019. Accessed 2 September 2019. twitter.com/ProfJackie/status/1082993588319985664.

Kim, Dorothy. 2017. "Teaching Medieval Studies in a Time of White Supremacy." *In the Middle* (blog). Accessed 2 September 2019.

inthemedievalmiddle.com/2017/08/teaching-medieval-studies-in-time-of.html.

Klein, Lauren, and Matthew Gold. 2019. "Introduction." In *Debates in the Digital Humanities.* Minneapolis, MN: University of Minnesota Press. dhdebates.gc.cuny.edu/read/untitled-f2acf72c-a469-49d8-be35-67f9ac1e3a60/section/0cd11777-7d1b-4f2c-8fdf-4704e827c2c2.

"Looking Forward: New Directions in Early Modern Race Studies." 2019. Plenary Panel Session presented at the 47th Annual Meeting of the Shakespeare Association of America. Organizer: Peter Erickson. Chair: Ayanna Thompson. Speakers: Bernadette Andrea, David Sterling Brown, Kim F. Hall. Washington, D.C., 19 April 2019. Accessed 6 June 2021. shakespeareassociation.org/saa-archives/audios/.

Mandell, Laura C., Clemens Neudecker, Apostolos Antonacopoulos, Elizabeth Grumbach, Loretta Auvil, Matthew J. Christy, Jacob A. Heil, and Todd Samuelson. 2015. "Navigating the Storm: IMPACT, EMOP, and Agile Steering Standards." *Digital Scholarship in the Humanities* 32 (1): 189–94. doi.org/10.1093/llc/fqv062.

Mapes, Kristen. 2019. "A Sort of Theme I Am Gathering from #ACH2019 so far is a Call for Slow DH, for Spending Time with Archives and Data and Material and the People within Them." Tweet. *@kmapesy*. 25 July 2019. Accessed 3 September 2019. twitter.com/kmapesy/status/1154395656464818176.

Martin, Kim, Beth Compton, and Ryan Hunt. 2017. "Disrupting Dichotomies: Mobilizing Digital Humanities with the MakerBus." In *Making Things and Drawing Boundaries*, edited by Jentery Sayers. Minneapolis, MN: University of Minnesota Press. dhdebates.gc.cuny.edu/read/untitled-aa1769f2-6c55-485a-81af-ea82cce86966/section/2256896b-9de5-478f-90b3-44d85e494483#ch29.

Milbank, Dana. 2019. "Opinion | Trump's Wall Isn't Evil. It's Medieval." *Washington Post*, 9 January 2019. Opinions. washingtonpost.com/opinions/trumps-wall-isnt-evil-its-medieval/2019/01/09/80dfa20a-1458-11e9-90a8-136fa44b80ba_story.html.

Morse, Heidi. 2018. "Classics and the Alt-Right: Historicizing Visual Rhetorics of White Supremacy – Learn Speak Act." *LearnSpeakAct* (blog). 2018. Accessed 2 September 2019. sites.lsa.umich.edu/learn-speak-act/2018/02/15/classics-and-the-alt-right/.

Nowviskie, Bethany. 2019. "Capacity through Care." In *Debates in the Digital Humanities* 2019, edited by Matthew K. Gold and Lauren F. Klein. Minneapolis, MN: University of Minnesota Press. dhdebates.gc.cuny.edu/read/untitled-f2acf72c-a469-49d8-be35-67f9ac1e3a60/section/3a53cbc1-5eee-421a-a4f6-82bb5dfb1c17#ch37.

Perry, David. 2019. "The Wall Isn't Medieval." *CNN Opinion*, 2019. Accessed 14 August 2019. cnn.com/2019/01/11/opinions/donald-trump-wall-is-not-medieval-perry/index.html.

"Public Humanities." 2019. In *Wikipedia*. Accessed 2 September 2019. en.wikipedia.org/w/index.php?title=Public_humanities.

RaceB4Race Executive Board. 2020. "It's Time to End the Publishing Gatekeeping!" Last modified 11 June 2020. medium.com/the-sundial-acmrs/its-time-to-end-the-publishing-gatekeeping-75207525f587.

ReKN Bibliography. Accessed 14 August 2019. rekn.itercommunity.org.

Risam, Roopika. 2018. "Decolonizing the Digital Humanities in Theory and Practice." In *The Routledge Companion to Media Studies and Digital Humanities*, edited by Jentery Sayers, 78–86. New York: Routledge. digitalcommons.salemstate.edu/english_facpub/7.

Schroeder, Robyn. 2017. "What Is Public Humanities? – Day of Public Humanities." Accessed 2 September 2019. dayofph.wordpress.com/what-is-public-humanities/.

Siemens, Raymond, Karen Armstrong, Constance Crompton, and The Devonshire MS Editorial Group, eds. n.d. *A Social Edition of the Devonshire MS | (BL Add 17,492)*. Accessed 2 September 2019. dms.itercommunity.org/.

Spiro, Lisa. 2012. "'This Is Why We Fight': Defining the Values of the Digital Humanities." In *Debates in the Digital Humanities*, edited by Matthew K. Gold. Minneapolis: University of Minnesota Press. dhdebates.gc.cuny.edu/read/untitled-88c11800-9446-469b-a3be-3fdb36bfbd1e/section/9e014167-c688-43ab-8b12-0f6746095335.

Stevens, Nikki, and Jacqueline Wernimont. 2018. "Seeing 21st Century Data Bleed through the 15th Century Wound Man." *IEEE Technology and Society Magazine* 37 (4): 46–54. doi.org/10.1109/MTS.2018.2876214.

Stommel, Jesse. 2015. "The Public Digital Humanities." *Disrupting the Digital Humanities* (blog). 9 January 2015. Accessed 2 September 2019. disruptingdh.com/the-public-digital-humanities/.

Ullyot, Michael. 2019. "Iter at 20: A Look Forward." Blog. Accessed 2 September 2019. ullyot.ucalgaryblogs.ca/2019/03/16/iter/.

Way, Geoffrey, Michael Noschka, and Devori Kimbro. n.d. "Remixing the Humanities." Accessed 2 September 2019. spreaker.com/show/remixing-the-humanities.

Zuckerberg, Donna. 2018. *Not All Dead White Men: Classics and Misogyny in the Digital Age.* Cambridge, MA: Harvard University Press.

———. n.d. "About EIDOLON." *EIDOLON.* Accessed 2 September 2019. eidolon.pub/about.

Building *A Social Edition of the Devonshire Manuscript*[1]

Ray Siemens
University of Victoria
siemens@uvic.ca

Constance Crompton
University of Ottawa

Daniel Powell
Legislative Assembly of British Columbia

Alyssa Arbuckle
University of Victoria

Maggie Shirley
Kootenay Gallery of Art

and the Devonshire Manuscript Editorial Group

The Multivalent Text of the Devonshire Manuscript

A Social Edition of the Devonshire Manuscript is an unconventional text: it blends traditional scholarly editing practices and standards with comparatively recent digital social media environments. In doing so, the edition aims to reflect both contemporary editorial theory, which recognizes the inherently social form and formation of texts, and the writerly and readerly practices that shaped the original production of the Devonshire Manuscript (London, British Library, MS Add. 17492). Dating from the 1530s to the 1540s, the Devonshire Manuscript is a multiauthored verse miscellany compiled by a number of sixteenth-century contributors.[2] As an inherently collaborative document, the manuscript calls for a social investigation of its production. In this chapter, we detail the content, context, process, and implications of *A*

[1] This chapter is republished with minor revisions from *Digital Scholarly Editing: Theories and Practices*, ed. Matthew James Driscoll and Elena Pierazzo (Cambridge: Open Book Publishers, 2016), 137–60, books.openedition.org/obp/3409, and which in turn reprints, with permission, an article in the journal *Renaissance and Reformation/Renaissance et Réforme* 30.4 (2015): 131–56.

[2] Following Beal's definition of a verse miscellany as "a manuscript, a compilation of predominantly verse texts, or extracts from verse texts, by different authors and usually gleaned from different sources" (Beal 2008, 429). In *A Dictionary of English Manuscript Terminology*, Beal lists the Devonshire Manuscript as a pertinent example of a verse miscellany (2008, 430).

ISBN 978-1-64959-063-3 (paper) ISBN 978-1-64959-064-0 (pdf) ISBN 978-1-64959-065-7 (epub)
New Technologies in Medieval and Renaissance Studies 11 (2025) 99–123

Social Edition of the Devonshire Manuscript (en.wikibooks.org/wiki/The_Devonshire_Manuscript). We will begin with an exploration of the textual, paratextual, and non-textual content of the Devonshire Manuscript. In section 2, we will focus on the process of building a social edition of the manuscript. To conclude, we will ruminate on the affordances of digital editing. Overall, we will consider how publishing in Wikibooks emphasizes the collaborative, social ethos of the Devonshire Manuscript itself, and how in doing so we attempt to model the *social scholarly edition.*[3]

The Devonshire Manuscript, acquired in 1848 by the British Museum, contains approximately two hundred items (the total sum of complete lyrics, verse fragments, excerpts from longer works, anagrams, and other ephemeral jottings) bound in a handwritten volume and inscribed in over a dozen hands by a coterie of men and women gathered around the court of Queen Anne Boleyn.[4] Despite growing scholarly interest in the Devonshire Manuscript, no critical editions existed during the production of *A Social Edition of the Devonshire Manuscript.*[5] The manuscript has long been valued as a source of Sir Thomas Wyatt's poetry; 129 of the two hundred items in the manuscript were composed (although not copied) by him. These verses, in turn, have been transcribed and published by Agnes K. Foxwell (1913), Kenneth Muir (1949), and Muir and Patricia Thomson (1969) in their respective editions of Wyatt's poetry.[6] As scholar Arthur F. Marotti argues, however, the author-centered focus of these editions distorts the character of the Devonshire Manuscript in two ways: "first, it unjustifiably draws the work of other writers into the Wyatt canon, and, second, it prevents an appreciation of the collection as a document illustrating some of the uses of lyric verse within an actual social environment" (Marotti 1995, 40).[7] The Devonshire

[3] Wikibooks is a Wikimedia project that continues the aim of Wikipedia; namely, to encourage, develop, and disseminate knowledge in the public sphere. Wikibooks differs from other Wikimedia projects in that it is primarily designed for facilitating collaborative open-content textbook building.

[4] On the origins, early history and enumeration of the Devonshire Manuscript, see especially Harrier 1975, 23–54; Southall 1964, 142–43; and Remley 1994, 41, 47–48. See also Baron 1994, 318–35, and Heale 1995, 297–301.

[5] Heale's edition (2012) is based on a regularized version of the Devonshire Manuscript Editorial Group transcriptions of the manuscript.

[6] Many of the remaining poems, unattributed to Wyatt, have been transcribed and published in Muir 1947. George Frederick Nott's important early two-volume edition (1815) does not include diplomatic transcriptions of verses.

[7] Nott's misguided statement, that the manuscript "contains Wyatt's pieces almost

Manuscript is much more than an important witness in the Wyatt canon; it is also a snapshot into the scribal practices of male and female lyricists, scribes, and compilers in the Henrician court.

A Social Edition of the Devonshire Manuscript seeks to publish the contents of the original manuscript in their entirety, move beyond the limitations of an author-centered focus on Wyatt's contributions, and concentrate on the social, literary, and historical contexts in which the volume is situated as a unified whole. In doing so, we remain mindful of the editorial theories championed by D. F. McKenzie and Jerome McGann (among others) that expand the notion of textual production beyond a simple consideration of authorial intention. For McGann (1988, 79–82), these "nonauthorial textual determinants" should be considered alongside authorial presence to include in our critical gaze "other persons or groups involved in the initial process of production," as well as the phases, stages, means, modes, and materials of this initial production process (McGann 1983). D. F. McKenzie's call for a "sociology of texts" (1986) further extends this concept of textual production by arguing for the significance of the material form of a text and its ability to affect the text's meaning. These theories have prompted critics to re-evaluate the notion of authorship in order to account for non-authorial (but nevertheless deeply significant) organizers, contributors, and collaborators. Marotti's assertion, that "literary production, reproduction and reception are all socially mediated, the resulting texts demanding attention in their own right and not just as legitimate or illegitimate variants from authorial archetypes," also reflects the changing landscape of editorial theory (Marotti 1995, 212). In keeping with McGann, McKenzie, and Marotti, *A Social Edition of the Devonshire Manuscript* aims to preserve the socially mediated textual and extra-textual elements of the manuscript that have been elided or ignored in previous works. These ostensible "paratexts" make significant contributions to the meaning and appreciation of the manuscript miscellany and its constituent parts: annotations, glosses, names, ciphers, and various jottings. The telling proximity of one work to another, significant gatherings of materials, illustrations entered into the manuscript alongside the text, and so forth all shape the way we understand the manuscript but are often ignored when preparing scholarly editions.[8] To accomplish this goal, we have pre-

exclusively" (1815, vii), or Muir's comment, "it is not always easy to decide whether a poem is written by a successful imitator or by Wyatt himself in an uninspired mood" (1949, 253), are characteristic of the sort of dismissive author-centric views taken to task by Marotti (1995).

[8] We have interpreted "paratext" broadly, as articulated in Genette 1997.

pared a diplomatic transcription of the complete Devonshire Manuscript with extensive scholarly apparatus.

The manuscript collection consists of short, courtly verses by Sir Thomas Wyatt (129 items, sixty-six unique to the manuscript) and Henry Howard, Earl of Surrey (one item); verses attributed to Lady Margaret Douglas (two items), Richard Hattfield (two items), Mary Fitzroy (née Howard) (one item), Lord Thomas Howard (three items), Sir Edmund Knyvett (two items), Sir Anthony Lee (one item; "A. I." has three items), and Henry Stewart, Lord Darnley (one item); transcribed portions of medieval verse by Geoffrey Chaucer (eleven items), Thomas Hoccleve (three items), and Richard Roos (two items); transcriptions of the work of others or original works by prominent court figures such as Mary Shelton, Lady Margaret Douglas, Mary (Howard) Fitzroy, Lord Thomas Howard, and possibly Queen Anne Boleyn. Alongside these are some thirty unidentified or unattributed pieces.[9] These multiple contributors often comment on and evaluate each other's work through marginal notation and drawing, in-line interjection, exchanging epistolary verse, and selectively altering transcribed texts.

A Social Edition of the Devonshire Manuscript follows Helen Baron's attribution of hands in the Devonshire Manuscript.[10] Of the roughly twenty hands, some are even and regular while others are idiosyncratic and variable. Historically, the exceptional difficulty of transcribing the Devonshire Manuscript has impeded widespread research on the text. Approximately 140 entries are copies of extant or contemporary works and bear the signs of copying. The majority of the pieces may reflect the work of local amanuenses and

---

[9] Scholars have only cautiously asserted an approximate number of items preserved in the Devonshire Manuscript: "the number of poems in the manuscript can only be given as approximately 184" (Southall 1964, 143); "the manuscript preserves about 185 items of verse, but it is impossible to obtain an exact figure as many of these are fragments, medieval extracts or the like, and others are divided up differently by various editors" (Remley 1994, 47). Seaton (1956) identified the medieval origin of the Richard Roos texts. Harrier (1956) first noted the use of William Thynne's 1532 edition of Chaucer as the source for that poet's verse in the Devonshire Manuscript.

[10] See en.wikibooks.org/wiki/The_Devonshire_Manuscript/Detailed_Hand_List_Hand_1 (accessed 2 December 2021). The most recent examination of the hands in D is that of Baron (1994). See also the earlier findings in Bond (1871). Where the transcribers differ from Baron's attribution, the project's identification is noted in the underlying TEI markup, hcmc.uvic.ca/~etcl/Devonshire_Manuscript_poems.zip (site discontinued, now available here: etcl.uvic.ca/devonshireMS/Devonshire_Manuscript_poems.zip).

secretaries with little professional regard for the expected standards of a presentation-copy manuscript. A full half of the manuscript's scribes (Hands 1, 3, 4, 5, 6, 8, 9, 10, 11, and Mary Howard Fitzroy) dedicate themselves to copying extant pieces; another five (Hands 1.1, 2, 7, Thomas Howard 2, and Margaret Douglas) enter a mix of extant material and material that appears unique to the manuscript. The remaining five (Hands 12, 13, Henry Stuart, Mary Shelton, and Thomas Howard 1) enter solely original materials. The work of the ten hands entering potentially original material to the manuscript amounts to forty-five pieces (fifteen identified and/or attributed). The many layers and authors render the Devonshire Manuscript an ideal text for experimentation in social editing.

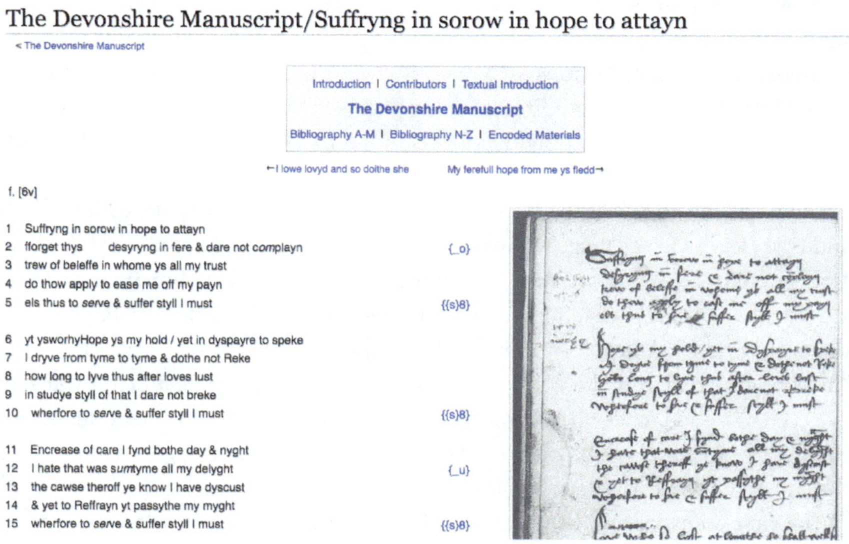

Figure 4.1. "Suffryng in sorow in hope to attayn" (fol. 6v) in *A Social Edition of the Devonshire Manuscript*. Wikibooks edition.

The manuscript itself bears traces of the original contributors' editorial processes. Besides writing epistolary verse, contributors to the manuscript interacted with one another through annotation. Occasionally, these marginal responses appear quite personal in nature. They include responses that evaluate the quality of certain lines or cross out one word and insert another. In doing so, the annotations reveal the compilers' social engagement and editorial collaboration. For example, the text of the poem "Suffryng in sorow in hope to attayn" (fols. 6v–7r; see Figure 4.1) is annotated in the left margin.

A hand identified as Lady Margaret Douglas's writes "fforget thys," to which a hand identified as Mary Shelton's responds, "yt ys wor[t]hy" (fol. 6v). The poem is written in a male voice appealing for the love of a lady. "Suffryng in sorow" and "desyryng in fere," the poet pleads for his unnamed addressee to "ease me off my payn" (fol. 6v, lines 1–2, 4).

While its authorship remains debated, the acrostic of the verse suggests that Shelton is the intended recipient—the first letter of its seven stanzas spells out "SHELTVN."[11] The scribal annotations, which may only refer to the quality of the verse, might therefore take on a more profound and personal meaning, as Douglas recommends rejecting the poem and its suit ("fforget thys"), but Shelton contradicts this advice with "('yt ys wor[t]hy')." At the end of the poem, Shelton adds a comment that has been variously transcribed as "ondesyard sarwes / reqwer no hyar," "ondesyrid favours / deserv no hyer," or perhaps "ondesyard fansies / requier no hyar."[12] The transcription poses an interesting editorial crux: "sarwes" might be read as "service" or "sorrows."[13] Likewise, "hyar" may be read as "hire" or "ear."[14] Although

[11] The poem is entered in the Devonshire Manuscript by an unidentified hand (H2) and is preserved in the Blage Manuscript (Trinity College, Dublin, MS 160, fol. 159r). Modern editors of Wyatt's poems commonly attribute the poem to him (Foxwell 1913, 257–58; Muir 1949, 96–97; Muir and Thomson 1969, 176–77; Nott 1815, 590). However, this attribution has not been universally accepted: Harrier argues that the poem "must be excluded from the Wyatt canon" since it "may be by Thomas Clere" (Harrier 1975, 41, 45), and Daalder (1975) silently excludes the poem from his edition. Boffey (1996, 173) has argued the author is Shelton, mistaking Shelton's signed comment at the end of the poem as an attribution.

[12] The first transcription as per Baron, (1994, 331); Remley gives "ondesyerd" in "Mary Shelton" (1994, 50). The second as per Foxwell (1913, 258). The third as per Heale (2012, 301). Heale (1998, 43) also gives "ondesiard fansies / requier no hiar" and "ondesyred fansies / require no hyar" (Heale 2004, 21).

[13] "Searwes" (device) is also possible, but unlikely. Alternatively rendering the word as "fansies" or "favours" is less problematic, but equally less probable.

[14] Zitner argues, "Whether Mary Shelton was saying that undesired service (attention) required no hire or that undesired sorrows required no ear, the response is pretty much the same in tone and substance" (1983, 513). While this comment may be a "remarkable example of an overtly critical rejoinder to a courtly lyric" written in the spirit described by Zitner, Remley argues that "it seems equally probable that her words are meant ironically," that they offer a "private recognition of the absurd spectacle of a man determined to get his way through protestations of extreme humility" (1994, 50). Similarly, Heale contends such "unsympathetic replies may be part of the

the precise intentions behind Shelton's annotations and commentary remain obscure, their potential importance to the meaning and interpretation of the verse cannot be disputed.

The Devonshire Manuscript embodies its compositional origins and circulation within the early Tudor court of Henry VIII, a body that was profoundly concerned with public and private performances of political loyalty and submission.[15] As Marotti notes, courtly manuscript miscellanies and poetic anthologies "represent the meeting ground of literary production and social practices" (1995, 212). The Devonshire Manuscript contains numerous examples of Marotti's assertion, especially in the form of epistolary verse and scribal annotation. Proximity and placement of poems often bear further significance. The poem "My ferefull hope from me ys fledd" (fol. 7v), signed "fynys quod n[o]b[od]y," is answered by the poem immediately following on the facing leaf, "Yowre ferefull hope cannot prevayle" (fol. 8r), in turn signed "fynys quod s[omebody]." While this kind of playful imitation and formal echoing does not strictly rely on the relative proximity of the poems in the manuscript, the effect is more immediately apparent and more visually striking when the poems are placed, as they are, on facing leaves.[16] Poetry became yet another venue for the performance of public and private roles within the royal court, and the Devonshire Manuscript reflects this oscillation between public and private, personal and communal: within it, the private became public, the public was treated as private, and all was deeply political. In addition to examining the volume as "a medium of social intercourse," other aspects of the Devonshire Manuscript—its multi-layered and multi-authored composition, its early history and transmission, the ways in which its contents engage with and comment directly on contemporary political and social issues—invite further investigation and demand consideration when making critical assessments (Love and Marotti 2002, 63).

---

conventional exchange of courtly verse" and might be offered in jest, as "such jesting offered some opportunities for female subject positions that seem to have appealed to the women using the manuscript" (2004, 21).

[15] Fox writes, "One striking phenomenon about early Tudor literature is that it was almost invariably concerned with politics, either directly or indirectly, and that this political bearing had a major impact on the nature of its literary forms" (1989, 3).

[16] The teasing blend of jest and earnestness in this pair of unattributed poems points to the role of much of the content in the manuscript as participating in the courtly "game of love." See Stevens 1979, 154–202; Boase 1977; Burnley 1998; and O'Donoghue 1982.

Like any of the other "nonauthorial" textual determinants described above, compilation is an act of mediation. The selection of verses to be recorded, the manner in which they were entered, and their position relative to one another all contribute to the meaning of the texts both individually and as a collection. Verses entered into the manuscript may have been selected on the basis of their popularity at court—perhaps accounting for the disproportionate number of Wyatt poems represented—or for more personal reasons; other verses were not simply selected and copied, but adapted and altered to suit specific purposes. The work of feminist literary critics and historians to rediscover texts by women and revise the canon of Western literature has further exposed the role of gender in the material and institutional conditions of textual production.[17]

To investigate the role of women in the production and circulation of literary works effectively, and building on the work of McGann (1983) and McKenzie (1986), Margaret J. M. Ezell has persuasively proposed that the definition of "authorship" needs to be re-examined and broadened (2002, 79). Ezell's study of women's miscellanies demonstrates that these acts of preservation and compilation often serve to reinforce religious and political loyalties and to "cement social bonds during times of duress" within female literary circles (2002, 86). In a similar vein, Elizabeth Clarke notes that "compilation, rather than authorship of the writing in a document," was the "dominant literary activity among women who could read and write" in the early modern period (2000, 53). This is certainly true in the case of the Devonshire Manuscript, where women were, for the most part, directly responsible for the compilation and copying of the predominantly male-authored contents of the anthology. Some of the lyrics demonstrate close female friendship—Mary Shelton and Margaret Douglas kept close company, evidenced by the fact that Shelton's hand often immediately follows Douglas's—and these lyrics are now understood to have a definite subversive meaning for a select group of individuals (Baron 1994, 328).[18]

---

[17] Representative studies include Beilin (1987); Ezell (1993 and 1999); Lewalski (1993); Walker (1996); and Wall (1993). See also the following representative essay collections: Haselkorn and Travitsky (1990); Hannay (1985); Woods and Hannay (2000); Wilcox (1996); Burke, Donawerth, Dove, and Nelson (2000).

[18] Kathryn DeZur notes that early modern women's participation in circulating love lyrics might also indicate "a possible site of resistance to the idealized cultural paradigm of women as chaste, silent, and obedient" (2004, 111). The Continental trend of courtly love made it fashionable for noble ladies at Henry VIII's court to compile miscellanies. Regardless, DeZur emphasizes that the tension between Christian val-

The Devonshire Manuscript is a rich, complex document. With its collection of courtly lyrics, pastiche of medieval and contemporary poetry, density of textual voices, and often-uncertain authorship and attribution, the manuscript demonstrates how textual production and interpretation were foundational to those living within the Tudor court. By paying heed to the various texts in and around the document—the annotations, order of leaves and social context—one may obtain a fuller understanding of the source text and its various actors. We believe that the physical and social elements of the Devonshire Manuscript lend themselves to digital editing and publication processes that more readily represent these aspects than a print environment can. *A Social Edition of the Devonshire Manuscript* focuses on the editorial and scribal practices that inform the context and production of the Devonshire Manuscript. By shifting our own editorial process into an environment representative of the inherent sociality of texts, *A Social Edition of the Devonshire Manuscript* hearkens back to the multi-author roots of the text itself. In the following section, we focus on the specifics of *A Social Edition of the Devonshire Manuscript*, exploring the benefits (and drawbacks) of building a scholarly edition on the Wikibooks platform.

Building a Social Edition

A Social Edition of the Devonshire Manuscript manifests Ray Siemens's earlier argument that social media environments might enable new editing practices (Siemens et al. 2012, 445–61).[19] In order to build an edition of an early modern text on the principles of open access and editorial transparency (in both production and dissemination), we have integrated scholarly content with environments maintained by the social and social-editorial communities already existent on the web—most notably on Wikibooks, a cross-section of intellectual research activity and the social media practices that define Web 2.0. Early on, Web 2.0 was described as Internet technologies that allow users to be active authors rather than simply readers or consumers of web content (DiNucci 1999, 220–22). Now, the term is most frequently associated with social media platforms (e.g., Facebook and Twitter) and blog applications (e.g., WordPress and wikis). In an experimental spirit, we have extended the editorial conversation into multiple pre-existing Web 2.0 and social media platforms, including Twitter, blogs, Wikibook discussion

---

ues and courtly expectations meant that a woman's demeanour was always under scrutiny (2004, 111).

[19] Ray Siemens, with Meagan Timney, Cara Leitch, Corina Koolen, and Alex Garnett, and with the ETCL, INKE, and PKP Research Groups.

pages, dedicated Renaissance and early modern online community spaces, and Skype-enabled interviews with our advisory group. As Tim Berners-Lee (the inventor of the World Wide Web as we know it) remarks, the Internet was originally developed for workers to collaborate and access source documents; with wiki and Web 2.0 technology, it is now returning to its roots (Mahoney 2011). Wikibooks emphasizes the importance of multi-authored and multi-edited endeavours. In doing so, the platform exemplifies McGann, McKenzie, and Marotti's earlier assertions that texts are created by a community of individuals. In what follows, we offer a brief overview of the process and thinking that led to the Wikibook instantiation of the manuscript as *A Social Edition of the Devonshire Manuscript* (see Figure 4.2).

Perhaps more than any other editorial choice, the iterative publication of *A Social Edition of the Devonshire Manuscript* departed most clearly from traditional scholarly editing practices. In effect, we have published (or are in the perpetual process of publishing) versions of the edition in multiple media: a fixed PDF version, distributed to the project's advisory board, and a version housed on the publicly-editable Wikibooks. We are also currently working with multiple publishing partners to produce a second online edition, an e-reader edition, and a print edition to meet the needs of a broad and varied readership.[20] These versions were planned to inform and influence each other's development, with cross-pollination of editorial input across platforms. Although they did so, each medium also engendered difficulties in communication, coordination, and expectations to be overcome or accommodated—with varying results.

The Wikibook edition's features stretch the limits of a print edition to the breaking point—especially in sheer size. Even if the manuscript facsimile pages and the XML files were excluded, *A Social Edition of the Devonshire Manuscript* would run to over five hundred standard print pages. In addition to a general and textual introduction, the online edition includes extensive hand sample tables that open our palaeographic attribution process to public scrutiny, witnesses that reflect the poem's textual legacy, biographies and genealogical diagrams that clarify the relationship between the manuscript's sixteenth century compiler-authors, and an extensive bibliography of quoted and related sources. Courtesy of Adam Matthew Digital, we have

---

[20] Since the original publication of this article, the ebook (ISBN 978-0-86698-518-5) and print version (ISBN 978-0-86698-517-8) were published by Iter Press and the Arizona Center for Medieval and Renaissance Studies (Toronto and Tempe, 2015), distributed via University of Chicago Press.

also included the facsimile image of each page of the manuscript. The discussion sections on each page, a feature unique to Wikimedia projects, promote conversation on various aspects of the poem at hand. In this way, the Wikibook edition extends the social context of the Devonshire Manuscript by providing a space for ongoing discussion, collaboration, and negotiation.

Figure 4.2. *A Social Edition of the Devonshire Manuscript* home page.

Editorial work on *A Social Edition of the Devonshire Manuscript* began long before we selected Wikibooks as a publication platform. In 2001, work on a digital edition of the manuscript began with a more recognizably traditional scholarly activity: primary source transcription. The transcription of the manuscript is based on examination of both the original document and a microfilm of the Devonshire Manuscript provided by the British Library. Members of the Devonshire Manuscript Editorial Group (or DMSEG, a team made up of up of scholars, postdoctoral fellows, graduate researchers, and programmers,[21] working with two publishers,[22] an editorial board,[23] and self-selected members of the public) prepared and transcribed (in a blind process) two independent paper copies from the microfilm. The transcribers collated the two paper copies manually as they were unable to perform a collation by electronic means using standard techniques; transcription of the *Devonshire Manuscript* is notoriously challenging, as the manuscript was inscribed by nineteen different hands, the majority of which used non-professional secretary script. The resultant rough transcription was resolved as far as possible using expanded paper prints and enlarged images. In general, their transcriptions were in accord with one another. Remaining areas of uncertainty were resolved with manual reference to the original document itself, housed at the British Library. This final, collated transcription forms the textual basis for *A Social Edition of the Devonshire Manuscript.*[24]

Guided by two principles, the team then encoded the text in XML according to the Text Encoding Initiative (TEI) Guidelines.[25] The first principle was

---

[21] Ray Siemens, Karin Armstrong, Barbara Bond, Constance Crompton, Terra Dickson, Johanne Paquette, Jonathan Podracky, Ingrid Weber, Cara Leitch, Melanie Chernyk, Brett D. Hirsch, Daniel Powell, Alyssa Anne McLeod, Alyssa Arbuckle, Jonathan Gibson, Chris Gaudet, Eric Haswell, Arianna Ciula, Daniel Starza-Smith, and James Cummings, with Martin Holmes, Greg Newton, Paul Remley, Erik Kwakkel, Aimie Shirkie, and the INKE research group.

[22] Iter, a not-for-profit consortium dedicated to the development and distribution of scholarly medieval and Renaissance online resources, in partnership with Medieval and Renaissance Texts and Studies and Adam Matthew Digital, a digital academic publisher.

[23] Robert E. Bjork (director, Arizona Center for Medieval and Renaissance Studies, Arizona State University), William R. Bowen (chair; director, Iter, University of Toronto Scarborough), Michael Ullyot (University of Calgary), Diane Jakacki (Georgia Institute of Technology), Jessica Murphy (University of Texas at Dallas), Jason Boyd (Ryerson University), Elizabeth Heale (University of Reading), Steven W. May (Georgetown College), Arthur F. Marotti (Wayne State University), Jennifer Summit (Stanford University), Jonathan Gibson (Queen Mary, University of London), John Lavagnino (King's College London), and Katherine Rowe (Bryn Mawr College).

[24] For further information on the collation process, including collation tools used, see Siemens with Leitch (2009).

[25] TEI provides a standard for encoding electronic texts. By encoding a text in XML

consistency: even if the team discovered one of their previous choices to be less than optimal, they continued in that pattern until the text was complete. Rather than employ varying practices, consistently encoding the entire manuscript in XML allowed for global changes that could be, and indeed were, made after the conclusion of the initial encoding.[26] The second principle was accountability: as the team encoded, they maintained regular documentation to ensure that neither the original encoder nor any subsequent encoder would lack a basis from which to proceed. Another successful practice was to encode the manuscript by building layers of TEI in phases. The manuscript was completely encoded at a conservative level before commencing the second phase. The second layer of encoding, complete with annotations and regularizations, deepened, clarified, and augmented the first. Although the project began in 2001, the implementation of the social edition method discussed here started with the formation of an advisory group in 2010. This provided a unique opportunity to invite potential critics to shape the process and the products associated with the social edition. As the final step before moving the edition into Wikibooks, the members of the DMSEG working in the Electronic Textual Cultures Lab (ETCL) at the University of Victoria prepared a static digital edition of the manuscript. This edition served as a base text against which our international advisory group of early modern and Renaissance scholars could compare the Wikibook edition as it evolved.[27]

Before deciding on Wikibooks as a platform, the team had considered hosting the edition on a stand-alone site. In response to public interest in the project, coupled with the team's investment in emerging public knowledge communities, we devised an editorial experiment: as a control we produced a static PDF version of the edition, and as a variable we moved the same content onto a Wikimedia platform. Most famous for Wikipedia, Wikimedia is a small, non-profit foundation, with fewer than 150 employees responsible for management, fundraising, and technological development. Volunteer editors contribute and moderate the content of the projects. We considered Wikisource, Wikibooks, and Wikipedia as platforms, eventually deciding to mount our edition in Wikibooks. Acknowledging the dedicated community already engaged in Wikimedia, we sought to discover Wikibooks' affordances

---

under TEI guidelines, one renders the text substantially more searchable, categorizable, and preservable.

[26] Please note that these global changes were questions not of transcription but of encoding patterns and standards.

[27] For a more in-detail description of transcription, collation, and encoding practices, please see Siemens, Bond, and Armstrong 2008.

for the scholar. Even though Wikipedia has more editors, Wikibooks is purposefully structured to support the book-like form. And although Wikisource appears as a more appropriate environment for a scholarly edition, publishing *A Social Edition of the Devonshire Manuscript* on Wikisource would have prevented the inclusion of any and all scholarly material outside the transcription itself—including palaeographic expansions and bibliographies. With a book-like research environment as our end goal, we produced an edition in Wikibooks that is scholarly and peer reviewed in a traditional sense, but also enables citizen scholars to access, contribute, and annotate material. Crucially, Wikibooks also archives each change in content, allowing us to track reversions and revisions to the text.

In order to keep the editorial and encoding process transparent, the Wikibook edition includes links to the baseline XML-encoded transcription.[28] Thus, in addition to being able to use the XML for their own projects, readers can see the encoder's TEI-based editorial choices. Others are able to download this XML and continue working with the document, potentially allowing the project to evolve in unanticipated ways. With the firm foundation of documented encoding, all those working with the document can refer to, build on, or adapt the project's foundation. The markup did not simply help the team keep track of the process; it also facilitated an ongoing scholarly conversation about the text. Readers can compare our transcriptions to the facsimiles included on each page of the Wikibooks edition and are free to contest (and even alter) our regularizations or corrections.

In November 2011, ETCL-based members of the DMSEG began converting the TEI-encoded text into Wikimarkup, the Wikitext language. The team then moved the text, appendices, glosses, commentary, and textual notes into Wikibooks, thereby providing a flexible collaboration environment for stakeholders inside and outside the lab. Wikibooks, like Wikimedia and institutional scholarship at large, has its own self-governing editorial culture, and *A Social Edition of the Devonshire Manuscript* received promising attention from Wikibooks' existing editorial community. Since then, the ETCL team has amplified the Wikibook with additional images of the manuscript, witness transcriptions, an extensive bibliography, and the XML files containing the encoded transcription of the manuscript. Consequently, the Wikibook became an edition as well as a research environment for both early modern scholars and Tudor enthusiasts. Various authors have written on the value of employing wikis as collaborative research or authoring platforms. Best

[28] hcmc.uvic.ca/~etcl/Devonshire_Manuscript_poems.zip (site discontinued and now available here: etcl.uvic.ca/devonshireMS/Devonshire_Manuscript_poems.zip).

practice standards and protocols have developed as an increasing number of practitioners become versed in Wikipedia, and we have consciously developed *A Social Edition of the Devonshire Manuscript*, a scholarly Wikibook edition, with these priorities and standards in mind.[29]

The Wikibook form gives us the opportunity to recognize and assign credit for important editorial work that extends beyond the creation of original content. Activities like discussion and feedback are central to scholarly revision and authorship, but can be difficult to monitor and quantify within a large project. A print edition often only acknowledges these forms of labour with a line or two on the acknowledgments page. Originally, we considered the discussion pages ideal for this type of scholarly discussion and editorial record keeping. Like a private wiki community, however, Wikibooks bears its own social conventions. Through conversation with an established Wikibooks editor we realized that the Wikibooks discussion pages are used more often for personal commentary and disputes than for editorial suggestions. Reminiscent of Douglas's note in the margin of "Suffryng in sorrow in hope to attyn" (fols. 6v–7r) to "fforget thys," and Shelton's contradiction "yt ys wor[t] hy," the Wikibooks discussion pages are predominantly venues for editors to offer one another personal support (or criticism) rather than to discuss content analytically.

Thus, rather than rely on the discussion pages for editorial decisions, we made the most substantive changes in Wikibooks based on Skype and Iter interactions with our advisory group. Although our hope had been to have the advisors edit directly in Wikibooks, some found the technological threshold for contributing too high, and it became more practical to have the ETCL team make the proposed changes in the Wikibook. We responded to the advisors' recommendations in near-real time, adding (among other suggestions) navigation menus and images requested through our ongoing consultation. Many avenues for editorial conversation are necessary in order to foster the sense of a community that, as one of our advisors noted, is "virtually there, as if everyone is crowded around a page, putting their two cents in on matters great and small." Even when those giving editorial direction do not

[29] Leuf and Cunningham (2001), authors of the first book on wikis, recognize that a wiki must fit the culture of the user community for it to be successful. Tonkin (2005) advises that a collaborative authoring wiki should include the following: a page locking system to deter simultaneous editing, a versioning system to track changes and the ability to lock editing on a page in the case of an edit war, as well as an efficient search function, and navigation, categorization, and file management abilities.

undertake the technical implementation, multiple social media platforms can facilitate social editing. Relying solely on one single communications platform could potentially impede the success of an evolving social edition.

Each social media platform attracts and enables specific types of interaction. Using social media allows us to integrate a new step into the editorial process—a step that fills the gap between an edition's initial planning stages and its concluding peer review. Producing an edition "live" in consultation with various groups across multiple media allows for a publication that can quickly and productively meet the needs of its readers. Employing and participating in various platforms alerted us to different priorities across platforms, as well as forcing us to think through how we might create a multispatial experience for safe, productive, and equitable interactions. In addition to producing an edition that allows for multiple editorial perspectives, the DMSEG gathered responses to the social edition-building methodology. In the interest of refining the process and expounding on its utility for collaborative editors in the Web 2.0 environment, the ETCL team used a combination of methods to gather data on the social edition building process. We conducted qualitative interviews with members of our advisory group to solicit their perspectives on the content of the evolving and fixed editions, as well as on issues of credit, peer review, and collaborative editing. We also enumerated interaction in Wikibooks. Furthermore, we invited feedback via Twitter, guest blog posts, and Iter's social media space. Rather than solicit anonymous reader reports from our advisors, we brought them into conversation with one another over the fixed edition and the evolving Wikibooks edition. We facilitated this conversation in a social media space housed by Iter, which serves a broad community of early modern and Renaissance associations and scholars. In many cases, their suggestions have already been incorporated into the Wikibooks publication; those that have not will be integrated into a final, socially mediated edition of the Devonshire Manuscript for print and e-publication with Iter and Medieval and Renaissance Texts and Studies (MRTS).

Considered as a whole, *A Social Edition of the Devonshire Manuscript* suggests that social media technologies can be harnessed for productive interaction and discussion by those scholars invested in a content area or project, but that they do require comprehensive oversight by dedicated staff to develop and maintain participation in knowledge construction and dissemination. Social scholarly editions represent a step toward diversifying and democratizing knowledge, and the Wikimedia suite of platforms is an established environment for this sort of work. Todd Presner reiterates this concept by considering Wikipedia as a model for the future of humanities research.

Presner deems Wikipedia "a truly innovative, global, multilingual, collaborative knowledge-generating community and platform for authoring, editing, distributing and versioning knowledge" (2010). Larger than a mere technological innovation, wikis represent a change in the philosophy and practice of knowledge creation. With this end in mind, we have published scholarly content in Wikibooks, an editable environment that allows for multithreaded conversation maintained by lay knowledge communities on the web. We hope that *A Social Edition of the Devonshire Manuscript* continues to serve all of the varying communities currently involved in the project: academic and non-academic alike.

Conclusion: Digital Affordances for Academic and Non-Academic Editing

The Devonshire Manuscript's historically social structure and content informed our choice of Wikibooks as a publication venue. Recently emerged social media environments, including the Wikimedia suite, shape the way academic and citizen scholars work by providing new tools and platforms to perform scholarly activities. These technological innovations encourage academic researchers to open up scholarship and ask questions not previously possible. The intersection of social media and the scholarly edition has a destabilizing effect, as it facilitates a model of textual interaction and intervention that represents the scholarly text as a process rather than a product. Moreover, these significant conceptual shifts in research, writing, and editorial practices have provoked various reconsiderations of the ethos and methods inherent in academic scholarship in particular, and knowledge creation in general. For instance, the open source movement has morphed through its open scholarship instantiation to develop a new breed of academic: the open scholar.[30] According to Terry Anderson, open scholars "create; use and contribute open educational resources; self archive; apply their research; do open research; filter and share with others; support emerging open learning alternatives; publish in open access journals; comment openly on the works of others; build networks" (quoted in Mahony 2011).[31] True

[30] Tapscott and Williams (2010) outline five levels of open scholarship: 1) course content exchange; 2) course content collaboration; 3) course content co-innovation; 4) knowledge co-creation; and 5) collaborative learning connection.

[31] Garnett and Ecclesfield (2012) discuss the Open Scholar philosophy further. Not to be confused with the Drupal software Open Scholar. Garnett and Ecclesfield (2012) reference *Academic Evolution*, a blog formerly run by Gideon Burton, who states: "the Open Scholar is someone who makes their intellectual projects and processes digitally visible and who invites and encourages ongoing criticism of their work and second-

openness requires adopting values that the nature and scale of the electronic medium necessitates (i.e., collaboration and innovation across backgrounds, skill levels, and disciplines).[32] These concepts vary considerably from the closed publication and professional cultures that have previously pervaded the university as an institution.

Technological advances potently shape how individuals and communities create new knowledge. As such, it behooves scholars to think through the affordances and implications of any collaborative publishing platform, space for social knowledge creation or multi-authored environment. Incorporating social media allowances and Web 2.0 practices into a scholarly edition recasts the primary editor as a facilitator, rather than progenitor, of textual knowledge creation. Conventionally, a single-authority editor determines and shapes what is important to the reader, focuses the editorial and analytical lens and ultimately exerts immense control over reader experience. A social media framework for the electronic scholarly edition pushes the boundaries of authority, shifting power from a single editor to a community of readers. As Kathleen Fitzpatrick writes, introducing different modes of reading and interpreting that take advantage of the capabilities of digital networks allows for new knowledge to develop:

> Scholars operate in a range of conversations, from classroom conversations with students to conference conversations with colleagues; scholars need to have available to them not simply the library model of texts circulating amongst individual readers but also the coffee house model of public reading and debate. This interconnection of individual nodes into a collective fabric is, of course, the strength of the network, which not only physically binds individual machines but also has the ability to bring together the users of those machines, at their separate workstations, into one communal whole. (Fitzpatrick 2007)

The social edition models a new kind of scholarly discourse network that hopes to eschew traditional, institutionally reinforced, hierarchical structures, and relies instead upon those that are community generated.

---

ary uses of any or all parts of it at any stage of its development" (academicevolution.com/2009/08/the-open-scholar.html; accessed 2 December 2021).

[32] Looking further than a mere series of activities, Charles Vest predicts the development of a meta-university: "a transcendent, accessible, empowering, dynamic, communally constructed framework of open materials and platforms on which much of higher education worldwide can be constructed or enhanced" (Vest 2006, 18).

A Social Edition of the Devonshire Manuscript brings communities together to engage in conversation around a text formed and reformed through an ongoing, iterative, public editorial process. A central aim of the project was to facilitate knowledge transfer and creation between multiple editorial communities with varying values and priorities. Ray Siemens has called for scholars "to extend our understanding of the scholarly edition in light of new models of edition production that embrace social networking and its commensurate tools," and to develop "the social edition as an extension of the traditions in which it is situated and which it has the potential to inform productively" (Siemens et al. 2012, 447). Bringing practice to theory, we have modelled the social scholarly edition. We have worked as a team to extend scholarly best practice and open-access methodology to collaborative editing in Web 2.0 environments. We have chosen to build an edition on Wikibooks, alongside (and with help from) the dedicated Wikibooks community. Our goal, manifested by community engagement via Wikibooks, Twitter, blogs, and an Iter Drupal-based social media space, is to use existing social media tools to change the role of the scholarly editor from the *sole authority* on the text to a *facilitator* who brings traditional and citizen scholars into collaboration through ongoing editorial conversation. By privileging process over product, the DMSEG aims to render transparent the production of an online edition of the Devonshire Manuscript.

The edition-building process situated our text at the intersection of academic and wiki culture. As we traversed this admittedly new and multidisciplinary ground, we sought advice and feedback from a variety of sources. We developed the public editing process to encourage communication between editorial communities while at the same time preserving the peer review process. Such open communication notwithstanding, conflicts in editorial norms exist, as standards and expectations concerning tone, feedback, and content vary widely across our multiple communities. *A Social Edition of the Devonshire Manuscript* brings overlapping groups of partners and stakeholders together in a way that a traditional print edition cannot. The first group (the partners) consists of scholars and publishers invested in the shifting landscape of scholarly collaboration and dissemination: project advisors, publishing partners at Iter and Medieval and Renaissance Texts and Studies (MRTS), digital content partners at Adam Matthew Digital, and members of the Digital Humanities community at the University of Alberta, who provided us with a tool to visualize Wikibooks contributions. The second group (the stakeholders) consists of individuals invested in early modern studies: project advisors, Wikimedia stakeholders, bloggers, and traditional and citizen scholars on Twitter. Trusting the content contributed by partners and stakeholders means not only trusting both groups but, perhaps more importantly, trusting our exploration of editable publication venues. In light of our experience with the iterative production of the social edition, we would argue for the importance of incorporating various social platforms and venues that enable conversation across previously divergent lines of knowledge production.

A Social Edition of the Devonshire Manuscript is designed to fill the void that Ezell notes has been left by the lack of effort made to "Catalogue and reconstruct patterns in women's manuscript texts to provide an inclusive overview of literary activities rather than isolated, individual authors" (Ezell 1999, 23). Concurrently, the DMSEG planned the form of the social edition in response to Greg Crane and others' exhortation of the "need to shift from lone editorials and monumental editions to editors [. . .] who coordinate contributions from many sources and oversee living editions" (Crane 2010, 81–97). The editorial communities that have grown up around social media sites like Wikibooks indicate a public desire to expand knowledge communities using accessible social technologies. Using the Devonshire Manuscript as a prototype, we have devised a method that addresses the questions that a social edition raises. Namely, how do we effectively integrate multiple communities with varying cultures and editorial standards while pushing the boundaries of editorial authority? How do we employ multiple social media platforms with varying degrees of openness to ensure a safe space for multiple individuals and opinions? And how do we shift the power from a single editor, who shapes the reading of any given text, to a group of readers whose interactions and interpretations form a new method of making meaning out of the source material? It is our hope that this model of the social scholarly edition successfully straddles various communities of scholars and modes of creating and disseminating knowledge. *A Social Edition of the Devonshire Manuscript* represents the range of possibilities for social scholarly editing across contemporary editorial communities—communities that need not be limited by social, geographic, or institutional boundaries.

WORKS CITED

Baron, Helen. 1994. "Mary (Howard) Fitzroy's Hand in the Devonshire Manuscript." *Review of English Studies* 45: 318–35.

Beal, Peter. 2008. *A Dictionary of English Manuscript Terminology, 1450–2000*. Oxford: Oxford University Press.

Beilin, Elaine V. 1987. *Redeeming Eve: Women Writers of the English Renaissance.* Princeton: Princeton University Press.

Boase, Roger. 1977. *The Origin and Meaning of Courtly Love: A Critical Study of European Scholarship*. Manchester: Manchester University Press.

Boffey, Julia. 1996. "Women Authors and Women's Literacy in Fourteenth- and Fifteenth-Century England." In *Women and Literature in Britain 1150–1500*, edited by Carol M. Meale, 159–82. Cambridge: Cambridge University Press.

Bond, Edward A. 1871. "Wyatt's Poems." *Athenaeum*, 27: 654–55.

Burke, Mary E., Jane Donawerth, Linda L. Dove, and Karen Nelson, eds. 2000. *Women, Writing, and the Reproduction of Culture in Tudor and Stuart Britain.* Syracuse: Syracuse University Press.

Burnley, David. 1998. *Courtliness and Literature in Medieval England.* New York: Longman.

Clarke, Elizabeth. 2000. "Women's Manuscript Miscellanies in Early Modern England." In *Teaching Tudor and Stuart Women Writers*, edited by Susanne Woods and Margaret P. Hannay, 52–60. New York: Modern Language Association.

Crane, Greg. 2010. "Give Us Editors! Re-inventing the Edition and Re-thinking the Humanities." In *Online Humanities Scholarship: The Shape of Things to Come*, edited by Jerome McGann, 81–97. Houston: Rice University Press. cnx.org/contents/XfgqFrtg@2/Give-us-editors-Re-inventing-t.

Daalder, Joost. 1975. *Collected Poems.* Oxford: Oxford University Press.

DeZur, Kathryn. 2004. "'Vaine Books' and Early Modern Women Readers." In *Reading and Literacy in the Middle Ages and Renaissance*, edited by Ian Frederick Moulton, 105–25. Turnhout: Brepols.

DiNucci, Darcy. 1999. "Fragmented Future." *Print* 53 (4): 220–22.

Driscoll, Matthew James, and Elena Pierazzo, eds. 2016. *Digital Scholarly Editing: Theories and Practices.* Cambridge: Open Book Publishers. books.openedition.org/obp/3409.

Ezell, Margaret J. M. 1993. *Writing Women's Literary History.* Baltimore: Johns Hopkins University Press.

———. 1999. *Social Authorship and the Advent of Print.* Baltimore: Johns Hopkins University Press.

———. 2002. "Women and Writing." In *A Companion to Early Modern Women's Writing*, edited by Anita Pacheco, 77–94. Oxford: Blackwell.

Fitzpatrick, Kathleen. 2007. "CommentPress: New (Social) Structures for New (Networked) Texts." *Journal of Electronic Publishing* 10 (3): dx.doi.org/10.3998/3336451.0010.305.

Fox, Alistair. 1989. *Politics and Literature in the Reigns of Henry VII and Henry VIII.* Oxford: Basil Blackwell.

Foxwell, Agnes K., ed. 1913. *The Poems of Sir Thomas Wiat.* London: University of London Press.

Garnett, Fred, and Nigel Ecclesfield. 2012. "Towards a Framework for Co-Creating Open Scholarship." *Research in Learning Technology* 19. journal.alt.ac.uk/index.php/rlt/article/view/724.

Genette, Gérard. 1997. *Paratexts: Thresholds of Interpretation.* Translated by Jane E. Lewin. Cambridge: Cambridge University Press.

Hannay, Margaret P., ed. 1985. *Silent but for the Word: Tudor Women as Patrons, Translators, and Writers of Religious Works.* Kent: Kent State University Press.

Harrier, Richard C. 1956. "A Printed Source for the 'Devonshire Manuscript.'" *Review of English Studies* 11 (1960): 54.

———.1975. *The Canon of Sir Thomas Wyatt's Poetry*. Cambridge, MA: Harvard University Press.

Haselkorn, Anne M., and Betty S. Travitsky, eds. 1990. *The Renaissance Englishwoman in Print: Counterbalancing the Canon.* Amherst: University of Massachusetts Press.

Heale, Elizabeth. 1995. "Women and the Courtly Love Lyric: The Devonshire MS (BL Additional 17492)." *Modern Language Review* 90 (2): 297–301.

———. 1998. *Wyatt, Surrey and Early Tudor Poetry.* London: Longman.

———. 2004."'Desiring Women Writing': Female Voices and Courtly 'Balets' in Some Early Tudor Manuscript Albums." In *Early Modern Women's Manuscript Writing: Selected Papers from the Trinity/Trent Colloquium,* edited by Victoria Elizabeth Burke and Jonathan Gibson, 9–31. Farnham: Ashgate.

———. 2012. *The Devonshire Manuscript: A Women's Book of Courtly Poetry*. Toronto: Iter and Centre for Reformation and Renaissance Studies.

Leuf, Bo, and Ward Cunningham. 2001. *The Wiki Way*. Boston: Addison-Wesley Professional.

Lewalski, Barbara K. 1993. *Writing Women in Jacobean England*. Cambridge, MA: Harvard University Press.

Love, Harold, and Arthur F. Marotti. 2002. "Manuscript Transmission and Circulation." In *The Cambridge History of Early Modern English Literature*, edited by David Loewenstein and Janel Mueller, 55–80. Cambridge: Cambridge University Press.

Mahony, Simon. 2011. "Research Communities and Open Collaboration: The Example of the Digital Classicist Wiki." *Digital Medievalist* 6. digitalmedievalist.org/journal/6/mahony (site discontinued). Now available: web.archive.org/web/20110309202132/www.digitalmedievalist.org/journal/6/mahony.

Marotti, Arthur F. 1995. *Manuscript, Print, and the English Renaissance Lyric*. Ithaca: Cornell University Press.

McGann, Jerome. 1983. *A Critique of Modern Textual Criticism*. Chicago: Chicago University Press.

———. 1988. "The Monks and the Giants: Textual and Bibliographical Studies and the Interpretation of Literary Works." In *The Beauty of Inflections: Literary Investigations in Historical Method and Theory*, 79–82. Oxford: Oxford University Press.

McKenzie, D. F. 1986. *Bibliography and the Sociology of Texts*. London: British Library.

Muir, Kenneth. 1947. "Unpublished Poems in the Devonshire Manuscript." *Proceedings of the Leeds Philosophical and Literary Society* 6: 253–82.

———, ed. 1949. *Collected Poems of Sir Thomas Wyatt*. London: Routledge and Kegan Paul.

Muir, Kenneth, and Patricia Thomson, eds. 1969. *Collected Poems of Sir Thomas Wyatt*. Liverpool: Liverpool University Press.

Nott, George Frederick. 1815. *The Works of Henry Howard, Earl of Surrey, and of Sir Thomas Wyatt, the Elder*. London: T. Bensley.

O'Donoghue, Bernard. 1982. *The Courtly Love Tradition*. Manchester: Manchester University Press.

Presner, Todd. 2010. "Digital Humanities 2.0: A Report on Knowledge." *Connexions*, 18 April 2010. cnx.org/contents/J0K7N3xH@6/Digital-Humanities-20-A-Report.

Remley, Paul. 1994. "Mary Shelton and Her Tudor Literary Milieu." In *Rethinking the Henrician Era: Essays on Early Tudor Texts and Contexts*, edited by Peter C. Herman, 40–77. Urbana: University of Illinois Press.

Seaton, Ethel. 1956. "The Devonshire Manuscript and its Medieval Fragments." *Review of English Studies* 7: 55–56.

Siemens, Ray, Barbara Bond, and Karin Armstrong. 2008. "The Devil is in the Details: An Electronic Edition of the Devonshire MS (British Library Additional MS 17,492), its Encoding and Prototyping." In *New Technologies and Renaissance Studies*, edited by William R. Bowen and Ray Siemens, 261–99. Tempe: Arizona Center for Medieval and Renaissance Studies.

Siemens, Ray, with Caroline Leitch. 2009. "Editing the Early Modern Miscellany: Modelling and Knowledge (Re) Presentation as a Context for the Contemporary Editor." In *New Ways of Looking at Old Texts IV*, edited by Michael Denbo, 115–30. Tempe: Renaissance English Text Society.

Siemens, Ray, Meagan Timney, Cara Leitch, Corina Koolen, and Alex Garnett. 2012. "Toward Modeling the Social Edition: An Approach to Understanding the Electronic Scholarly Edition in the Context of New and Emerging Social Media." *Literary and Linguistic Computing* 27 (4): 445–61.

Southall, Raymond. 1964. "The Devonshire Manuscript Collection of Early Tudor Poetry, 1532–41." *Review of English Studies* 15: 142–50.

Stevens, John. 1979. *Music and Poetry in the Early Tudor Court*. Cambridge: Cambridge University Press.

Tapscott, Don, and Anthony D. Williams. 2010. "Innovating the 21st-Century University: It's Time!" *Educause Review* 45 (1): 16–29.

Tonkin, Emma. 2005. "Making the Case for a Wiki." *Ariadne,* 30 January 2005. ariadne.ac.uk/issue42/tonkin.

Vest, Charles M. 2006. "Open Content and the Emerging Global Meta-University." *Educause Review* 41 (3): 18–30. er.educause.edu/articles/2006/1/open-content-and-the-emerging-global-metauniversity.

Walker, Kim. 1996. *Women Writers of the English Renaissance.* New York: Twayne.

Wall, Wendy. 1993. *The Imprint of Gender: Authorship and Publication in the English Renaissance.* Ithaca, NY: Cornell University Press.

Wilcox, Helen, ed. 1996. *Women and Literature in Britain, 1500–1700.* Cambridge: Cambridge University Press.

Woods, Susanne, and Margaret P. Hannay, eds. 2000. *Teaching Tudor and Stuart Women Writers.* New York: Modern Language Association.

Zitner, S. P. 1983. "Truth and Mourning in a Sonnet by Surrey." *English Literary History* 50 (3): 509–29.

GEMMS (Gateway to Early Modern Manuscript Sermons): Developing a Community of Sermon Scholars

Anne James
University of Regina

Jeanne Shami
University of Regina

GEMMS (Gateway to Early Modern Manuscript Sermons) is a fully searchable bibliographic database containing metadata about early modern English sermons in manuscript (1530–1715). This resource (https://gemms.usask.ca/) facilitates access to manuscript sermons and sermon notes that are vital to providing a fuller picture of early modern preaching than that presented solely by printed sermons but are scattered through numerous archives, primarily in the United Kingdom (UK) and North America, and seldom fully cataloged.[1] The first stage of the project (2014–19) focused on the creation of a viable data set using metadata collected and entered by the principal investigators (PIs) and graduate research assistants (GRAs). Its second phase focuses on developing an international community of researchers from a variety of disciplines by enabling user contributions of metadata through what Mark Hedges and Stuart Dunn refer to as "community sourcing" (2018, 17); ensuring stability and long-term viability of the resource; and exploring research opportunities created by the data set.[2] This essay outlines the challenges and opportunities of creating a community of both occasional and committed contributors from a multi-disciplinary group of users including early modern social, political, and religious historians, literary scholars, theologians, book historians, church historians, and genealogists.

---

[1] As in the case of other performative genres, the printed record tells an incomplete story. Many preachers preached from notes, only writing out their sermons later, frequently editing or expanding them. The various forms of preachers' notes, auditors' notes, and readers' notes can fill in many gaps in our understanding of the sermons as events or occasions rather than only as texts. See, for example, the following discussions that focus on the performative nature of sermons and on sermon notes as the record of those performances: Hunt 2010; Spurr 2013; Hughes 2014; Craig 2011; Verweij 2016. For an overview of the experience of the sermon, see Shami 2017, 195–200.

[2] Hunyadi (2012) notes that increasing interdisciplinarity in humanities research makes collaboration among researchers even more essential (93).

ISBN 978-1-64959-063-3 (paper) ISBN 978-1-64959-064-0 (pdf) ISBN 978-1-64959-065-7 (epub)
New Technologies in Medieval and Renaissance Studies 11 (2025) 125–143

Background and Context

The first phase of the GEMMS project involved intensive metadata collection by the PIs as well as by several GRAs based in Britain, with metadata being input both by the researchers and by Iter fellowship holders based in Toronto, supervised by a research associate (RA). The database and website were developed and maintained in their early stages by the Humanities and Fine Arts Digital Research Centre (DRC) at the University of Saskatchewan before moving to Iter Community for ongoing hosting and maintenance; now, the site is back at the University of Saskatchewan.This model enabled the amassing of a significant amount of metadata—records of almost twenty-one thousand sermons from over 1,270 manuscripts as of February 2021—as well as the creation of a functional website and database, but has been viable only with substantial funding by the Social Sciences and Humanities Research Council of Canada (SSHRC). This funding was renewed for an additional four years in 2019, which is enabling the collection of additional metadata; identification of preachers and locations; cross-referencing of various witnesses of the same sermon, including printed editions; enhancement of metadata through contributors' additions, including transcriptions, notes, keywords, images; and improving search functionality. With the possible exception of ongoing support for maintenance, it is highly unlikely that any further grant moneys will be received after 2023. As Camille Villa notes, "funding proposals in the digital humanities are structured so as to offer limited resources for technical support after the conclusion of project development" (2015). Ongoing content creation becomes increasingly difficult without financial support, and many projects are archived or disappear altogether.[3] The project's long-term sustainability consequently requires the development during the second grant phase of a model that relies upon a high level of cooperation and collaboration both within the research team and with users and contributors. Collaboration is also crucial to achieving the project's ultimate goal, which is not simply better access to sermons in manuscript but increased understanding of early modern sermons culture. The question remains, then, of how improved access to manuscript sermons enhances or changes our understanding of specific types or occasions of sermons or furthers our biographical, social, ecclesiological, and political knowledge of early modern England. This question can only be answered by developing a dynamic and

[3] The problems of ending projects for which funding is no longer available without losing access to their intellectual content and search functions have only recently begun to be explored. See Smithies et al. (2019), and the University of Victoria's "Endings Project: Building Sustainable Digital Humanities Projects" (endings.uvic.ca).

collaborative community of those who read and use sermons for a variety of purposes, and who are inspired by the quality and freshness of the metadata GEMMS has made accessible to apply this data to new research questions.[4]

The kind of sermons network we envision builds on a distinction first articulated by Jeremy Roschelle and Stephanie D. Teasley between cooperation, which involves a "division of labor among participants [. . .] where each person is responsible for solving a portion of the problem" (1995, 70), and collaboration, "a coordinated, synchronous activity that is a result of a continued attempt to construct and maintain a shared conception of a problem" (70). Building a collaborative community requires more understanding of the entire process by all of the participants, supported by robust interpersonal communication. Accordingly, developing and sustaining a collaborative model needs to occur at two levels: within the research team and in the research team's relationships with external contributors.

Building a Collaborative Research Team

The research team initially functioned as a hierarchical structure that assigned primary responsibilities for the collecting, inputting, and checking of metadata to specific individuals within the team. The PIs collected data in the form of notes and photographs taken at archives, which was input and checked by the GRAs and Iter fellows under the supervision of the RA. Two collaborators were responsible for the database and website development. This created an efficient workflow that supported the initial growth of the project. As GRAs and Iter fellows developed expertise in various areas, however, they began contributing beyond their original roles, and the structure became more fluid.

Lynne Siemens and the INKE research group have noted that the process by which teams progress from their formative structure to a "mature and effective collaboration" (2014, 2) is not well understood. Unlike projects in which GRAs are hired for relatively straightforward tasks of data entry, this project from the beginning required students to have advanced palaeographic skills, some knowledge of the Bible, and strong critical thinking skills. Knowledge of Latin and Greek was an asset, but not required. Early modern sermon manuscripts, particularly those containing notes taken by auditors at sermons,

[4] 2014–19. Principal investigators: Jeanne Shami and Anne James. Collaborators: Jon Bath and Brent Nelson. RA: Jennifer Farooq. GRAs: Lucy Busfield (Walton), Robert Imes, Catherine Evans, and Hannah Yip. Iter fellows: Benjamin Durham, David Robinson, Adam Richter, and Brandon Taylor.

are often barely legible or written in difficult hands. Preachers' names are frequently abbreviated, and names of some communities have changed over time. As GRAs in the UK were subsequently hired to collect and enter data, additional skills were required. Manuscripts may contain materials related to sermons, such as biblical exegesis or commentary, that are difficult to distinguish from sermons, and traces of sermons exist in a variety of forms. Consequently, GRAs have been required to identify or disambiguate little-known people and places using a variety of sources; connect manuscripts with print sources; solve puzzles presented by notes and photographs taken by the PIs in archives; and make judgments about the types of materials they are looking at in archives based on the project's taxonomy of sermon types.[5] This level of intellectual effort differentiates the tasks of GRAs involved in GEMMS from those involved in some other types of projects, such as correcting Optical Character Recognition (OCR).

As GRAs and Iter fellows gained these skills, they were asked to write blog posts using their archival discoveries as springboards to individual research contributions. Their blogs, ranging from "Science in Early Modern Sermons" to analysis of a single preacher's digital archive (John Davenport), have publicized our project and advanced their own research interests. At the Canada Milton Seminar 2018, two Iter fellows launched GEMMS, earning an invitation to present again in 2019.[6] One critique of digital humanities projects has noted that students working on large digital projects may only have opportunities for these kinds of contributions, which lack the prestige of peer-reviewed presentations or publications (Anderson et al. 2016). In contrast, these GRAs have used their participation in the project to advance their own scholarship and enhance their CVs. For example, while collecting metadata, a UK GRA discovered a number of lay sermons, a category not included in our taxonomy, and one that deserves discussion by sermons scholars. Two GRAs received fellowships to pursue their research at American libraries. One helped to organize a one-day workshop ("Early Modern Sermons: Performances and Afterlives") at the University of Sheffield in November 2018 that brought together leading British scholars, a host of students, and

[5] The taxonomy includes three separate categories: sermon types (complete sermons, drafts and outlines, notes, and transcriptions), each of which may be subdivided by their creators (preachers, readers, and auditors), sermon genres (farewell, charity, anniversary, university, and many others), and occasions, whether liturgical, civil, or political. On the process of classifying the various traces of sermons in manuscript sources, see also Morrissey 2017.

[6] Presenters were Adam Richter and David Robinson.

local audience members, in which GEMMS was a much-discussed resource in almost every session, and which one PI was also able to attend. On the strength of her paper at that workshop, the other was invited to present a plenary talk about GEMMS at the Conference on Sermon Studies in Dublin in September 2019.[7] The talk was given jointly with the RA, allowing these two members of the team to work collegially and to speak face to face, an opportunity often lacking for geographically scattered members of digital project teams.[8] Likewise, students have taken initiative to enhance their skills in digital humanities using GEMMS data. While we welcome the ways in which students are developing their skills and portfolios, we are aware of current concerns regarding the ownership of intellectual property for students working on digital projects for which they are receiving financial reward (Hedges and Dunn 2018, 114–16). Katrina Anderson, Lindsey Bannister, Janey Dodd, Deanna Fong, Michelle Levy, and Lindsey Seatter (2016) have shown that students' perceptions of their roles as collaborators on these projects may be very different from those of the PIs, and we recognize the importance of maintaining a dialogue with student researchers to ensure that they recognize not only the value they contribute to the project but also how it develops their professional and academic profiles. As the project evolves in the next phase, it is poised to see the development of relationships that are "networked" rather than strictly hierarchical (Siemens and the INKE Research Group, 2014), as students contribute intellectual content as well as collect and process metadata.

The GEMMS research team is geographically distributed on two continents, which has provided increased opportunities for team members while posing some challenges for communication and collaboration. In the initial grant period, the two principal investigators (PIs) were at one institution, the University of Regina, while two collaborators at the University of Saskatchewan primarily worked on developing the website and the database at the DRC.[9]

---

[7] UK GRAs Hannah Yip and Catherine Evans; RA Jennifer Farooq.

[8] Siemens and the INKE Research Group (2014, 6) notes that in the case of INKE (Implementing New Knowledge Environments), meetings between GRAs and PIs at conferences and other gatherings helped GRAs to see themselves as collaborators rather than as merely assistants. See also Siemens 2015.

[9] SSHRC defines a collaborator as "an individual, participating in a grant application, who may make a significant contribution to the intellectual direction of the research or research-related activity, and who may play a significant role in the conduct of the research or research-related activity" (sshrc-crsh.gc.ca/funding-financement/programs-programmes/definitions-eng.aspx). Collaborators, however, are not entitled

In the second phase, a new collaborator based in Newfoundland has joined the team. Throughout the project, we have been fortunate to have Iter fellows based at the University of Toronto, the RA in the Toronto area, and GRAs working both in Canada and the UK. Hiring research assistants in the UK is cost efficient and contributes to the training and development of new researchers, but it limits opportunities for face-to-face communication with the PIs and RA. Although the RA has been able to offer face-to-face training for the Iter fellows, the UK research assistants received training via teleconferencing software. The increasing development of videoconferencing platforms improves communications but does not entirely replace the benefits of in-person meetings. The RA acts as liaison between the GRAs and the PIs regarding training and assignments of tasks, but to date most communication has been between individuals rather than the entire team and has been conducted largely by email.

In the first grant period, communication between those focusing on the content (the PIs and the GRAs) and the two collaborators providing the DH expertise (one primarily responsible for the creation of the database and website at the DRC) tended to be sporadic. It was conducted primarily with the RA as the liaison between the PIs and the DH collaborators, and most frequently focused on developing search functions and solving problems as they arose. During that phase, the database and website developer, Jon Bath, moved into a faculty position. Although he continues to consult on the project, he was unable to remain actively involved as a collaborator in the second phase. The other collaborator, Brent Nelson, has moved into a new role as a PI, and a collaborator with expertise in data visualization, Matthew Milner, has joined the project as we move into the second phase and begin to concentrate on research applications. A GRA at the University of Saskatchewan will also have an opportunity to integrate subject knowledge with DH experience by working on the project. Technical support and programming for the database's transition to the Drupal platform will be delivered by the University of Saskatchewan Library IT department as part of the services offered by the DRC in support of faculty research. Increased connection with the library, which now houses the DRC, is important in terms of sustainability, as libraries are primary dispensers and preservers of digital scholarly content in universities. In initial meetings, DRC and library IT staff indicate that they see working on the transition of GEMMS to Drupal not only as a task that will make this resource more sustainable, but also as a learning opportunity that will enable them to plan similar transitions for a variety of other DH projects.

to SSHRC funding for research activities.

As part of this phase, a more robust dialogue will need to develop within the entire project team in order to address longer-term issues including ongoing maintenance and stability as well as documentation of the stages of the project to create a record that can be used not only for this project but as part of the developing discourse about ending or archiving projects to ensure that data remains available to users. Recent research on the problems of long-term sustainability of major projects after their completion points to the importance of fully integrating research and technical aspects (Smithies et al. 2019; endings.uvic.ca; digitalhumanities.berkeley.edu/) and of maintaining appropriate levels of documentation. Like many projects, ours did not begin with the end in mind, but we need to ensure that our future development is cognizant of it. As the author of the Berkeley blog notes,

> few DH projects will ever achieve the level of support or traffic that requires having full-time support staff dedicated to the maintenance of that project. Realistically, the maintenance of inactive or archived projects will fall to a staff member at an IT department, the institution's library, or a DH center who juggles maintenance for a portfolio of projects alongside their day-to-day responsibilities (digitalhumanities.berkeley.edu/).

The experience of King's College, London, indicates that reclaiming projects that have fallen too far behind technically may be prohibitively expensive or offer too many security vulnerabilities to be viable (Smithies et al. 2019).

Developing a Community through Group-Sourcing

Collaboration among team members is not sufficient to create a resource that aspires to some degree of comprehensiveness, nor does it resolve the problem of maintaining the project in the long-term without the current level of funding. Moreover, one of this project's goals from the outset was to create a community of sermon scholars who would collectively consider some of the ongoing questions in sermons scholarship, such as the classification of sermons and their various traces. Resolving these problems requires finding means of collaborating with those not formally involved in the project: engaging users to become contributors and correctors of data, as well as creating partnerships with the institutions where the data is held. GEMMS falls between the ends of the spectrum usually recognized in discussions of group- or crowd-sourcing: a small, dedicated online community of contributors with expertise on a particular subject at one end and a large and constantly fluctuating body of contributors with few interpersonal connections at the other.[10]

---

[10] Hedges and Dunn (2012) use the examples of two "citizen science" projects, Marine

Enrique Estellés-Arolas and Fernando González-Ladrón-de-Guevara define crowdsourcing as "a participative distributed online process that allows the undertaking of a task for the resolution of a problem" (2012, 196). As Trevor Owens observes,

> Most successful crowdsourcing projects are not about large anonymous masses of people. They are not about crowds. They are about inviting participation from interested and engaged members of the public. These projects can continue a long-standing tradition of volunteerism and involvement of citizens in the creation and continued development of public goods. (Owens 2012)

According to Daren C. Brabham, Kurt M. Ribisi, Thomas R. Kirchner, and Jay M. Bernhardt (2012), four types of projects are suitable for crowdsourcing, including "Knowledge Discovery and Management," where the crowd collects information that is known to exist but is scattered in various locations, and puts it into a controlled format and location (182). The GEMMS project fits into this category, as those who visit archives and libraries in the course of their research and have a knowledge of these materials are well placed to add records to the database so that they can be accessed by others within and outside the community. In order to unlock the potential for the project to benefit from these contributors, however, we need to have the ability to identify, call, encourage, and reward a group of both occasional and dedicated contributors; a stable and secure platform as well as mechanisms for ensuring quality control; and administrative support.

Motivating contributors has been studied extensively.[11] Studies of crowdsourcing generally distinguish between intrinsic and extrinsic motivation, and most conclude that intrinsic motivation is key to high involvement and

---

Lives (ML) (marinelives.org/wiki/MarineLives) and Old Weather (OW) (oldweather.org), to illustrate these two poles. While ML "targets the subset of potential participants who are sufficiently dedicated to learn the required skills, commit their time, and persist when they encounter problems," OW recruits large numbers of volunteers, only a few of whom contribute extensively. They note, however, "that in some projects it is possible for participants to move on to a different level, and to carry out more complex tasks; examples of this are the ships' histories created in OW" (12). Rockwell (2012) describes a similar range of projects.

[11] These include Ryan and Deci (2000) and Hedges and Dunn (2012, 2018). Hedges and Dunn consolidate previous research into a wide range of projects—academic and non-academic—and provide examples of the full range of motivations, examining projects where motivations are complex and evolving.

high quality of participation. Intrinsic motivation "is defined as the doing of an activity for its inherent satisfactions rather than for some separable consequence" (Ryan and Deci 2000, 56). People may be intrinsically motivated to the extent that they feel competent, autonomous, and related to others they admire or to a larger, important cause. However, it is likely that most contributors will require some extrinsic motivation, such as social recognition or a benefit not available to those outside the group. Ryan and Deci conclude that the ideal in crowdsourcing is "to promote the autonomous regulation of extrinsically motivated behaviors" (2000, 64) that leads to a sense of belonging and recognizes the individual's competence, thus enabling greater intrinsic motivation. Hedges and Dunn concur, concluding that

> Emergence of more collaborative and co-productive forms of crowdsourcing has led to increased focus on "community motivations, around creation of benefits for the common good—to human knowledge or a cultural commons—*and* on a more profound engagement with the subject and a closer involvement of contributors in defining and doing research. (2018, 103)

While the relatively small group of researchers who focus on sermons tend to know each other, at least by repute, many other researchers, academic and non-academic, use sermons occasionally in their work or may encounter them while searching for other materials. These individuals work in a variety of disciplines, including theology, literature, and history (political, social, family, and ecclesiastical). Our initial call for participation was delivered primarily to the most dedicated sermons researchers through social media and our website in 2018, after developing an online form on which contributors could record and submit their data to be entered by GEMMS researchers. Ongoing encouragement on social media and even a recent simplification of the form have elicited few contributors despite almost unanimous support for the resource from sermons scholars.

If we compare our project to the crowdsourced John Donne Society Digital Prose project (donneprose.blogspot.com), we can see some difficulties we face as well as their potential solutions. The Digital Prose project involves creating a digital archive of John Donne's prose works both by correcting OCR and by digitizing exemplars not previously digitized in order to provide reliable texts of Donne's prose works. This project began with a call for volunteers from a relatively small and clearly defined group—the John Donne Society. This group already possessed a strong interest in the work to be done, as they recognized its utility for both their own projects and their research community. In other words, this group had a high degree of intrinsic motivation. The task was clearly defined, and participants could choose their level of participation. In addition, the task itself required little training beyond a basic understanding of Extensible Language Markup (XML), was relatively straightforward and repetitive, and could be done from a laptop anywhere. While the work requires close attention to detail, content knowledge is not essential. Social recognition is offered through a listing of volunteers on the website. In addition, the project was used in teaching settings, enabling a large number of student contributions. Despite these advantages, however, the project has had difficulty completing tasks and has had few "supercontributors," those who provide the most contributions.

In contrast, GEMMS attempts to tap into a more varied demographic that includes not only academic researchers from a variety of disciplines but also non-academic researchers with specific interests in church history, local history, and genealogy. This means that there is no existing organization of sermons scholars comparable to the John Donne Society, which tends to make the social rewards of contributing less evident to potential contributors. The work also requires more intellectual effort—deciphering handwriting that is often difficult; checking biblical references when they are unclear; and differentiating various types of sermon traces, such as whether notes were made by preachers, auditors, or readers—and can only be done by visiting an archive. Even the minimum amount of data we are requesting requires a significant time commitment when researchers' time in archives is often limited. One might anticipate that dedicated sermons scholars would have the most reason to contribute as they are likely to reap the most benefit from the database; however, these individuals may not wish to publicize their findings until they have examined them and possibly used them in their own work (Hedges and Dunn 2018, 115). For most academic researchers in these fields, individual publication has typically been the standard for hiring, promotion, and tenure. While contributors' names are linked to records, institutional recognition for this kind of contribution, which tends to be seen as simply an extension of traditional collegiality, is often lacking. The only major contributor to date is not a full-time academic, suggesting that sharing data may be easier for those less dependent upon professional benefits. Moreover, users already have free and full access to the content of the database whether they contribute or not, and as Estellés-Arolas and González-Ladrón-de-Guevara note, "the use of a free service cannot be considered recompense" (2012, 195).

Possible solutions to these barriers to contribution include simplifying the process of submitting metadata by offering an option for contributors to simply submit an email including the basic data and a photograph of the title page (where permitted by the archive) and having the information entered by the GRAs. Enhanced social recognition through blog posts dedicated to the contributions senior scholars have made to sermons scholarship might be motivating factors for some. Similar rewards could be available to those who contribute data to the project, even if their contributions are small.[12] However, engaging potential contributors, including well-known sermon scholars, in conversations about the kind of contributions they would be willing to make is necessary for us to learn how important recognition is to them, and whether factors such as time constraints pose more significant barriers. Workshops and conferences that showcase the research opportunities afforded by the database, as well as for teaching seminars, provide opportunities to meet with interested researchers face-to-face, a supplement to online communication processes that Siemens emphasizes as crucial to providing space for conversations that allow for innovation, creative breakthroughs, and problem solving (2014, 6–7). With few extrinsic rewards, we must demonstrate the intrinsic rewards of sharing information and ensure that contributors recognize that the project is not simply about collecting data but about engaging with fundamental questions that affect all of our scholarship in this field. As Hedges and Dunn observe, "Participants need to be able to see both *why* an institution or project is involving them—the overall goal—and *how* their contributions are used to help achieve that goal, if they are to participate fully in this common purpose" (2018, 109).

Engaging occasional users of sermons poses more complex problems. Simply connecting with these individuals will require a variety of strategies that may include working with groups such as local history and genealogy societies and libraries that serve them. As Rose Holley notes in her report of crowdsourced OCR correction, genealogists are "highly motivated to learn new skills in order to get the information they need. They also have a sense of responsibility towards other genealogists to help not only themselves but other people where possible. They realise the importance of information resources and researchers connecting with each other" (2010, 19). Many have an extensive knowledge of archival research, particularly in their local archives, and are connected to networks of other researchers through regional or local organizations.

---

[12] Rockwell emphasizes the importance of not neglecting "the long tail of participants who just want to give a little time," observing that not only do "their contributions add up," but they are also valuable "word-of-mouth advertising" (2012, 147).

Largely missing from our current collaborative model are librarians and archivists, who have been almost universally interested in and supportive of this project, allowing us access to their materials and working spaces. We need to find ways to engage them—along with institutions such as Dr. Williams's Library, New College Library (Edinburgh), and Westminster College (Cambridge) Library—more actively in this project, first by making contact and then by demonstrating how contributing to the project can benefit their institutions. Social recognition of these institutions can help to draw interest from other libraries and archives. Attending events as well as making contacts through social media may help to increase our engagement with this community and allow us to demonstrate the mutual benefits of collaboration. Many archival collections remain uncataloged due to limited budgets and staffing. By adding metadata for these collections to the database, archivists can make their collections more accessible, perhaps leading to increased awareness and use of their resources, and even potential increases in funding and staffing. For example, we were able to secure a short-term appointment for a recent PhD graduate, Helen Kemp, to enter metadata from Thomas Plume's Library, a private library in Maldon, Essex, which she had collected in the course of her doctoral research. This example, although requiring grant funding, demonstrates how such relationships can be mutually beneficial. However, in recruiting librarians and archivists, we also need to be aware of the institutional realities they face. While they support increased access, they may not have the staff to cope with additional uses of their collections: not only in-person visits but also requests for information or images, the provision of which is a significant cost in staff time to small institutions. We need to ensure that we offer them participation at a level that is manageable for them.

While concerns have been raised regarding the quality of data supplied by crowdsourcing, this has proven to be less of a problem than anticipated.[13] If contributors recognize that they have a vested interest in high quality data in the database, and that their names will be attached to their contributions, there is less likelihood of incorrect data. Moreover, it is important to define tasks precisely. As Hedges and Dunn (2018) note, the more precisely defined a task is, the more successful it will be (where it's "easier not to be wrong"

[13] This issue is covered in various contexts in Hedges and Dunn (2018, 75–76). However, the authors conclude that "To achieve a useful and/or usable academic outcome, it is necessary to correctly match the processes to be undertaken to the asset in question, to select the right kind of task by which those processes will be carried out and to be clear about what the intended output is to be" (103).

[103]). While we are unable to check contributed data against the original manuscripts, we will need a system that will enable us to ensure that all the essential information has been provided, and this system may well entail recruitment of contributors who can fulfill the important role of correcting existing data. Mistakes are common when transcribing difficult handwriting, and, in a closely written sermon notebook, the end of one sermon and the beginning of the next may easily be missed. Offering corrections could form part of some sort of discussion board, a function that Hedges and Dunn suggest can help to develop a sense of community and "shared purpose" among contributors (2018, 23). It is important to recognize, however, that such a process also requires the availability of researchers to check and make applicable corrections as well as to moderate forum communications.

Julia Flanders points out that collaboration also involves collecting and processing data that can be reused by other projects (2012, 68). Recently, one of our Iter fellows, who has been responsible for researching biographies of preachers, independently began plotting geographical locations for a particular group of preachers on the digital Agas map created by the Map of Early Modern London at the University of Victoria (mapoflondon.uvic.ca/map.htm). Opportunities for more formal collaborations with projects dealing with early modern England can enable productive sharing of data. Our newest collaborator is one of the creators of NanoHistory, which "allows users to track historical people, organizations, places, things, and their interaction over time" by allowing "users to pull data from existing resources" and to integrate it with their own (nanohistory.org/about/). These kinds of collaborations between projects allow scholars to develop connections between various kinds of activities, including the relationships between preaching, printing, and other means of sermon transmission; the spatial and temporal formations of denominational clusters; and interactions between preaching occasions and other civil and ecclesiastical events. While sermons have been recognized as an influential genre in this period, there is still much to discover about the ways in which they circulated among communities.

Collaboration with Iter Community

GEMMS has been part of Iter Community from its inception, and Iter's role in providing stability for GEMMS, and in expanding the network of people, projects, and institutions with which GEMMS interacts, has been significant. Stability and an expanding network, however, present some challenges. Paradoxically, stability on the one hand and an expanding network on the other might be mutually destructive rather than mutually constructive, and

GEMMS must address this paradox in its second phase as it seeks to reposition itself within the overwhelming multitude and variety of digital resources available for early modern studies.

There is no doubt that the stability provided by Iter hosting was key to the success of GEMMS's initial SSHRC grant (2014–19). SSHRC adjudicators and reviewers have become cautious, if not suspicious, of the publication of personal websites, hosted on university servers. It's possible that the credibility of individual websites is an issue, especially if they have not been reviewed, but the larger issue appears to be their sustainability and their ability to communicate with larger research communities. Databases as research publications, and not simply tools, challenge the values of committee members, while websites as add-ons to research projects are often dismissed or trivialized as they tend to fall into disuse, or are left to die on servers after people who have designed and created them retire, die, lose funding, or move on to other projects. The creators of the Renaissance Knowledge Network identified this as the first issue facing Renaissance scholars: "There exist a plethora of resources, designed and built at great cost to funders and universities, but they are difficult to locate, do not speak to one another, and are underused in scholarship" (Powell et al. 2015, 2–3). Consequently, demonstrating that the stability afforded by Iter would allow GEMMS to develop as a digital resource beyond current funding cycles, and beyond the changing circumstances of the PIs, was of primary importance in simply getting the project started.

The Iter fellows who joined the project in a joint-funded initiative, along with our other GRAs, have contributed to the stability of the project and constitute a small, core community of paid collaborators within a growing network of user/contributors. They have exceeded expectations over an expanding range of tasks: entering metadata from manuscripts (often practically illegible, or written in a difficult hand), identifying little-known persons and locations, connecting manuscripts to print sources, solving puzzles presented by our archival notes and photographs, all while setting a high standard of accuracy. Their social media contributions and presentations have provided research and professionalization opportunities for them as well as publicity for the project. In 2018, the database and website were moved to Iter's servers, with the project accessible directly from the Iter Press page (itergateway.org/iter-press/Database). Being part of Iter Press gave the project additional visibility for Renaissance scholars, as well as offering technical stability.

However, "Storage is not synonymous with sustainability": "What sustains a scholarly text [or database] is the community that is built around it, the way that its ideas are taken up by other scholarship, and the way that it circulates among scholars, students, and the general public" (Bowen et al. 2014, 7). The project is ultimately valuable only if such circulation occurs. But for that to happen, this community has to be visible as part of a large and stable consortium of resources, researchers, and users.

The current reality, however, is far more chaotic. Several initiatives are seeking to integrate and provide open access to resources for early modern scholarship such as GEMMS, but integration of resources is an ongoing challenge not only for GEMMS but for all of the initiatives currently vying for attention in the digital universe. Instead of a vibrant, coherent, mutually-supportive network, we are bombarded by many siloed projects, not all of them equally stable or useful, and few of them peer-reviewed after their initial launch. In fact, the proliferation of unevaluated projects may actually be obstructing collaboration.

Finding GEMMS, for example, is not as easy as it should be. Scholars going to the Renaissance Knowledge Network (ReKN, rekn.org), for example, for a single point of entry into an entire world of scholarly activity, specialized for and oriented for scholars of the Renaissance, will not find GEMMS, unless they already know that it is under the Iter umbrella. It is not included under "Databases" because it is a finding aid rather than a database repository containing primary source content. Nor is it classified as a Map or an Archive. And it is not included as a Catalog, except as it is an invisible part of Iter Gateway. The reasons for the low profile are complex, but rest partly on GEMMS's self-definition as a bibliographical database, an entity which does not fall easily within the ontology of ReKN's research resources, or those of other aggregating consortia. Most significantly, GEMMS is not a database of textual content (images and transcriptions of the sermons and sermon notes themselves), a feature requested by users and likely to increase usage exponentially were we to provide it. This is simply not going to happen in the near future. Leaving aside the prohibitive obstacles to such an enterprise, we believe that the quality of research is enhanced by actual contact with manuscripts as material objects. In addition, a resource such as GEMMS that increases exponentially the known body of materials available will have to work hard to overcome the current taste for targeted, limited engagements with resources, leading to quick publication. Telling a researcher that there are hundreds of funeral sermons, most of which have never been printed, scattered across two continents, for example, will discourage many from tackling the genre comprehensively until images and/or transcriptions are readily available. And yet, although GEMMS is not a digital humanities content database, it is more than a library catalog or finding aid. Our challenge is to use the next five years to find out how to turn these apparent limitations into strengths.

As we've charted the first five years for GEMMS, then, we are convinced that the sheer complexity of the network of resources for Renaissance studies can create as much fragmentation and isolation as it does collaboration. As part of Iter's acknowledged and well-recognized infrastructure, however, we are confident it is possible for GEMMS to interact with a diverse, expanding, but integrated collective. In the next stage of the process, we hope the connection with Iter will lead to peer review of GEMMS in journals such as *Early Modern Digital Review*, an online, open-access, and refereed journal publishing high-quality reviews of digital projects related to early modern society and culture, committed to productive evaluation of both established digital resources and recent tools and projects (emdr.itercommunity.org). Such academic review will enhance GEMMS's visibility and its scholarly credibility. Since the writing of this essay, GEMMS has moved to the University of Saskatchewan and is no longer part of Iter Community. We are grateful for Iter's continued support in effecting this transition.

As we enter our second phase, the biggest challenges to building the collaborative community we imagine are, first, access, and second, articulation of our core mission. GEMMS is open, available, and stable—but how do people find out about it? How do they apply it to their research? How does it engage users and contributors? As we attempt to grow our group-sourcing initiative, we are working on the premise that no one umbrella organization—at least not yet—is able to provide the hub, and generate the collaborations, that can enrich our understanding of sermon culture and potentially sustain GEMMS with minimal funding. Only human connections can do that.

WORKS CITED

Anderson, Katrina, Lindsey Bannister, Janey Dodd, Deanna Fong, Michelle Levy, and Lindsey Seatter. 2016. "Student Labour and Training in Digital Humanities." *Digital Humanities Quarterly* 10 (1): digitalhumanities.org/dhq/vol/10/1/000233/000233.html.

Bowen, William R., Constance Crompton, and Matthew Hiebert. 2014. "Iter Community: Prototyping an Environment for Social Knowledge

Creation and Communication." *Scholarly and Research Communication* 5 (4): 9 pp. doi.org/10.22230/src.2014v5n4a193.

Brabham, Daren C., Kurt M. Ribisi, Thomas R. Kirchner, and Jay M. Bernhardt. 2012. "Crowdsourcing Applications for Public Health." *American Journal of Preventative Medicine* 46 (2): 179–87. doi.org/10.1016/j.amepre.2013.10.016.

Craig, John. 2011. "Sermon Reception." In *The Oxford Handbook of the Early Modern Sermon*, edited by P. McCullough, H. Adlington, and E. Rhatigan, 178–97. Oxford: Oxford University Press.

Estellés-Arolas, Enrique, and Fernando González-Ladrón-de-Guevara. 2012. "Towards an Integrated Crowdsourcing Definition." *Journal of Information Science* 38 (2): 189–200. doi.org/10.1177/0165551512437638.

Flanders, Julia. 2012. "Collaboration and Dissent: Challenges of Collaborative Standards for Digital Humanities." *Collaborative Research in the Digital Humanities: A Volume in Honour of Harold Short, on the Occasion of his 65th Birthday and his Retirement, September 2010*, edited by Marilyn Deegan, Willard McCarty, and Harold Short, 76–80. Farnham: Ashgate.

Hedges, Mark, and Stuart Dunn. 2012. *Crowd-Sourcing Scoping Study: Engaging the Crowd with Humanities Research.* stuartdunn.files.wordpress.com/2013/04/crowdsourcing-connected-communities.pdf.

———. 2018. *Academic Crowdsourcing in the Humanities: Crowds, Communities and Co-Production.* Oxford: Chandos.

Holley, Rose. 2010. "Crowdsourcing: How and Why should Libraries do it?" *D-Lib Magazine* 16 (3/4): doi.org/10.1045/march2010-holley.

Hughes, Ann. 2014. "Preachers and Hearers in Revolutionary London: Contextualising Parliamentary Fast Sermons." *Transactions of the Royal Historical Society* 24 (December): 55–77. doi.org/10.1017/S0080440114000036.

Hunt, Arnold. 2010. *The Art of Hearing: English Preachers and Their Audiences, 1590–1640.* Cambridge: Cambridge University Press.

Hunyadi, Laszlo. 2012. "Collaboration in Virtual Space in Digital Humanities." In *Collaborative Research in the Digital Humanities: A Volume in Honour of Harold Short, on the Occasion of his 65th Birthday and his Retirement, September 2010*, edited by Willard McCarty, Marilyn Deegan, and Harold Short, 93–104. Farnham: Ashgate.

Morrissey, Mary. 2017. "Sermon Notes and Manuscript Communities." *Huntington Library Quarterly* 80 (2): 293–307. doi.org/10. 1353/hlq.2017.0017.

Owens, Trevor. 2012. "The Crowd and the Library." 20 May 2012. trevorowens.org/2012/05/the-crowd-and-the-library/.

Powell, Daniel, Raymond G. Siemens, William R. Bowen, Matthew Hiebert, and Lindsey Seatter. 2015. "Transformation through Integration: The Renaissance Knowledge Network (ReKN) and a Next Wave of Scholarly Publication." *Scholarly and Research Communication* 6 (2), 17 pp. doi.org/10.22230/src.2015v6n2a199.

Rockwell, Geoffrey. 2012. "Crowdsourcing the Humanities: Social Research and Collaboration." In *Collaborative Research in the Digital Humanities: A Volume in Honour of Harold Short, on the Occasion of his 65th Birthday and his Retirement, September 2010*, edited by Willard McCarty, Marilyn Deegan, and Harold Short, 135–54. Farnham: Ashgate.

Roschelle, Jeremy, and Stephanie D. Teasley. 1995. "The Construction of Shared Knowledge in Collaborative Problem Solving." *Computer Supported Collaborative Learning*, edited by C. O'Malley, 69–97. NATO ASI Series (Series F: Computer and Systems Sciences) 128. New York: Springer. doi.org/10.1007/978-3-642-85098-1_5.

Ryan, Richard M., and Edward L. Deci. 2000. "Intrinsic and Extrinsic Motivations: Classic Definitions and New Directions." *Contemporary Educational Psychology* 25 (1): 54–67. doi.org/10.1006/ceps.1999.1020.

Shami, Jeanne. 2017. "The Sermon." In *The Oxford Handbook of Early Modern English Literature and Religion*, edited by A. Hiscock and H. Wilcox, 185–206. Oxford: Oxford University Press.

Siemens, Lynne. 2015. "'More Hands' Means 'More Ideas': Collaboration in the Humanities." *Humanities* 4: 353–68. doi.org/10.3390/h4030353.

Siemens, Lynne, and the INKE Research Group. 2014. "Research Collaboration as 'Layers of Engagement': INKE in Year Four." *Scholarly and Research Communication* 5 (4): 1–12. doi.org/10.22230/src.2014v5n4a181.

Smithies, James, Carina Westling, Anna-Maria Sichani, Pam Mellen, and Arianna Ciula. 2019. "Managing 100 Digital Humanities Projects: Digital Scholarship & Archiving in King's Digital Lab." *Digital Humanities Quarterly* 13 (1): digitalhumanities.org/dhq/vol/13/1/000411/000411.html.

Spurr, John. 2013. *The Laity and Preaching in Post-Reformation England.* London: Dr. Williams's Trust.

Verweij, Sebastiaan. 2016. "Sermon Notes from John Donne in the Manuscripts of Francis Russell, Fourth Earl of Bedford." *English Literary Renaissance* 46 (2): 278–313.

Villa, Camille. 2015. "The Cost of Customization: Building, Maintaining, and Sustaining DH Projects." Digital Humanities at Berkeley. digitalhumanities.berkeley.edu/blog/15/04/23/cost-customization-building-maintaining-and-sustaining-dh-projects.

Towards a Model of the Network Edition

Kyle Dase
University of Saskatchewan

Digital editions, by one name or another, have been a part of medieval and Renaissance studies for over two decades. The methodology behind such projects has shifted considerably over that time: from Peter Robinson's edition of *The Wife of Bath's Prologue* on CD-ROM (1996), to the online hypertext editions of the late 90s and early 2000s, to the collaborative crowdsourcing and social projects such as Transcribe Bentham and *A Social Edition of the Devonshire Manuscript* (see Siemens et al. in this volume), projects have pushed the boundaries of what an edition can be and of the relationships between editors, readers, and texts. As an extension of this trend, I propose a new type of edition that pushes these boundaries further: a dynamic hypertext edition that incorporates an interactive network graph as its interface. This network edition allows for a new kind of computer-assisted reading where a reader navigates the text via network paths, emphasizing both the social nature of texts and the relationships between texts and those who produce them.[1]

The first section of this chapter maps the trajectory and trends of core principles in digital scholarly editing and more recent developments in projects featuring network visualization in Renaissance studies in order to demonstrate the potential for merging these practices in a network edition. To this end, I conduct several case studies of select digital humanities (DH) projects in medieval and Renaissance studies in an effort to understand how each explores and tests the relationships between editors, readers, and texts in a distinct way while maintaining certain common principles of freedom and accessibility that scholars have advocated for from the outset of early modern digital studies.

[1] For the purposes of this essay, a network can best be understood as an interconnected or related set of entities (in this context, entities are usually people and/or their letters, poems, and other works). A network graph, then, is a diagrammatic depiction of such entities and their relationships. Finally, network paths or pathways are those trails a user creates when navigating an interactive edition or project.

ISBN 978-1-64959-063-3 (paper) ISBN 978-1-64959-064-0 (pdf) ISBN 978-1-64959-065-7 (epub)
New Technologies in Medieval and Renaissance Studies 11 (2025) 145–170

In identifying the core principles and innovations in each project, I highlight those principles that repeat themselves in digital studies and have been productive in their practical application. Certain ideological principles such as transparency, accessibility, and collaboration are at the center of DH rhetoric, and determining how practical applications of digital studies interact, problematize, or even resist these principles can point us to areas where consistent developments are being made or tensions still reside in the discipline.

The second part of this chapter observes the rise of digital network projects or projects that employ network visualization and analysis as their primary perspective for investigating texts.[2] I examine Shakeosphere, Six Degrees of Francis Bacon, and Mapping the Republic of Letters, as well as the research outputs scholars have generated through these projects as a means of understanding the appeal of these tools and their associated methodologies. While these research outcomes frequently consist of close reading combined with analysis of their visualizations, the projects themselves are often divorced from the texts and contexts they represent.

Finally, I propose a method for incorporating these network visualization tools into an editorial framework and argue that the recent increase in accessibility and utility of network visualization and network analysis tools could allow for their integration into the context of a digital edition not as a simple accessory in a dynamic edition but as the primary interface for interacting with the edition. However, such an interface comes with its own problems as well, and issues of transparency and accountability require new consideration in this form of data visualization. I explore how the network projects mentioned above, particularly Six Degrees of Francis Bacon, have attempted to account for these new issues.

I then outline two instances where the network edition could have considerable advantages over its more orthodox counterparts: a more traditional subject, as in an edition of John Donne's verse letters, and a "coterie edition" that centers on the kind of literary exchange one finds within Katherine Philips's Society of Friendship.

My hope is that this framework can maintain the legacy of transparency, accountability, and accessibility found from the outset of digital and online editions while adding data visualization resources into the toolkit of the editor,

---

[2] For use of the term "digital network project" in early modern studies, see Alison Langmead, Jessica M. Otis, Christopher N. Warren, Scott B. Weingart, and Lisa D. Zilinksi (2016).

ultimately allowing them to better represent certain readings and circumstances of texts that have previously been overlooked or underrepresented.

Digital Textual Editing: Hypertext, Diplomacy, and Biases

Early discourses about textual editing using digital tools consist largely of a discussion about how exactly this new medium might change the way we edit texts. In *Hypertext: The Convergence of Contemporary Critical Theory and Technology*, George Landow describes an optimistic camp that sees a new degree of freedom in hypertext editions (1992, 87).[3] Landow sees a number of possible reasons for such optimism, and at least one is a shift in the reader's relationship with the text and its author: "a certain aspect of authorial control has vanished, or rather been ceded to the reader" (1992, 85–87). In an article describing the implications of his digital edition of *The Wife of Bath's Prologue* on CD-ROM, Peter Robinson suggests the sheer volume of available material and the mutability of that information permits the reader to create their own reading as they select different material in a new method where "the balance of power in editing has shifted [. . .] to presenting the text as a series of manuscript objects" (1993, 11). Robinson claims it unlikely that "the same critic will read it the same way on any two occasions" (1994, 11), let alone that any two critics will produce the same reading. The edition deconstructs the traditional relationship between editor and reader, allowing a user to rearrange and compile the nearly sixty manuscript and print witnesses within the digital edition into countless possible arrangements. Such an approach augments the editor's role to incorporate tasks we might typically associate with an archivist or compiler, insofar as they provide "a presentation of the manuscripts" (Robinson 1994, 11). But it also transfers an editorial task to the reader who must now manipulate the edition to develop close readings of a text with an incredible amount of variation that formerly lay obscured behind editorial authority.

Ian Small finds the optimism of hypertext critics problematic and states that there is an inherent problem in the assumption that the computer provides editors with "a new kind of freedom [. . .] from the restrictions imposed by value-judgments of individual editors" (1993, 24). In particular, Small is concerned with the presentation of curated material as an unfiltered archive,

---

3 For Landow's description of hypertextual critics in contrast to critical theorists, see the following passage: "writers on hypertext are downright celebratory [. . .] the vocabulary of freedom, energy, and empowerment marks writings on hypertextuality. [. . .] Writers on hypertext, in contrast, glory in possibility, excited by the future of textuality, knowledge, and writing" (Landow 1992, 87).

a mistake he accuses The Rossetti Archive of committing (1993, 29). He sees a great danger in this assumption given the nature of hypertext and digital editions to obfuscate the value-laden nature of the editorial decisions contained within:

> The only change which the computer brings about is to *increase* the available number of relevant facts at our disposal; but it has not made them any less selective or any less value-laden [. . .] the Rossetti hypertext project will certainly allow the reader to access much more information about text production than can be made available in a book. But all of this "new" information is still only a tiny fraction of the *possible* information; and [. . .] still remains as steeped in value as in any book edition. [. . .] However, the value-judgments whereby this information *is* produced have tended to become more obscure than ever. (Small 1993, 29)

Robinson provides a counternarrative to Small's concerns as he offers that the reader "may test every stage of our reconstruction of the transmission history of the text. They will have the same tools that we have; they may use these to confirm or deny our reconstruction" (Robinson 1993, 10–11). The greater role transparency plays, the less one needs be concerned about the value-laden judgments given that the reader can trace editorial decisions themselves. In other words, borrowing the terms of Krista Stinne Greve Rasmussen, the reader moves from their traditional role to become both a user and a co-worker, not just dependent upon the editor for "reliable academic versions of literary works" but interested in "the relation between the work's numerous texts and versions" as a user and actively contributing "to the scholarly enterprise . . . tak[ing] part in the editorial work at some level" as a co-worker (Rasmussen 2016, 127). This distinction is useful as it highlights the reader's shift in roles: gaining greater access and the transparency of the editor's decisions but also having to bear the burden of evaluating those decisions, and even the edition's construction, themselves.

Robinson also goes on to acknowledge that this presents a fundamental shift in editorial theory as the traditional roles of editors and readers blur (1993, 11).[4] The freedom from bias in editing is an illusion, as Small claims, but the freedom to take on a portion of the editorial role in one's own reading is the new reality. A trend to make more editorial resources available to the reader and to develop a degree of reader agency in the editorial process is at the center of this development.

---

[4] Robinson elaborates: "This edition, then, is redefining what we do as editors. It will also, we think, redefine what readers do" (1993, 11).

Some editors saw online editions as an opportunity to be more transparent in their process. In the introduction to his hypertext edition of *The Seafarer*, Corey Owen urges editors to "make their biases as transparent as possible" and claims he offers "as many relevant documents as possible" in an effort to amend the issues outlined by Small (Owen 1999). Owen argues that hypertext cannot act as a pure medium that provides a transparent text in the same way Beatrice Warde first hypothesized of traditional editing in *The Crystal Goblet* (1956), but it can allow editors to add transparency to the process of curating texts. Transferring the notion of transparency from text to editor alleviates one issue Small raises, but even though an editor's choices might be transparent, "it has not made them any less selective or any less value-laden" (Small 1993, 29). Moreover, as Kathleen Fitzpatrick points out, the realities of an online, digital medium reorients not only the way that readers relate to their editors, but how they might relate to each other: "Given [. . .] that many can not only read a text individually but also interact with the same text at the same time, developers of textual technologies would do well to think about ways to situate those texts within a community, and to promote communal discussion and debate within those texts' frames" (2007). What Fitzpatrick outlines here is the digital edition's capacity to be more than an isolated experience. Instead, it can be a hub for many different readers to share their experiences with an edition as well.

Both Small's issue with an editor's selective judgment and Fitzpatrick's keen observation of how online texts could potentially facilitate not only reading but discussion of a text are addressed, at least in part, through the concept of the social edition, where Landow's celebratory attitude towards the shift of authorial control is taken even further by disseminating that control among a larger number of individuals.

Social Editions as Transparent and Public: A Social Edition of the Devonshire Manuscript

When we discuss making an edition or text "social" in textual editing, there are several definitions one could employ and not all of them are related to digital projects. The notion of social texts has existed in textual scholarship since the 1970s, while the social edition is a relatively new phenomenon introduced by the Devonshire MS project in the early 2010s.[5] The former conceptualizes text in a way that acknowledges how the many institutions and readers surrounding a text affect the modern reader, rather than framing

[5] For an overview of the term "social" in textual editing and its uses in the field, see Robinson (2016).

a text as the product of a lone author. The latter is a concept for an edition that incorporates collaborative technologies for tasks such as transcription (Robinson 2016). Moreover, social editing, a collaborative process of editing texts using a method such as crowdsourcing, is a distinct, albeit related term that often plays a role in social editions.

The Devonshire Manuscript Project Team outlines a typology for electronic editions, classifying the "dynamic text," "hypertextual edition," and "dynamic edition" (Siemens et al. 2012). The dynamic edition is the most important for our purposes, as it consists of a dynamic text, which is itself a combination of an "edited electronic text" with "analytical tools," with the features of a hypertext edition "plus automated means of discovering and interrelating external resources" (Siemens et al. 2012, 446). These features not only interrupt the linearity of traditional reading, but automate "reading-related functions that would likely not be carried out without the assistance of the computer" on account of the implausible amount of time required to complete them manually (Siemens et al. 2012, 447). The various available resources and pathways change the model of the edition: "In essence, the dynamic edition structures and treats the text as a database" (Siemens et al. 2012, 447). This database structure is the means by which the dynamic edition facilitates the automation and exploration that give the reader access to content with greater ease than print (Siemens et al. 2012, 446). As we will see, a network edition is a means of changing one's perspective of this database structure in a way that highlights readings in a relational model.

While their definition of the dynamic edition outlines the current state of electronic scholarly editions, The Devonshire Manuscript Project Team also identifies a need to incorporate new understandings of the electronic edition based on the development of new social tools: "While the electronic medium is most certainly a productive space in which to present and analyze editions, it is increasingly difficult to ignore the influence of new and emerging possibilities for the electronic scholarly edition in the current phase in the social formation of the web" (Siemens et al. 2012, 446). The team proposes and models the social edition as a way of better comprehending the impact that large scale online collaboration can have on digital textual editing. A social edition depends upon a scholarly "community of practice" or a group of people engaged in different types of collaboration "extended to include public expertise while still valuing the experience, resources, and tools already in place" (Siemens et al. 2012, 450). The result is an expansion of Landow's claim that hypertext cedes control to the reader, as a social edition "pushes the boundaries of authority further, shifting power from a single editor, who shapes the reading of any given text, to a group of readers comprising a community whose interpretations themselves form a new method of making meaning out of the material" (Siemens et al. 2012, 453). In principle then, the social edition relies upon an already established community that opens its doors to outsiders to participate in activities that, in the case of electronic scholarly editions, are regulated by a set of scholarly values. In practice, this requires meticulous attention to principles of accessibility and transparency.

A practical application of the social model outlined above is *A Social Edition of the Devonshire Manuscript* (en.wikibooks.org/wiki/The_Devonshire_Manuscript; see Figure 4.2 in Siemens et al. in this volume): a digital, social edition housed on the Wikibooks platform that allows any individual with access to the Internet to edit the text of the edition of a sixteenth-century manuscript that is "the first sustained example of men and women writing together in the English tradition" (Siemens, Armstrong, and Crompton 2015, 1).[6] The editorial team of this edition situates this practice within developments of contemporary editorial theory as well as the unique circumstances of the Devonshire Manuscript's production:

> [The edition] blends traditional scholarly editing practices and standards with comparatively recent digital social media environments. In doing so, the edition aims to reflect both contemporary editorial theory, which recognizes the inherently social form and formation of texts, as well as the writerly and readerly practices that shaped the original production of the Devonshire Manuscript. (Siemens et al. in this volume, 99)

The well-documented social nature of this manuscript makes it uniquely suited to the social model of the edition, and the process of collaboration that produces the edition mimics the production of the manuscript itself. *A Social Edition of the Devonshire Manuscript* rectifies the "author-centred" focus of earlier editions that "distorts the character of the Devonshire Manuscript" (Siemens et al. in this volume, 100).

The core editorial collaborators of this project define a social edition as "a work that brings communities together to engage in conversation around a text formed and reformed through an ongoing, iterative, public editorial process" (Siemens, Armstrong, and Crompton 2015, 3). This definition is linked to the earlier idea of a "social text," mentioned above, as it incorporates the

[6] The material cited here from Siemens, Armstrong, and Crompton (2015) can also at present be consulted in the Wikibooks edition of *A Social Edition of the Devonshire Manuscript* (en.wikibooks.org/wiki/The_Devonshire_Manuscript).

notion of a text as the product of multiple agents rather than a lone author. The project also resists Small's criticisms of "selective" and "value-laden" editorial decisions by means of the transparency encouraged in early hypertext editions that make their materials available as well as in their declared practice of editing as an "ongoing, iterative, public editorial process" (Siemens, Armstrong, and Crompton 2015, 3). Any endeavor that permits and promotes public interaction must, in its very nature, strive to be transparent in its editorial decisions to facilitate the interventions of members outside the traditionally established community. Indeed, hosting an online edition within a platform such as Wikibooks ensures that the continuous, accessible nature of the project and its meticulous log of every change to the text promote ongoing accountability among its core group of editors by recording each intervention with the text. Beyond a clear log of contributor intervention, the edition also provides facsimiles of the manuscript in question as well as a link to high resolution images in the British Library's manuscript viewer and other supplementary materials that complement the manuscript text.

However, points of contention remain. Generally, the social approach raises concerns about attribution and authorship in terms of whether citation of a contributor fully constitutes giving credit in exchange for labor. The more interesting implications for this chapter are where one draws the line of editorial control. Even though the social edition invites contributions from any individual, the editors from that original scholarly community of practice still establish the original, value-laden principles by which new engagement is evaluated, and maintain the ability to roll back or change any contributions. A certain amount of gatekeeping remains in such projects at a practical level. Still, this iteration of the social edition disseminates editorial authority among the greatest number of people possible, addressing Small's criticisms by "free[ing] readers from the authority of those who hold cultural power" as well as any edition reasonably can (1993, 27).

Curation and Exploration in The Pulter Project

Another example of a project in Renaissance studies that implements both the dynamicity of hypertext and the innovation of social editions, *The Pulter Project: Poet in the Making* (Knight and Wall 2018, pulterproject.northwestern.edu) is a recent, ongoing digital edition of a manuscript containing the poems of Renaissance poet Hester Pulter, led by its general editors, Leah Knight and Wendy Wall. The edition utilizes many of the features already discussed in an effort to correct the exclusion of Pulter's work from the literary canon as well as Pulter's exclusion from other intellectual spaces in scholarly discourse (e.g., experimental science). *The Pulter Project* contains a link to the University of Leeds Library's high resolution images of the manuscript in question; a more general edition, in what they call the Elemental Editions of the poems, that provides only "minimal annotation"; and Amplified Editions, imaginative editions held to a scholarly standard through peer review but encouraged to push beyond the Elemental Editions in "their overall interpretation and/or editorial apparatus"[7] (see Figure 6.1). *The Pulter Project* also contains "curations" and "explorations." A curation is a kind of commentary that includes audio or text from various analogues or sources "that invite contemplation of different ways in which a particular poem might be contextualized" (Knight and Wall 2018, "Curations"). Knight and Wall see this as a means to push interdisciplinary and intertextual readings for a single poem and "suggest intertextual comparisons, contextualizations, analogues, source studies, and further reading on related topics."[8] "Explorations" are similar to "curations," except that they relate to multiple poems from the project "in order to articulate and exhibit their relations with each other and possibly with other materials" (Knight and Wall 2018, "Contributions"). These are versions of hypertext being used to its potential: rather than simply mention an image or sound, these editorial works directly engage the reader with other texts related to the poem or poems. Just one example, Lara Dodds's exploration of "Hester Pulter and the Imagined Worlds of Astronomy and Poetry" (2018), invites readers to contemplate the relationship between the new model of the cosmos, the ambitions of Milton's Satan in *Paradise Lost*, Donne's contemplation of "new Philosophy" in *The First Anniversary*, the various perspectives of photographs taken from space, and Pulter's own poetic notions of perspective and space in two of her poems. Knight and Wall invite contributors to create their own "curations," "explorations," and "further amplified editions" which, if accepted by peer review, will be featured as part of *The Pulter Project* (Knight and Wall 2018, "Contributions"). Their first contributions were subject only to internal review, but these and others are now subject to an external peer-review process. While the project may not permit contributions as seamlessly as *A Social Edition of the Devonshire Manuscript*, it still participates with readers in a social way that invites their insight and contribution to the edition as a whole.

[7] Wendy Wall and Leah Knight, email message to author, August 10, 2019.

[8] Ibid.

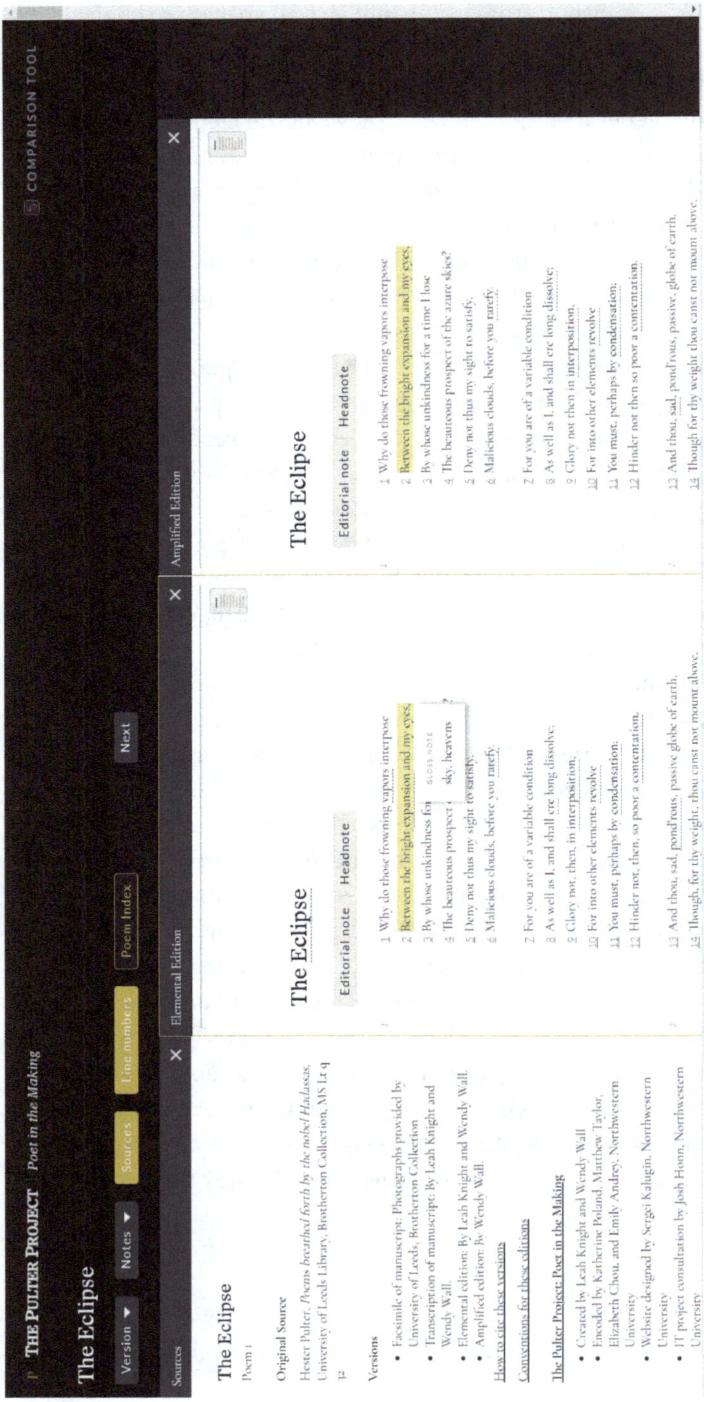

Figure 6.1. Elemental and Amplified edition of "The Eclipse" from *The Pulter Project*.

The project also leverages the relative ubiquity of online access to promote an understudied Renaissance author. While another online edition of Shakespeare's works may only add to the Bard's prominence, the inclusion of Hester Pulter as an easily accessible Renaissance author is a significant contribution and a compelling case for the impact of online accessibility.[9] Pulter's poetry has been limited to a single 2014 edition by Alice Eardley and is likely to suffer from "the unreliability of continuity and short print runs of academic presses" that compounds the utility of their digital edition in addition to its many features and resources that a traditional print publication could not replicate with any ease (Knight and Wall 2018, "Why Did We Build This?").

The Pulter Project also aims to retain the transparency valued from the outset of electronic editions and espouses that editorial principle in their mission statement: "*The Pulter Project* seeks to pull back the editorial curtain to reveal to readers the often invisible decisions underwriting the making of poetry and poets" (Knight and Wall 2018, "Why did we Build This?"). The project accomplishes this by "present[ing] a set of possible texts and interpretations, enfolded within a framework that transparently exposes what is at stake in making editorial choices" (Knight and Wall 2018, "Why did we Build This?"). This is an analog of the transparency of process theorized in hypertexts of the late 1990s and early 2000s, expanded as a hub for multiple authors to perform their transparent curation in a single virtual space. *The Pulter Project* extends that transparency—usually applied only to the process of textual editing—from the poems to the poet herself as part of the establishment of canon. Pulter's position as a relatively unknown poet who has been excluded from the literary canon creates a unique opportunity, as Knight and Wall describe:

> Pulter's manuscript affords scholars of literary history the rare opportunity to reflect on the creation of a writer's profile in the making. The Pulter Project is therefore designed to encourage the process of scholarly reception to unfold mindfully and abundantly, in part by generating a space in which competing models for curating and editing her work are made available for future students and scholars. (2018, "Why Did We Build This?")

The editors of *The Pulter Project* have managed to join multi-authored social collaboration and the transparency of process framed in the editorial work of early online editions into an edition that incorporates interdisciplinary perspectives upon a single subject with peer-reviewed accountability. In short, *The Pulter Project* takes many of the most advantageous features of

[9] For a closer analysis of how the proliferation of certain authors in the digital space affects the canon, see Laura Estill's chapter in this volume.

the projects and editions discussed above and employs them to highlight the poetry and life of an individual whom traditional academic pursuits had dismissed to the margins—in an edition that extends to the reader not only a degree of ceded authorial control but also a modicum of power in (re-) establishing the literary canon.[10] How the advisory board moderates control in this ongoing project will have a significant effect on the process and perspectives through which Pulter's work enters that literary canon.

The digital projects outlined above employ distinct methods but maintain recurring principles: each edition has constituted some reduction of the control a traditional editor has over their text. Key tenets in this process tend to be transparency and, by extension, accessibility and accountability. These projects implement features that further transparency, accessibility, and accountability, deconstructing the traditional editorial role as an authority that presents a finished product in the text and instead incorporating the reader into the process of constituting the text to varying degrees. With this in mind, we now turn our attention to the rise in digital network projects in early modern studies, how their users and creators use them to produce traditional research, and their potential applications in digital editorial practice as the tools to produce these projects become more accessible and their benefits become more apparent in the context of the principles mentioned above.

Network Visualization and the Trajectory of Digital Editions

Network visualization and analysis has become a popular tool in the digital humanities. For scholars who study the early modern period, there are several major DH projects that either incorporate network visualization or analysis or make it the primary means of investigation in their research. The three projects examined here are representative of a larger trend that seems likely to grow: Mapping the Republic of Letters features an interactive

[10] Likewise, those practicing digital humanities in early modern studies currently have a unique opportunity to leverage scholarly work on less-studied women authors to a similar end by building upon the considerable scholarship that already exists. For just a few examples of scholars bringing the work of early modern women authors to the fore, see Margaret Ezell 2002, Laura Mandell 2003, and Jacqueline Wernimont and Julia Flanders 2010. Digital humanities scholars, especially digital scholarly editors, are especially well-situated to better incorporate such voices into the canon in the wake of digital endeavors like *The Pulter Project*, Women Writers Project (wwp.northeastern.edu), The Orlando Project (artsrn.ualberta.ca/orlando/), and The Material Cultures of Early Modern Women Writing created by The Early Modern Women Research Network (2017, hdl.handle.net/1959.13/1326860).

network visualization of the epistolary exchange in the early modern intellectual movement charted over a map of the world; Six Degrees of Francis Bacon represents the social network of early modern England in a digital network project that invites collaborative user contribution and pares down the scope of that massive network through user-created selections including various occupations, social circles, and political allegiances; and Shakeosphere: Mapping Early Modern Social Networks is a digital network project that presents the relationships between individuals involved in print production, from the introduction of the printing press in England to the end of the eighteenth century, as an interactive network graph. Each of these projects employs network visualization and analysis but provides different degrees of access to their datasets. Moreover, because they do not engage directly with the theoretical framework of electronic editions, values of transparency, though often engaged, are advocated in different terms. The following summary of each project serves to highlight how they function distinctly from one another, and a brief discussion of Blaine Greteman's article (2015) on Milton's *Epitaphium Damonis*—a Latin elegy lamenting the death of Milton's longtime friend Charles Diodati—demonstrates how network visualization tools can challenge us to engage with different paradigms of the author, rather than merely reinforce what we already know.

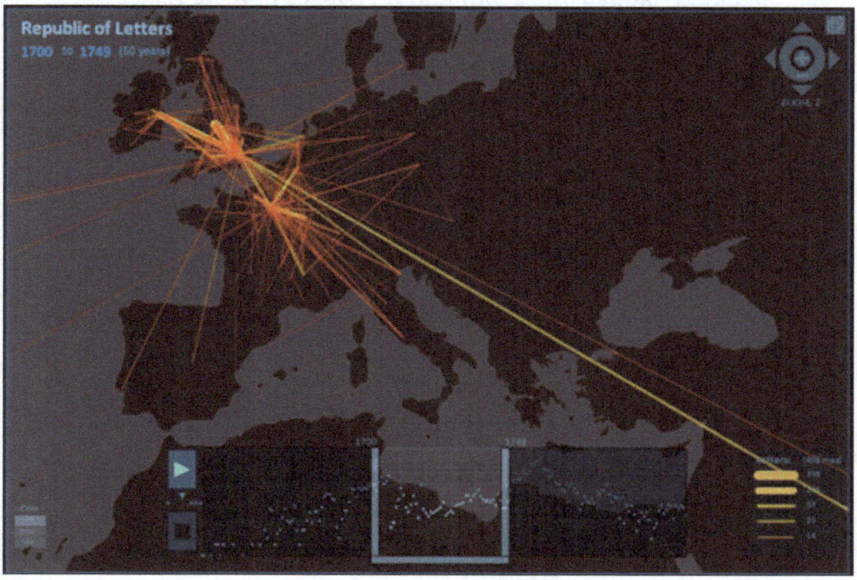

Figure 6.2. Geographical visualization generated by the Republic of Letters.

In 2009, Paula Findlen, Dan Edelstein, and Nicole Coleman began Stanford University's Mapping the Republic of Letters project (republicofletters.stanford.edu), which combines several important features into a single resource (Findlen, Edelstein, and Coleman 2013). Its network visualization ran on Adobe Flash Player (now obsolete) and allows the user to view the epistolary exchanges between cities throughout the Enlightenment. The interface contains a scale that allows one to filter correspondences between certain dates and generate them chronologically on a player (see Figure 6.2). In addition to the default view of connections between cities, there are filters that allow one to observe the flow and volume of letters as well. Perhaps its most impressive feature, pressing the Shift key and clicking any edge brings up a list of the correspondence that contributes to the size of that edge, and one can click any letter from that list to open a new tab to the letter's corresponding entry in the Electronic Enlightenment Project containing its metadata and, if one has access beyond the paywall, the text of the letter selected in the visualization. The webpage then provides links to the project's pages describing the recipient, correspondent, and locations involved that contain relevant biographical information or resources such as maps (McNamee 2018). Merging the Electronic Enlightenment Project's letters with a network visualization interface based on its metadata does more than just permit scholars to look at old material in a different light. It changes how we read by disrupting linearity and presenting new pathways of reading that allow for different avenues of investigation.[11] The result has been a series of case studies on specific actors in the network—such as Galileo, Benjamin Franklin, and Voltaire—that would not have been possible without the unique perspective Mapping the Republic of Letters provides.

[11] For some excellent examples of new patterns emerging from such research, see the following Vimeo channel: *Humanities + Design*. vimeo.com/athanasius (accessed 6 June 2021).

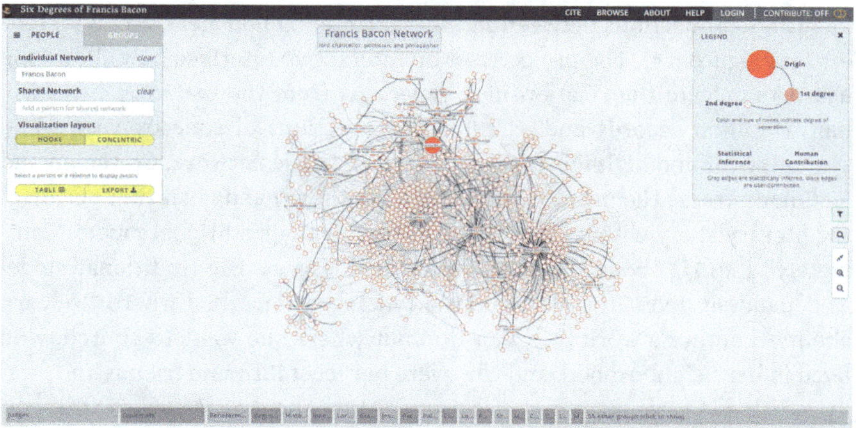

Figure 6.3. Francis Bacon's social network, from *Six Degrees of Francis Bacon.*

Six Degrees of Francis Bacon (sixdegreesoffrancisbacon.com) is a digital network project started at Carnegie Mellon that aims to be a "a digital reconstruction of the early modern social network" (Warren et al., n.d.; see Figure 6.3). It presents the adapted metadata of the *Oxford Dictionary of National Biography* (*ODNB*) in an interactive global network graph that invites user contributions and grants complete access to the project's own dataset.[12] The process by which the project team has extracted and visualized the *ODNB*'s data has provided insight into individuals who have gone largely unnoticed during traditional research methods but play significant roles in the larger social network of early modern England, such as Thomas Smelt and Edward Sylvester (Warren et al. 2016; Otis 2014). In many ways, the project has adapted the theoretical framework of the social edition to an interactive social network graph: the adapted *ODNB*, the curated product of a scholarly community of practice, has been opened to general collaboration and input that receives credit through logged attribution. The project even permits a user to download the graph's dataset either in its entirety or a refined selection. The project leaders have clearly demonstrated they value interoperability, accessibility, and transparency.

The University of Iowa's Shakeosphere project (shakeosphere.lib.uiowa.edu/), created by Blaine Greteman and David Eichmann, presents metadata from the English Short Title Catalogue (ETSC) in a social network graph that

[12] For an in-depth explanation of how the Six Degrees of Francis Bacon team transformed the *ODNB*'s metadata into a network graph, see Warren et al. 2016.

identifies connections between Authors, Printers, Publishers, and Booksellers (see Figure 6.4). The project uses an interactive interface that allows the user to navigate the relationships generated from the metadata of nearly half a million records and examine cross-sections of time by year while searching for and highlighting any individual in the network. Greteman and Eichmann frame the project within network theory and posit that performing literary study within this context "inverts" the traditional model "completely" (2015, "About *Shakeosphere*"). They describe the traditional model as dependent upon "the local and the synchronic" method where "to learn about an author's work [. . .] you find out where she went to church, who lived in her neighborhood, and who were her most intimate friends and family members" (Greteman and Eichmann 2015, "About *Shakeosphere*"). Traditional methods, Greteman and Eichmann argue, allow a scholar to find what they already know to be present, but make it difficult to see the role a work or author plays within a "broader communication network" such as that of early modern information (2015, "About *Shakeosphere*"). Social network visualization and analysis can better represent this data and provide a new perspective on early modern intellectual exchange:

> To understand where an author gets new ideas, and how he communicates those ideas powerfully and influentially, network theory suggests we need to understand not close personal attachments but weak ties—the distant, and sometimes fleeting connections we establish when we send a letter, hire a printer, or contract with a publisher. Shakeosphere will allow us to see those weak ties more clearly than ever before. (Greteman and Eichmann 2015, "About *Shakeosphere*")

Greteman incorporates the described approach in his article "Milton and the Early Modern Social Network: The Case of the *Epitaphium Daemonis*," to explore the influence that the network of early modern literary exchange had on the lament. Greteman emphasizes that no author, not even Milton, is truly isolated from the larger society that plays a role in how they formulate their work:

> [W]riting cannot be separated from the networks that make it possible and that it helps construct. Even if we imagine Milton at what may be his most solitary [. . .] we find him engaged in a complex network. It includes the book he reads, the editor and printer who produced it, the paper on which he writes, the shops where these items were purchased, the candle that provides his light, and the father who, in Milton's own account, "destined" him for this study (Greteman 2015, 80).

Greteman employs the network visualization and analysis available to him through the *Shakeosphere* project to argue for a reading of *Epitaphium Damonis* that employs Actor-Network Theory as an explanation of the poem's contemporaneity. He argues that, despite the many declarations of isolation in the poem itself, *Epitaphium Damonis* is an "intermediary" in a socio-literary exchange—between Milton, Diodati, and the other Italian poets from that literary circle—that identifies and celebrates many other intermediary works Milton received as part of those relationships (Greteman 2015, 88–89) Greteman's counterintuitive analysis of Milton's *Epitaphium Damonis* is, in part, the result of a visualization that promoted a social reading of the text as product of a network instead of the labor of a sole author. Greteman also uses network graphs to demonstrate that "Milton's social network was essential" to both the poem's composition and its material production (2015, 88–89). The more accessible such tools become, the greater the chance scholars will use them for important literary criticism that challenges our perceptions of early modern literature and its contexts.

Each of the projects mentioned above supplies valuable tools for network visualization that allow scholars to perform a new kind of analysis on early modern material and that have resulted in important academic contributions. However, these projects separate the metadata used in their visualizations from the texts they describe. Even in the case of Mapping the Republic of Letters, the letters from the Electronic Enlightenment are links to a separate, static project. The appeal of incorporating the perspectives of a network graph into an edition is in its ability to facilitate new readings, especially for those not directly involved in a project's creation and development who want to interact with the literature itself using network theory in tandem with close reading. This could prove particularly powerful for the exploration of literary texts.

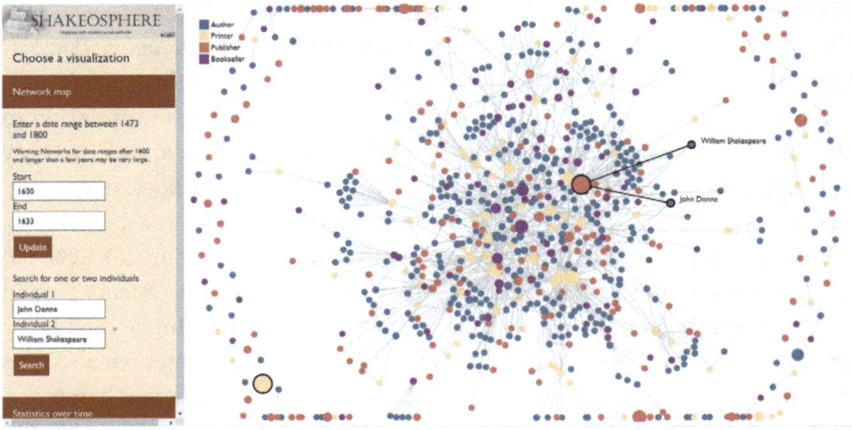

Figure 6.4. Shakeosphere visualization showing results for William Shakespeare and John Donne from 1630 to 1633.

Of course, just as Small observed of new editorial practices in digital editions, digital network projects come with new potential to obscure the value judgments incorporated into their editorial practices. In the projects mentioned above, a large blind spot of any visualization is the information that a dataset has ignored, underrepresented, or omitted. For instance, in the case of Six Degrees of Francis Bacon, the biases of the editors who created the *ODNB* are represented in the visualization of its metadata. As a result, women constitute less than 6 percent of the project's initial dataset (Warren et al. 2016; Weingart and Otis 2016). This is an issue with many projects built upon historical datasets and indicative of the need for editors to be transparent about their data and its compilers in addition to voicing awareness about how that data influences their visualizations, all while dedicating resources to round out gaps in that data over time.[13] Finally, such projects should always avoid the notion that their data constitutes an unfiltered archive that presents an objective dataset without biases or that a project's visualization is an unfiltered representation of that data.

Fortunately, we have already seen digital network projects that incorporate many features required for a network edition to follow the trajectory of

[13] See, for example, Six Degrees of Francis Bacon's event held on 23 January 2016: "Call for Participation: Networking Early Modern Women," accessed 20 September 2020, and "Midwives and Poets: What's in a Relation?" *Six Degrees of Francis Bacon Blog*, 9 March 2016, 6dfb.tumblr.com/post/140753600476/midwives-and-poets-whats-in-a-relation.

such principles advocated in electronic edition theory: Mapping the Republic of Letters has prototyped the direct linking of texts and visualizations, Greteman's work with Shakeosphere has demonstrated that such visualizations promote decentralized readings of even well-known authors; Six Degrees of Francis Bacon has an ongoing, collaborative interface that invites user contributions and facilitates ongoing accountability and transparency. An edition that incorporates these features—though it shares analogues with the editorial practices and outlooks mentioned at the beginning of this chapter—could cede editorial control to the reader in a new way, and even possibly to a greater degree, than previously established methods alone.

Whereas the first part of this chapter is concerned with charting the common values and trends between the two distinct practices of digital textual editing and the production of digital network projects, it concludes with a rationale and potential case for merging these two practices, arguing that the decentralized perspective of a network visualization can facilitate a reader's engagement with the text(s) in a new way that resembles the navigation of a network graph. Such an approach will not always be inherently valuable, but there are certain circumstances, such as the examples outlined below, where reading in such a way can give us a fuller understanding of the social context in which some texts were originally produced and circulated.

Network Visualization as Interface: The Network Edition

Ultimately, this chapter suggests that early modern digital network projects can be synthesized with long-established principles in electronic editing in order to create a network edition. The primary feature of a network edition is its implementation of network visualization(s) as the primary interface(s) for the user's engagement with an edition. The nodes and links in the network constitute the material of the edition, and relationships between these entities constitute relationships between texts and relevant elements, depending on what entity or entities the visualization prioritizes. If we can agree, as Landow and others have claimed, that hypertext creates a network and that our reading is a navigation of the database materials that make up that network, then a network edition provides an interface by which one can explore the hypertext from a bird's eye view to discover new pathways, connections, and patterns where each unique path is another configuration of the text (Landow 2006, 70–71).[14] In other terms, the network edition

[14] See also Landow 2006, 60–61. Note this passage: "Michael Heim, who believes loss of authorial power to be implicit in all electronic text, complains: 'Fragments, reused material, the trails and intricate pathways of "hypertext," as Ted Nelson terms it, all

makes possible a new method of computer-assisted reading: one where the act of 'reading' becomes a combination of exploring the pathways and entities of a network graph while engaging with the texts that make up that network. This network edition still retains similarities to the editions discussed above. For instance, it still deconstructs the traditional relationship between editors and readers, still places a greater degree of editorial control and responsibility in the reader's hands, and a reader is unlikely to read a network edition in the same way twice. But the reader's new perspective emphasizes the interrelated nature of the hypertext that makes up the edition and acknowledges a reader's position within a network of texts at any given moment of interaction.

Potential Applications and Their Advantages: John Donne's Verse Letters and Coterie Editions

Although a network edition certainly cannot be an optimal approach to all texts, one can imagine circumstances where such an interface could be a real advantage. In the case of a more traditional collection of poems, John Donne's verse letters are an excellent example. While context is important for any poem, the verse letters are especially beholden to their circumstances as products of epistolary exchange. Early critics' failure to recognize these poems as social texts led to a mischaracterization of their value and a neglect of the manuscript tradition that in turn resulted in editors' scathing remarks and an underrepresentation of the verse letters in Donne criticism.[15] In truth, the verse letters are highly dependent upon the relationships within Donne's coterie for which they were crafted: as interactions between friends they are personalized poems that require the context of those friendships in order to be well understood.[16] Moreover, the poems' distribution in manuscript saw

---

these advance the disintegration of the centering voice of contemplative thought. The arbitrariness and availability of database searching decreases the felt sense of an authorial control over what is written' (*Electric Language*, 220). A database search, in other words, permits the active reader to enter the author's text at any point and not at the point the author chose as the beginning" (Landow 2006, 129; quoting Heim 1987).

[15] In his introduction to the *Satires, Epigrams, and Verse Letters of John Donne*, W. Milgate called the verse letters "gauche" (1967, xxiv), while Patricia Thomson claimed in "Donne and the Poetry of Patronage: The Verse Letters" that "the desire to please brought out the worst in Donne" (1973, 280–81).

[16] Literary scholars such as John T. Shawcross, Margaret Maurer, Dennis Flynn, Ted-Larry Pebworth, and Claude J. Summers have challenged earlier attitudes towards

their circulation beyond individual friendships into a network of friends and friends of friends, making them coterie-constructed texts—more socially significant than the discreet instances of communication between two people.

Imagine an edition where the home page invites the reader to engage with one of multiple network visualizations, each focusing either on a different time or important coterie circle. Like the home page to many wikis, this could also include a random highlighted node or edge in the network, say Christopher Brooke or even the friendship between John Donne and Christopher Brooke. Entering one of these network visualizations presents a social network visualization similar to what one sees in projects such as Shakeosphere or Six Degrees of Francis Bacon. This includes nodes labeled as individuals but also edges that represent and indicate a relationship between nodes. Edges are color-coded to indicate the nature of a relationship (e.g., spouses, friends, patrons, beneficiaries, etc.) and edge thickness indicates the number of texts in the edition related to that relationship. Selecting any individual in the network highlights associated individuals of one degree while opening a window with tabs that contain an index of that individual's written works, a biography with links to other significant people in the network from the subject's life, and a list of notable relationships. From here, there are a range of options: selecting any given work (in this case a poem or letter) brings up its text while altering the network to highlight the parties relevant to or mentioned in the work; selecting any relationship edge in the network would, similarly to selecting a node, open a window with an index of works associated with that relationship, a full description of that relationship similar to the biography entry for individuals, and a list of others closely related to the members of that relationship. Finally, one could provide filters that highlight specific groups such as political factions (e.g., those affiliated with The Earl of Essex) or associations via patronage (e.g., the circle of patronage surrounding Lucy Russell, Countess of Bedford). One can easily see how such a network edition could highlight the relationships and community so central to Donne's verse letters, let alone the aid that various biographical and contextual materials could provide to the reader.

Perhaps an even more tantalizing prospect is the creation of a coterie edition: that is, a network edition that distributes its focus across a closely associated group of people rather than singling out an individual or set of texts. For

---

Donne's verse letters via readings informed by the poet's prose correspondence and relationships. Recent scholarship has demonstrated that the verse letters require particular attention to their coterie context and the relationships that inspired them. For a starting point of this discussion, see Maurer (1976).

instance, Katherine Philips's Society of Friendship could benefit greatly from such treatment. Whereas a network organized around a single author's set of socially constructed texts like Donne's verse letters might highlight the important social context for those texts, a coterie edition organized around a literary circle such as the Society of Friendship would focus on the larger network of texts and individuals who contributed to that context. Representing a coterie through a network interface has the advantage of decentralizing the reading of the texts associated with that coterie away from the editor's own biases as to who the core agents of that network are. In other words, where a traditional print or even a hypertext edition would have to prioritize a certain agent in the structure, at least in its interface, the network edition can present a visualization of the coterie as a whole.

Finally, there is an even greater potential for network and coterie editions. Alison Langmead, Jessica M. Otis, Christopher N. Warren, Scott B. Weingart, and Lisa D. Zilinksi have laid out a way forward for establishing the groundwork for the much more ambitious goal of one day "creating a network of early modern projects that could then be expanded into the larger humanities solar system" (Langmead et al. 2016, 33). A more modest application of the same ambition is to establish a common ontology and framework easily adaptable to different early modern coteries that could eventually connect. A network edition of Donne's verse letters would certainly overlap with the circle of literary patronage organized around Lucy, Countess of Bedford, for instance, and various literary circles of the early modern period connect through an individual such as Ben Jonson. In fact, Jonson is an excellent example. He participated in the coterie tradition, was friends with important Renaissance authors like Donne and Shakespeare, was a member of important patronage circles such as the Countess of Bedford's, and even founded his own literary group of poets and playwrights in the Sons of Ben. If a group of scholars were to create such individual coterie editions with a view to eventual interoperability, a community of coteries could eventually emerge that links our readings of the many literary circles of early modern England.

There is also a possibility that scholars might be able to leverage pre-existing, large corpora such as the Early English Books Online and its Text Creation Partnership: a project that has already released some thirty-five thousand "highly accurate, fully-searchable, SGML/XML-encoded texts" that are "currently available for access, distribution, use, or reuse by anyone" under a Creative Common license ("About EEBO-TCP"). The vast amount of metadata and text for all canonical literature in a single group of materials could be an excellent resource for starting a network edition. One could even conceive of using network visualizations to navigate such a large database. However, the curation and visualization of tens of thousands of entries would require careful consideration and resources beyond anything yet done in literary data visualization, and EEBO-TCP might best serve as a resource that provides easy access to base texts for works that have received less critical attention.

Even the proposition of merging smaller digital network editions may seem overly ambitious at the moment, but the current discussion around interoperability in digital network projects emphasizes that this is possible. Langmead et al. have already established there are methods by which early modern digital network projects can optimize their ontologies for interoperability, and they propose, among other developments, "a network of digital humanities network projects" and "example crosswalks between presented data sets" that would serve as a common lexicon of attributes among projects (Langmead et al. 2016, 33). Establishing common ontological properties for a small web of network editions is not such a tremendous task, relatively speaking, and a community of coterie editions that connect through common agents could eventually give way to considerably greater understanding of how the exchange of literary ideas and trends occurred in the Renaissance. In the meantime, combining methods from electronic editing and digital network graphs makes logical sense and allows readers to engage with texts through a new method of computer-assisted reading that advances the fundamental principles of editing and transparency that have been present since the outset of electronic editing: a noble aim in and of itself.

WORKS CITED

"About EEBO-TCP." Text Creation Partnership. Accessed 20 September 2020. textcreationpartnership.org/tcp-texts/eebo-tcp-early-english-books-online/.

"Call for Participation: Networking Early Modern Women." Six Degrees of Francis Bacon. Accessed 20 September 2020. networkingwomen.sixdegreesoffrancisbacon.com/.

Chaucer, Geoffrey. 1996. *The Wife of Bath's Prologue on CD-ROM*. Edited by Peter Robinson. Cambridge: Cambridge University Press.

Dodds, Lara. 2018. "Hester Pulter and the Imagined Worlds of Astronomy and Poetry." In *The Pulter Project: Poet in the Making*, edited by Leah Knight and Wendy Wall. pulterproject.northwestern.edu.

Ezell, Margaret. 2002. "Women and Writing." In *A Companion to Women's Writing*, edited by Anita Pacheco, 77–94. Malden, MA: Blackwell.

Findlen, Paula, Dan Edelstein, and Nicole Coleman. 2013. Mapping the Republic of Letters. Stanford: Stanford University. republicofletters.stanford.edu/.

Fitzpatrick, Kathleen. 2007. "CommentPress: New (Social) Structures for New (Networked) Texts." *Journal of Electronic Publishing* 10 (3): dx.doi.org/10.3998/3336451.0010.305.

Greteman, Blaine. 2015. "Milton and the Early Modern Social Network: The Case of the *Epitaphium Daemonis*." *Milton Quarterly* 49 (2): 79–95. doi.org/10.1111/milt.12126.

Greteman, Blaine, and David Eichmann. 2015. Shakeosphere: Mapping Early Modern Social Networks. Accessed 6 June 2021. shakeosphere.lib.uiowa.edu/.

Heim, Michael. 1987. *Electric Language: A Philosophical Study of Word Processing*. New Haven: Yale University Press.

Knight, Leah, and Wendy Wall, gen. eds. 2018. *The Pulter Project: Poet in the Making*. Accessed 6 June 2021. pulterproject.northwestern.edu.

Landow, George. 1992. *Hypertext: The Convergence of Contemporary Critical Theory and Technology*. Baltimore: Johns Hopkins University Press.

———. 1997. *Hypertext: The Convergence of Contemporary Critical Theory and Technology* 2.0. Baltimore: Johns Hopkins University Press.

———. 2006. *Hypertext 3.0: Critical Theory and New Media in an Era of Globalization: Critical Theory and New Media in a Global Era*. Baltimore: Johns Hopkins University Press.

Langmead, Alison, Jessica M. Otis, Christopher N. Warren, Scott B. Weingart, and Lisa D. Zilinksi. 2016. "Towards Interoperable Network Ontologies for the Digital Humanities." *International Journal of Humanities and Arts Computing* 10 (1): 22–35.

Mandell, Laura. 2003. "Introduction: The Poetess Tradition." *Romanticism on the Net* 29–30. doi.org/10.7202/007712ar.

Maurer, Margaret. 1976. "John Donne's Verse Letters." *Modern Language Quarterly* 37 (3): 234–59.

McNamee, Robert, dir. 2018. *Electronic Enlightenment Scholarly Edition of Correspondence,* Version 3.0. Oxford: University of Oxford. Accessed 6 June 2021.

Milgate, W., ed. 1967. *The Satires, Epigrams and Verse Letters of John Donne.* Oxford: Clarendon Press.

Otis, Jessica M. 2014. "Every One Was a Henry: Tales from the Raw NER Data." *Six Degrees of Francis Bacon Blog.* 20 October 2014. 6dfb.tumblr.com/post/100499157781/high-degree-nodes-tales-from-the-raw-ner-data.

Owen, Corey. 1999. *The Seafarer: A Hypertext Edition.* University of Saskatchewan. Accessed 6 June 2021. usask.ca/english/seafarer/TOC.htm.

Rasmussen, Krista Stinne Greve. 2016. "Reading or Using a Digital Edition? Reader Roles in Scholarly Editions." In *Digital Scholarly Editing: Theories and Practices*, edited by Elena Pierazzo and Matthew Driscoll, 119–33. Cambridge: Open Book Publishers.

Robinson, Peter. 1993. "Manuscript Politics." In *The Politics of the Electronic Text,* edited by Warren L. Chernaik, Caroline Davis, and Marilyn Deegan, 9–16. London: University of London Office for Humanities Communication.

———, ed. 1996. *The Wife of Bath's Prologue on CD-ROM*. By Geoffrey Chaucer. Cambridge: Cambridge University Press.

———. 2016. "Social Editions, Social Editing, Social Texts." *Digital Studies/Le champ numérique* 6. doi.org/10.16995/dscn.6.

Siemens, Raymond, Karen Armstrong, and Constance Crompton, eds. 2015. *A Social Edition of the Devonshire Manuscript (BL Add. MS 17,492).* Toronto: Iter / Tempe: Arizona Center for Medieval and Renaissance Studies.

Siemens, Raymond, Megan Timney, Cara Leitch, Corina Koolen, and Alex Garnett. 2012. "Toward Modeling the Social Edition: An Approach to Understanding the Electronic Scholarly Edition in the Context of New and Emerging Social Media." *Literary and Linguistic Computing* 27 (4): 445–61.

Small, Ian. 1993. "Text Editing and the Computer: Facts and Values." In *The Politics of the Electronic Text*, edited by Warren L. Chernaik, Caroline Davis, and Marilyn Deegan, 25–30. London: University of London Office for Humanities Communication.

Thomson, Patricia. 1973. "Donne and the Poetry of Patronage: The Verse Letters." In *John Donne: Essays in Celebration*, edited by A. J. Smith, 308–23. New York: Barnes and Noble.

Transcribe Bentham: A Participatory Initiative. Accessed 9 August 2019. transcribe-bentham.ucl.ac.uk/td/Transcribe_Bentham.

Warde, Beatrice. 1956. *The Crystal Goblet: Sixteen Essays on Typography*. Cleveland: World Publishing Company.

Warren, Christopher, Daniel Shore, Jessica Otis, Lawrence Wang, Mike Finegold, and Cosma Shalizi. 2016. "Six Degrees of Francis Bacon: A Statistical Method for Reconstructing Large Historical Social Networks." *Digital Humanities Quarterly* 10 (3): digitalhumanities.org/dhq/vol/10/3/000244/000244.html.

Warren, Christopher, Daniel Shore, Jessica Otis, and Scott Weingart. n.d. Six Degrees of Francis Bacon. Pittsburgh: Carnegie Mellon University. Accessed 9 August 2019. sixdegreesoffrancisbacon.com/.

Weingart, Scott, and Jessica M. Otis. 2016. "Gender Inclusivity in Six Degrees." *Six Degrees of Francis Bacon Blog*. 5 January 2016. 6dfb.tumblr.com/post/136678327006/gender-inclusivity-in-six-degrees.

Wernimont, Jacqueline, and Julia Flanders. 2010. "Feminism in the Age of Digital Archives: The Women Writers Project on JSTOR." *Tulsa Studies in Women's Literature* 29 (2): 425–35.

Extending the Contribution of Online Digital Projects about the Middle Ages and Renaissance: A Case Study of DEx: A Database of Dramatic Extracts

Luis Meneses
Vancouver Island University

The digital humanities are at a turning point where we should make a departure from the traditional analyses used in other disciplines, devising our own methods to address our research questions (Orlandi 2019). In my opinion, Iter Community is at the forefront of facilitating new methodologies in the digital humanities. Iter Community is a not-for-profit partnership between the Electronic Textual Cultures Lab (University of Victoria) and Iter (University of Toronto) that is dedicated to facilitating and supporting communication, collaboration, and digital project creation for research communities of the Middle Ages and the Renaissance. Iter Community aspires to support scholarly communication and information sharing, provide an incubator for digital projects, and offer website hosting and repository services. William Bowen provides a more detailed explanation of Iter's structure in this volume. While it is true that online digital projects have a limited useful life, often accompanied by research and updates from a primary investigator, there is a certain inherent fragility associated with our online digital projects as research tools. As a specific characteristic of these new methods of analysis, this fragility introduces additional complexities that threaten the completeness and sustainability of our work over time.

I have seen many successful projects in the digital humanities shift their focus from active development to data management. This change might be caused by internal reasons such as loss of funding, change in personnel, or simply decay in interest. Either way, it illustrates my main point: envisioning plans for the long-term maintenance of online digital projects is often overlooked. In this chapter, I propose to elaborate on the impact that online digital projects—using relatively new technologies—can have within Iter's context and how to extend their contribution towards research in the long term. It is a pressing issue, as online projects are often designed to run and be viewed on specific computer architectures that cannot be easily replicated.

ISBN 978-1-64959-063-3 (paper) ISBN 978-1-64959-064-0 (pdf) ISBN 978-1-64959-065-7 (epub)
New Technologies in Medieval and Renaissance Studies 11 (2025) 171–188

I am going to focus this chapter on the background, the current state, and the future of an Iter project as a case study. A Database for Dramatic Extracts (DEx) is an online, searchable database of extracts transcribed from seventeenth-century manuscripts ("DEx: A Database of Dramatic Extracts" 2019). DEx also aims to provide information to textual editors, literary scholars, and cultural historians interested in theater history, audience reception, early modern print and manuscript culture, and the history of reading. This interoperability as a medium to facilitate and afford the exchange of information is an integral part of DEx, which is quite important as it affects how users carry out their intended work and the scholarly inquiries that it can help answer.

Paul Conway has argued that "We are at the end of 'boutique' digital scanning projects for which the principal goal is [. . .] extraordinary attention to the unique properties of each artifact" (Conway 2010, 76). On the other hand, Laura Estill has contended that with early modern manuscripts, "boutique" projects are one of the best ways forward (Estill 2017). I agree with Estill's argument, and this brings me to the case study here. DEx is a boutique project that makes text manuscripts searchable with transcriptions, which is always the result of paying attention to each manuscript as a "unique artifact." More specifically, early modern readers and playgoers often kept commonplace books and miscellanies, where they would copy poems, aphorisms, letters, accounts, and any number of things (including selections from plays). The role of DEx as a boutique project is to help scholars find selections from plays copied into manuscripts. While contemporary readers often overlook lesser-known historical plays and playwrights, early modern readers did not make the same distinction.

It is fair to say that DEx has an interesting history, which includes a failed reimplementation and a successful migration that involved different institutions in two countries. Its history makes DEx a useful case study of why long-term maintenance plans should be considered throughout the lifecycle of an online digital project, and of how the impact of even a boutique project can extend beyond the intended audience. This analysis aims to help us understand the impact of applying new technologies in medieval and Renaissance studies, and to encourage the development of long-term maintenance and preservation strategies for online digital projects.

Context

DEx is not alone in its designation as a boutique project under Iter's umbrella. Iter supports collaborative partnership in the development and distribution of online resources by providing development, hosting, and repository services for digital projects through its Partnership Project Development Award. Other boutique projects previously hosted by Iter that focus on the unique properties of an artifact include:

a. *A Social Edition of the Devonshire Manuscript* brings communities together to engage in conversation around a text formed and reformed through an ongoing, iterative, public editorial process. Principal Investigator: Ray Siemens, University of Victoria. Formerly dms.itercommunity.org.

b. The Martin Marprelate Press offers a freshly edited collection of primary documents connected with the secret press that produced the Martin Marprelate tracts (1588–89): the notorious anti-episcopal satires that sparked the most famous pamphlet war of the English Renaissance. The depositions, examinations, investigative summaries, trial records, and other documents generated by the hunt for the Marprelate Press provide extraordinary evidence, unmatched for the period, for the day-to-day workings of an underground print campaign. Principal Investigator: Joseph Black, University of Massachusetts Amherst. Formerly marprelate.itercommunity.org.

c. GEA – Invisible Sienese Women made Visible aims to disseminate information about Sienese women and their families in the period of time (roughly 1450–1570) before and after the war against the Spanish troops that ended the Sienese independence after the Treaty of Cateau-Cambresis (1559) and subjugated Siena to Florence and to the rule of Cosimo I de' Medici. Principal Investigator: Elena Brizio, CET Florence. Formerly gea.itercommunity.org.

d. Gravell Watermark Archive is a collection of photographic reproductions of over seven thousand watermarks in paper made between 1400 and 1835, available as a searchable online electronic database. Principal Investigator: Daniel W. Mosser, Virginia Polytechnic Institute and State University. gravell.org.

e. Digital Acting Parts is an online environment that both mimics and enhances the early modern acting experience in order to facilitate actors learning their lines. Digital Acting Parts is the first project to give users an interactive experience with an early-modern-inspired "actor's part," which encourages both active reading and memorization, in turn leading to a better understanding of the texts themselves. Principal Investigator: Laura Estill, St. Francis Xavier University. Formerly dap.itercommunity.org/dap/ (decommissioned).

Background

Since the earliest uses of computers and computational techniques in the humanities at the end of the 1940s, scholars, projects, and research groups had to look for systems that could provide representations of data that the computer could process. When human beings read texts, they perceive both the information stored in the linguistic code of the text and the meta-information inferred from the appearance and interpretation of the text. One of the core specifications in DEx is that the play extracts are encoded using the guidelines provided by the Text Encoding Initiative (TEI). The TEI Guidelines specify encoding methods for machine-readable texts, mainly in the humanities, social sciences, and linguistics, that are defined as an application of the Extensible Markup Language (XML). XML is a markup language that defines a set of rules for encoding documents in a format that is both human- and machine-readable. XML is widely used for the definition of device- and system-independent methods of storing and processing texts in electronic form.

The first prototype for DEx (Estill 2013) was developed by Neal Audenaert at the Texas Center for Applied Technology (TCAT, tcat.tamu.edu/). Before working at TCAT, Audenaert was a researcher in the Center for the Study of Digital Libraries (CSDL) at the Department of Computer Science at Texas A&M University. Like many other digital humanities projects developed at the CSDL during this time (for example, the Nautical Archeology Digital Library and the Online Picasso Project), this first prototype was based on Java Servlets. A Servlet is a Java programming language class that is commonly used to extend the capabilities of servers that host applications accessed by means of a request-response programming model. I see this choice of technology as a direct consequence of two factors: first, the popularity that Java had in the mid 2000s; and second, the fact that the Department of Computer Science at Texas A&M was fully supporting Java and building their core courses on it. Java was a good decision for building the core architecture of DEx at the time, but the development of online projects has currently shifted towards practices involving more agile solutions. Due to this shift, decisions affecting the technology in early versions of DEx did not scale well over time.

In software development, a prototype is an initial or preliminary version of a computer program that serves as the starting point to develop further versions or iterations from it. A prototype is typically very different from its final version: as a consequence of the iterative process of development, errors in the software are fixed and new features are implemented. The development cycle of a project can last several months or years depending on its scope, culminating in a stable solution that is suitable for a production environment: a setting where software and other products are actually put into operation for their intended uses by end users.

Interestingly, DEx moved quickly from a prototype towards a production environment hosted at TCAT with the understanding that it would be later moved to Iter's servers. Figure 7.1 shows the manuscript browser for the Java-based implementation of DEx. DEx received very few updates over time and its core library dependencies became depreciated. This made the prototype impossible to update and the transfer to Iter's server infrastructure unfeasible. Attempts to replicate and move DEx to different servers also failed. Thus, the only viable solution at this point was to rebuild DEx from the ground up.

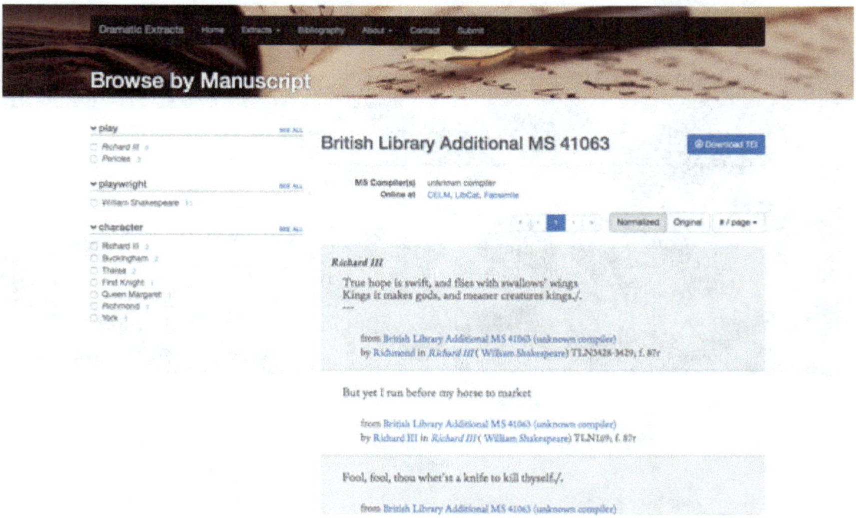

Figure 7.1. Manuscript browser in the Java-based implementation for DEx.

The next step was an attempt to reimplement DEx using WordPress ("Wordpress: Blog Tool, Publishing Platform, and CMS" 2019). In my opinion, this reimplementation failed because it involved inserting extracts in XML (a NoSQL database and an alternative to traditional relational databases) into MySQL (a relational database and a more traditional solution) which introduced unwanted redundancy and an additional level of complexity that was unnecessary. At this point, Iter contacted TCAT and asked them to package the server that hosted the Java implementation of DEx into a Docker container. A Docker container image is a lightweight, standalone, executable package of software that includes everything needed to run an application: code, runtime, system tools, system libraries and settings. This container was deployed into a virtual machine in Compute Canada. I used the image in the Docker container to create a model that I followed to create the new implementation for DEx.

Current Implementation

The current implementation of DEx can be accessed at dex.digitalearlymodern.com, and has two components: first, a WordPress instance that contains pages describing the site, along with forms to contact the principal investigators of the project and to submit additional dramatic extracts; and second, a dynamic database site that parses the extracts from the XML files. The template for the WordPress component was the only component that was salvaged and carried over from the previous failed reimplementation of DEx. Figure 7.2 shows the current WordPress component for DEx.

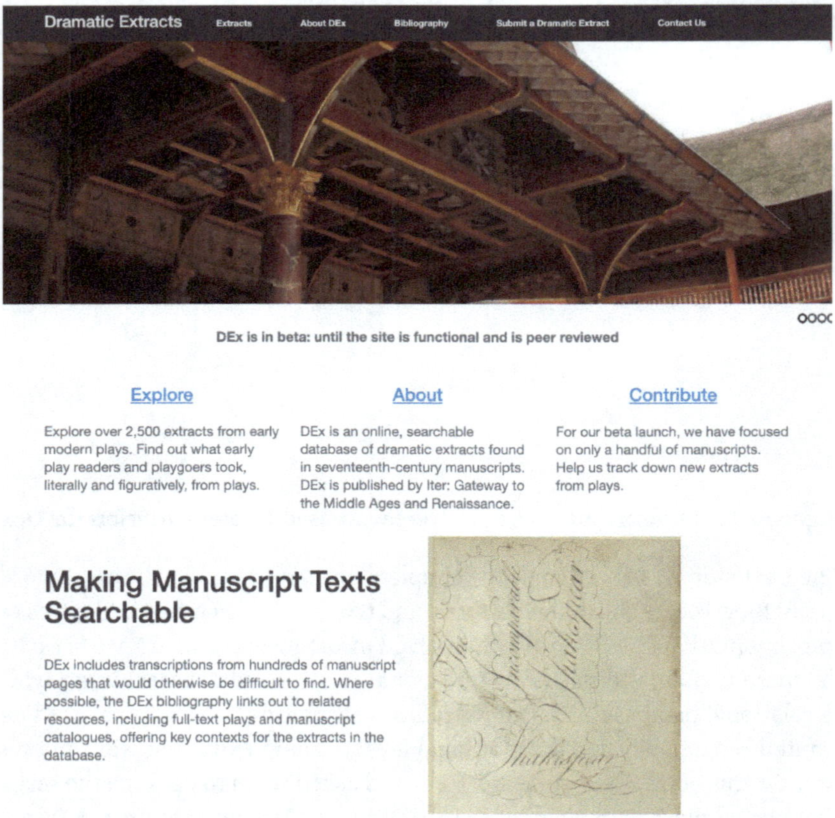

Figure 7.2. The current WordPress component for DEx.

The dynamic database site, which is referred to internally as Daikatana—a reference to John Romero's video game—reimplements the functionality of DEx using Python (van Rossum 1995) and relies on open source libraries. The XML files are parsed at runtime using Beautiful Soup, the webpages are rendered using Flask, and Whoosh provides the backend for the search engine. In this sense, the dynamic database site is a complete departure from the Java-based version of DEx, and it is unique in its architecture as it does not use a relational database. I expect that this reimplementation based on open source libraries will extend the shelf life of DEx considerably (Meneses and Furuta 2019). The real question (and the focus of this chapter) is how the technology decisions made in a software development cycle will increase the life of a finished product while also laying the foundation for its long-term preservation.

The XML Parser for DEx

The tools and software libraries used in the current version of DEx were chosen because of their reliability, ease of use, and reliance on open licenses. Reliable and easy to use software libraries were important since they would facilitate the long-term maintenance of the project and afford a shorter development cycle. An open license is a license agreement that contains provisions allowing other individuals to run programs for any purpose, study how they work, and change them to suit specific purposes. An open license also has the benefit of building a community by promoting the production of high-quality programs ("Open-Source Software Movement" 2017). Proprietary (also known as closed source) software libraries were not a particular problem in the previous versions of DEx, but they introduce potential challenges that I wanted to avoid altogether.

The dynamic parser uses Beautiful Soup (Richardson 2015) to parse the all the XML files in DEx. Beautiful Soup is a Python library for extracting data out of HTML and XML files. In a nutshell, Beautiful Soup works with parser libraries to provide Python idiomatic expressions for navigating, searching, and modifying the parse tree. The reasons for using this library in DEx are three-fold: First, I wanted to avoid the problems of inserting XML into the records of a relational database. Second, the software interfaces for Beautiful Soup are highly optimized and they commonly save developers hours or days of work. I had previous experience and knowledge from working with Beautiful Soup in similar digital humanities projects and was confident that its expressive interfaces were the right tool for this task. And third, Beautiful Soup is very fast and lenient when it uses lxml (lxml 2018) as its parser library. This speed allowed the parsing of all the XML files to be done at runtime. The parsed files are then stored into a Beautiful Soup object that is saved into a Python Pickle, which is a way to convert a Python object into a character stream. The idea is that this character stream contains all the information necessary to reconstruct the object in another Python script. Any object in Python can be pickled so that it can be saved to disk.

DEx runs as a Unix service that is deployed in a Web server. Each time the service is started, it checks for changes in the XML files by comparing the current set of files against a size signature. If changes are detected, the current Pickle file is overwritten by a new one containing a Beautiful Soup object with the data from the new set of XML files. On the other hand, if changes are not detected, the Unix service loads the current Pickle file into memory. This check was put in place to speed the availability of the service. Normally, loading a new set of files into DEx takes less than twenty seconds.

Despite all of its positive aspects and affordances, Beautiful Soup is a memory intensive library. In the specific case of DEx, loading all of the XML files into memory is possible because it is a boutique project that utilizes a discrete number of files. I am confident that the parser can be scaled to accommodate a larger number of files, but it is inevitable that the computer server where the application is hosted will require the allocation of larger resources.

The Templating Framework for DEx

DEx was built using Flask ("Flask: A Python Microframework" 2018): a web framework written in Python. Flask is often classified as a microframework because it does not require particular tools or libraries. It has no database abstraction layer, form validation, or any other components. Flask supports extensions that can add application features as if they were implemented in Flask itself.

Flask uses by default the Jinja2 templating system (Ronacher 2019). Jinja2 is one of the most used template engines for Python and is distributed under BSD license, which imposes minimal restrictions on the use and distribution of its covered software. Jinja2 is inspired by Django's templating system but extends it with an expressive language that gives template authors a more powerful set of tools. Taking advantage of this expressiveness, Flask afforded the deployment of a modular master template that allows a layout and structure to be extended into all the pages in the project. In turn, combining this templating system with the parser that I described in the previous section of this chapter allowed me to replicate the functionality and mimic the presentation of the extracts from the Java version of DEx. The current version of DEx has views for browsing extracts by manuscript, author, characters, and plays. The bibliography is parsed at runtime, and the spelling of the extracts can be toggled between their normalized and original versions. This functionality required specific CSS rules to be applied to a set of tags that were embedded in the parsed XML. Figure 7.3 shows the user interface for DEx displaying results by authors. Figures 7.4 and 7.5 show an example of an extract that was parsed in the previous and current versions of DEx.

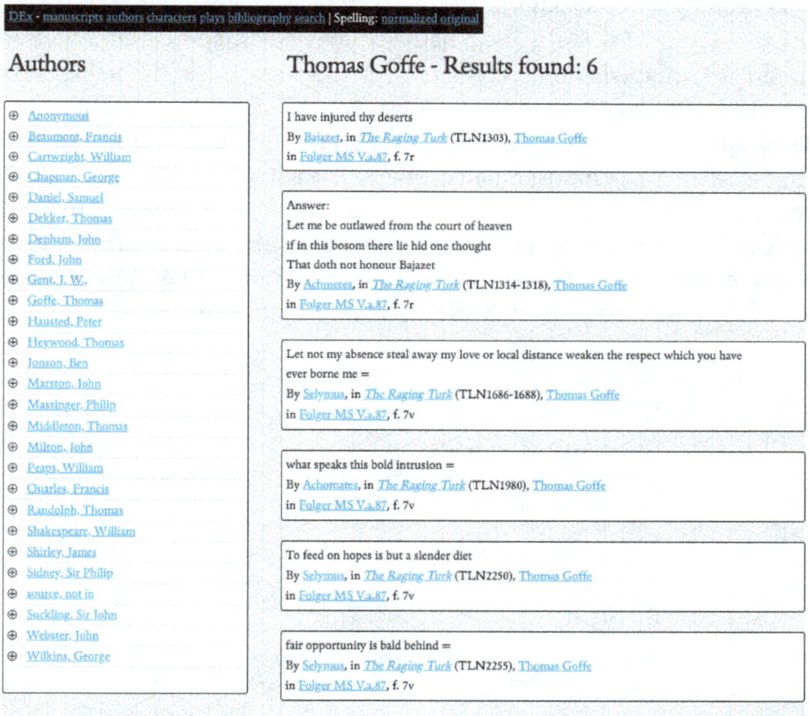

Figure 7.3. User interface for DEx displaying results by authors.

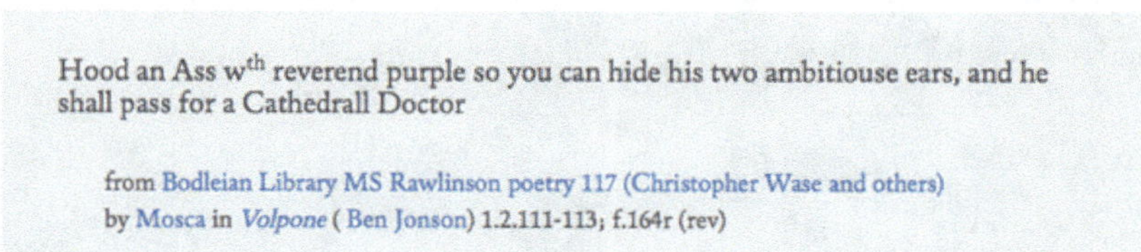

Figure 7.4. Example of an extract parsed in the Java version of DEx.

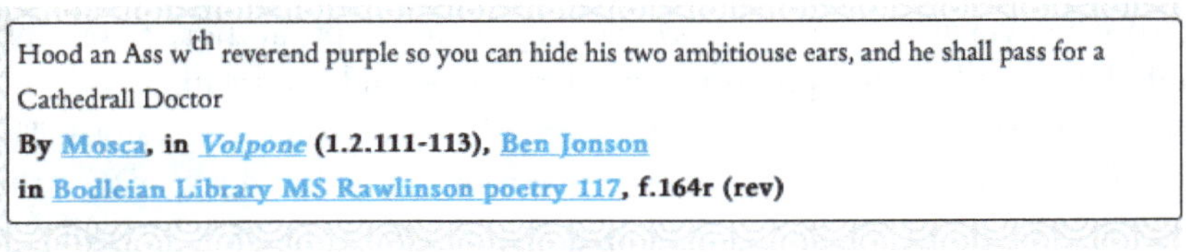

Figure 7.5. Example of an extract parsed in the current version of DEx.

A password protected administrative section was also built into the current version of DEx. Since Flask natively does not support user validation, I used Flask_simplelogin (Rocha 2017) for this task. Flask_simplelogin is an extension that provides the simplest way to add secure login capabilities to a Flask application, which was very appropriate since DEx does not require a complex framework for user management. The administrative section in DEx provides forms for uploading and deleting XML files and for restarting the application when needed. This functionality gives the principal investigators complete control over the content in the project. Figure 7.6 shows a screenshot of the password protected administrative section of DEx.

Figure 7.6. The password-protected administrative section of DEx.

Integrating a Search Engine with DEx

The search functionality in DEx is provided by Whoosh (Chaput 2017): a fast, pure Python search engine library that is distributed under a BSD license. Just like Apache Lucene (Apache Software Foundation 2011), almost none of the important behaviors in Whoosh are hard-coded. Indexing of text, the level of information stored for each term in each field, parsing of search queries, the types of queries allowed, scoring algorithms, etc. are all customizable, replaceable, and extensible. This flexibility afforded a robust integration into the Flask application and allowed the implementation of a schema that treats each extract as a document. Furthermore, if changes are found in the set of XML files when the service for DEx is restarted, the index for the search engine is rebuilt at runtime. Since the files are already parsed and ingested into a Beautiful Soup object, the time for rebuilding the search engine is negligible. The search engine also looks for results in all fields of the schema and supports wildcard expressions, discarding the need to implement additional features that are found in an "advanced" search. Figure 7.7 shows the search engine interface for DEx.

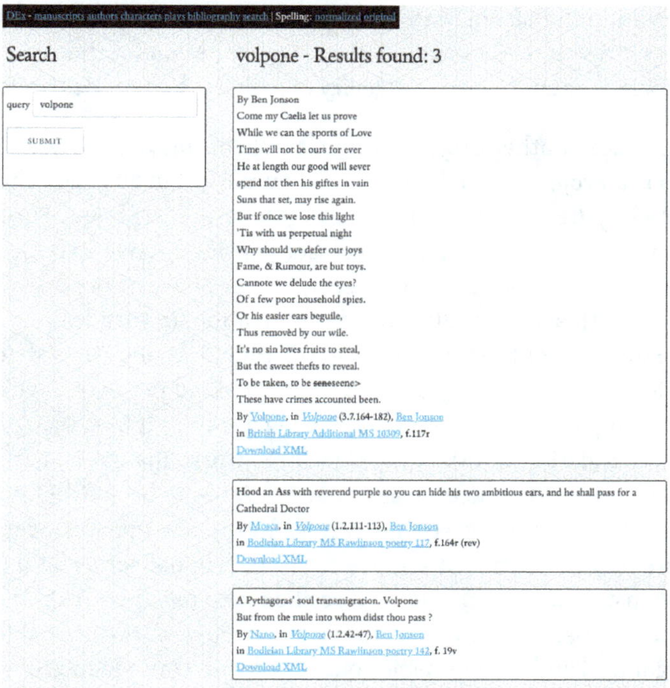

Figure 7.7. Search engine interface for DEx.

Reflections on the Completion of the Initial Development Cycle for DEx

One crucial aspect that led to the successful completion of the initial development cycle for DEx was the nature of the collaboration between an area expert (the principal investigator) and a methodology expert (the software developer). Constant communication through meetings and dialogue led to continuous revisions and improvements in each milestone of the software. In my opinion, this continuous consultation is a crucial aspect towards achieving productive development cycles for digital humanities projects that is often overlooked. In this sense, the principal investigator's familiarity with the capabilities and limitations of digital technologies and methods can make a clear difference and ultimately benefit the outset project.

In isolation, the applications and the use of the technology in the components in DEx are expected. The interaction of the components as a whole application and how they contribute towards the user experience are what make them novel. All the software and libraries used in DEx are distributed under an open license, which means that they can be freely used, distributed, and modified. In this sense, the choices I made in the software and technologies were very intentional. Software and libraries under open licenses are commonly supported by the community over longer periods of time and a crucial aspect towards extending the longevity of a digital humanities project.

I will introduce another project as an example of this longevity. Digital Acting Parts is a project that I created with Laura Estill in 2015 and that is now also hosted by Iter. Digital Acting Parts (Meneses, Estill, and Furuta 2015) is an online environment that gives users an interactive experience with an early-modern-inspired "actor's part," from Shakespeare's plays which encourages both active reading and memorization, in turn leading to a better understanding of the texts themselves. Digital Acting Parts shares some similarities with DEx as they are both Python based projects. Digital Acting Parts has a slightly different set of dependencies since it uses Django (Django Software Foundation 2016) as its Web framework. Django is a framework distributed under a BSD license and that continues to be actively supported. All in all, Digital Acting Parts has received very few updates over the last four years and has survived a move from its original server at a different academic institution. I attribute this resilience to two factors: 1) the dependency on open software, and 2) well-organized and maintainable source code. Organized and maintainable source code is a consequence of following the community's established conventions expressed in the style guide for Python Code (van Rossum 2001).

Using software under open license does have some drawbacks. For example, updates can take some time to be incorporated into the existing codebase, and software libraries are often replaced by those providing similar functionality. I cannot stress enough the special attention that must be paid by developers when choosing software and libraries, which can be inferred by the frequency and magnitude of updates made to a repository. In my opinion, this aspect is crucial towards ensuring the reliability of a digital humanities project over time.

Ensuring the Longevity of DEx

Previous studies have attempted to harness and manage the fragility of online resources (Bar-Yossef et al. 2004). I believe that the inherent characteristics of online digital humanities projects present an interesting and unique opportunity for inquiry for two reasons. First, the research aspect of the digital humanities makes it difficult to identify when projects have been abandoned. And second, digital humanities projects have a limited useful life, which may or may not be indicated by updates in the project's content and tools.

One aspect that I have been exploring recently is the packaging of Flask applications as standalone apps. This can be achieved by using PyFladesk (Moqadam 2019): a software library that creates a QWebview (a widget that is used to view and edit Web documents) and then runs a Flask application on it instead of rendering a view of the application in a Web browser. DEx is an optimal candidate for packaging as a standalone application, since it does not rely on queries to an external database to display its results. By default, PyFladesk allows every internal link to open inside the app and every external link to open in the default browser. External links in DEx can be considered negligible. The main idea behind this packaging is to ensure the longevity of a project by creating a software wrapper around it; in the future we may not have a Web server that can run Python applications, but we will have an emulator that can run bytecode for 686 processors. Figure 7.8 shows DEx running as a standalone application on Mac OS X 10.14.3.

Figure 7.8. DEx running as a standalone application on Mac OS X 10.14.3.

This alternate strategy for deployment and archival can also be applied to digital humanities projects that use a relational database. GEA – Invisible Sienese Women made Visible is an Iter project that reconstructs the history of the difficult times between the early 1500s and the 1560s as experienced through the lives of women. GEA focuses on their activities in the familial, social, and economic life of their natal and marital families; their role in the life of their children and relatives, in culture, in female artistic patronage, and also in the male political arena. Because of its scope, GEA presents a different scenario as it relies on MySQL (Oracle Corporation 2018): a relational database. GEA was built using SQLAlchemy ("SQLAlchemy - The Database Toolkit for Python" 2019): a Python SQL toolkit and Object Relational Mapper that provides an abstraction layer that gives application developers the full power and flexibility of SQL. Because of this abstraction, I can switch the database driver to SQLite (SQLite 2018) which allows the database to run locally within the application without sacrificing speed and reliability. Figure 7.9 shows GEA displaying test data and running as a standalone application on Mac OS X 10.14.3.

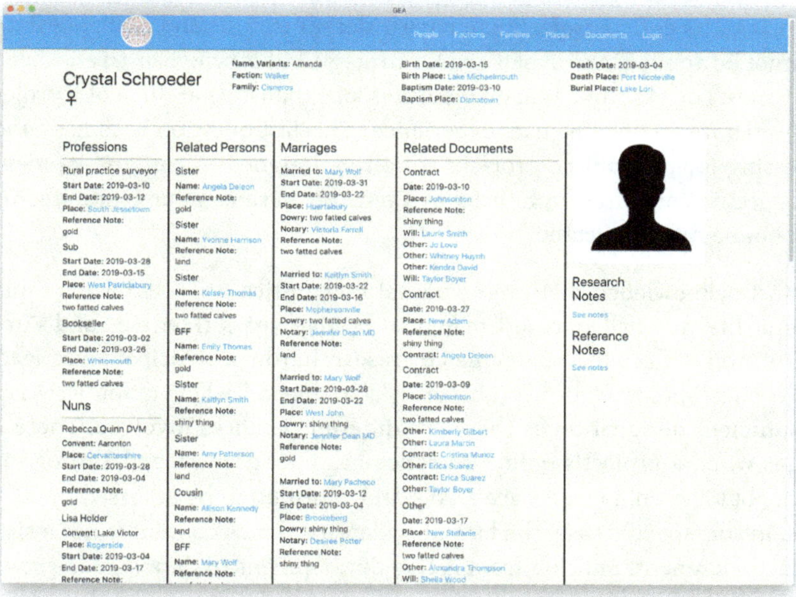

Figure 7.9. GEA displaying test data and running as a standalone application on Mac OS X 10.14.3.

This strategy for deployment also opens possibilities for running digital humanities projects on other devices (for example, cellphones or microcontrollers), different scenarios for testing, debugging, and replication, and implementing alternative deployment solutions that don't necessarily need to rely on a Web server. In this case, an executable file for an Iter project could be uploaded to an institutional repository or ingested into the Internet Archive, an important step towards ensuring their long-term preservation and availability as digital humanities projects.

Conclusions

In this paper I have described the steps I took towards extending the contribution of an online digital humanities project that deals with medieval and Renaissance studies. These steps include using open source libraries, utilizing community standards, and encapsulating server environments into standalone applications. The work I have outlined can be extended towards other digital humanities projects, where updating an existing codebase is not feasible.

I must voice my opinion on preservation strategies. I believe this is a complex issue as online projects can have different extents and a single solution cannot be applied. Archival is a valid strategy, but it brings forth another set of issues. For example: What constitutes an exhaustive archive of a project? How can we archive the user experience? This last question becomes a more pressing issue as online projects are often designed to run and be viewed on specific computer architectures. Some of these computer architectures cannot be fully replicated.

I must acknowledge that online digital humanities projects have a limited useful life, which I have estimated to be five years (Meneses and Furuta 2019), and it is often accompanied by research from a principal investigator. After this time, many projects become "abandoned," which is not necessarily a sufficient designation as there are different nuances involved. There are cases when a project's online presence has not received updates for some time, but the online tools are stable and continue to be accessed by its users. In this specific case, the lack of updates and new content is not a signal of abandonment. Shifting from active development to data management is also common after some time. These are clear examples of why the rules for traditional resources do not fully apply and why new metrics are needed to identify issues concerning online projects in the digital humanities.

As I stated in the introduction of this chapter, the creation and maintenance of online digital projects over time falls under Iter's mandate. In this chapter I have focused on how the technology decisions made in a software development cycle can increase the life of a software product while also laying the foundation for its long-term preservation. I have also outlined the lessons learned in a specific case that turned out to be a complicated process involving multiple variables that deal with both computer software and hardware. As a generalization, the projects hosted by Iter make research materials and documents related to the Middle Ages and the Renaissance accessible over the Web. While this allows the project's principal investigator to make inferences and reach conclusions, the applications are not computationally intensive. The foundations that we are establishing towards extending the contribution of online digital projects will become crucial and extremely valuable as we create our own methodologies in the digital humanities.

WORKS CITED

Apache Software Foundation. 2011. "Welcome to Apache Lucene." Accessed 29 March 2020. lucene.apache.org.

Bar-Yossef, Ziv, Andrei Z. Broder, Ravi Kumar, and Andrew Tomkins. 2004. "Sic Transit Gloria Telae: Towards an Understanding of the Web's Decay." In *Proceedings of the 13th International Conference on World Wide Web*, 328–37. WWW '04. New York: ACM. doi.org/10.1145/988672.988716.

Chaput, Matt. 2017. "Whoosh: Fast Pure-Python Full Text Indexing, Search and Spell Checking Library." Accessed 11 April 2021. pypi.python.org/pypi/Whoosh/.

Conway, Paul. 2010. "Preservation in the Age of Google: Digitization, Digital Preservation, and Dilemmas." *The Library Quarterly* 80 (1): 61–79. doi.org/10.1086/648463.

"DEx: A Database of Dramatic Extracts." 2019. Accessed 30 April 2021. Formerly dex.itercommunity.org/, now available at dex.digitalearlymodern.org.

Django Software Foundation. 2016. "The Web Framework for Perfectionists with Deadlines | Django." Accessed 20 February 2020. djangoproject.com.

Estill, Laura. 2013. "Introducing DEx: A Database of Dramatic Extracts." *Journal for Early Modern Cultural Studies* 13 (4): 128–30. doi.org/10.1353/jem.2013.0038.

———. 2017. "Making Manuscripts Searchable: DEx, a Database of Dramatic Extracts, Digital Publication, and Boutique Projects." Presented at the Digital Humanities 2017 conference, Montreal, Canada. August 8–11, 2017.

"Flask: A Python Microframework." 2018. Accessed 6 June 2021. flask.pocoo.org/.

lxml. 2018. "Lxml - Processing XML and HTML with Python." Accessed 6 June 2021. lxml.de/.

Meneses, Luis, Laura Estill, and Richard Furuta. 2015. "Digital Acting Parts: Learning and Understanding Shakespeare's Plays." Presented at the Joint CSDH/SCHN & ACH Digital Humanities Conference 2015, Calgary, Alberta, Canada. 30 May–1 June 2016.

Meneses, Luis, and Richard Furuta. 2019. "Shelf Life: Identifying the Abandonment of Online Digital Humanities Projects." *Digital Scholarship in the Humanities* 34 (1): 129–34. doi.org/10.1093/llc/fqy079.

Moqadam, Saeed. 2019. PyFladesk: Create Desktop Application by Using Flask and QtWebKit. Python. Accessed 6 June 2021. github.com/smoqadam/PyFladesk.

"Open-Source Software Movement." 2017. Wikipedia. Accessed 6 June 2021. en.wikipedia.org/wiki/Open-source-software_movement.

Oracle Corporation. 2018. "MySQL." Accessed 6 June 2021. mysql.com/.

Orlandi, Tito. 2019. "Reflections on the Development of Digital Humanities." Presented at the Digital Humanities 2019 conference, Utrecht, The Netherlands, 9–12 July 2019.

Richardson, Leonard. 2015. "Beautiful Soup: We Called Him Tortoise Because He Taught Us." Accessed 3 May 2021. crummy.com/software/BeautifulSoup/.

Rocha, Bruno. 2017. Flask_simplelogin: Flask Simple Login - Login Extension for Flask (version 0.0.6). Python. github.com/rochacbruno/flask_simplelogin.

Ronacher, Armin. 2019. "Jinja." Pallets. Accessed 6 June 2021. palletsprojects.com/p/jinja/.

van Rossum, Guido. 1995. "Python Tutorial, Technical Report CS-R9526." Amsterdam: Centrum voor Wikunde en Informatica (CWI). ir.cwi.nl/pub/5007/05007D.pdf.

———. 2001. "PEP 8 — Style Guide for Python Code." Python.Org. Accessed 6 June 2021. python.org/dev/peps/pep-0008/.

"SQLAlchemy - The Database Toolkit for Python." 2019. Accessed 6 June 2021. sqlalchemy.org/.

SQLite. 2018. "SQLite Home Page." Accessed 6 June 2021. sqlite.org/index.html.

"Wordpress: Blog Tool, Publishing Platform, and CMS." 2019. WordPress. Accessed 6 June 2021. wordpress.org/.

In Search of the Other Voice[1]

Margaret L. King
Brooklyn College and the Graduate Center, CUNY, emerita

In 1995, the two of us—Albert Rabil, Jr. and Margaret L. King—sitting in the attic study of Al's rambling old house, together launched the Other Voice in Early Modern Europe series to recover works by women, and by men about women, that had been neglected in scholarly discussions of the period 1300 to 1800. Both of us had written on such women—he on Laura Cereta, I on Isotta Nogarola, two then virtually unknown fifteenth-century female humanists—and knew there was more to be said. The University of Chicago Press agreed to take on a series projected to run about a dozen volumes: works of the early women humanists and humanist defenses of women, concentrating on what was later called the *querelle* tradition (the *querelle des femmes*, or "debate about women") that was a major literary strand running from the fifteenth to the seventeenth century.

With a harvest of new ideas generated in the 1990s and 2000s by Rabil's several summer NEH Institutes for Teachers and for Higher Education Faculty, the list was later expanded. Its original focus on the debate over women's moral and intellectual capacity broadened to include other works of a more literary, or devotional nature, or addressing such matters as medicine and philosophy, as the analysis of topics that follows will indicate. Chicago continued to sustain the series from 1996, when the first volume appeared (Rabil's translation of Henricus Cornelius Agrippa's *Declamation on the Nobility and Preeminence of the Female Sex*), until 2010.

When Chicago moved to drop the series after sixty volumes had been published, William Bowen at the University of Toronto, the director of Iter Inc. (housed in the University of Toronto Libraries), agreed to adopt it, and the Other Voice then moved to that most welcoming institution. Thus the

[1] I am grateful to Elizabeth Hageman, Other Voice editor for English volumes, and Margaret English-Haskin, project manager at Iter, Inc., for their invaluable and substantial contributions to this essay. I am grateful, as well, to the Canada Research Chair program and St Francis Xavier University's Digital Humanities Centre, which supported the creation by Kate Beers of the helpful figures in this chapter. With sadness I note the death of Albert Rabil, Jr., on January 8, 2021.

ISBN 978-1-64959-063-3 (paper) ISBN 978-1-64959-064-0 (pdf) ISBN 978-1-64959-065-7 (epub)
New Technologies in Medieval and Renaissance Studies 11 (2025) 189–216

Toronto series was born in 2007, with its first volumes published in 2009.[2] From that starting point through 2014, titles were published jointly by Iter and the Centre for Reformation and Renaissance Studies (CRRS) at Victoria University in the University of Toronto; from 2015 to 2020, they have been published jointly with the Arizona Center for Medieval and Renaissance Studies (ACMRS).[3] As successor to the Chicago series, the Toronto series as of this writing (mid-2019) has now published or has in press a further seventy-four volumes,[4] exceeding in its ten years of publication the total crop of Chicago titles (which came out at an average rate of four per year) over its fifteen years. In 2011, Elizabeth Hageman joined Rabil and me as editor of the Other Voice series with particular responsibility for English-language texts, thus extending the original mission to translate texts from Latin and modern European languages.

As a result of the initiative of the three editors, of the enthusiasm and labor of the contributors, and of the great generosity first of the Chicago and then of the Toronto publishers, and the dedication and expertise of their professional staffs, the Other Voice series now has (or will soon have) 134 volumes in circulation: sixty in the Chicago series and seventy-four (all those already published or currently in production) from Toronto.[5] More are coming. The Toronto series list on the Other Voice website (othervoiceineme.com/othervoice-toronto.html) currently runs to 138 titles, including those already in print.[6] By the time the publisher completes the list of titles remaining, and planned to be composed, submitted, vetted, and published, the total of Other Voice volumes will likely reach 175, or possibly 200. This is a substantial addition to the total roster of Renaissance and early modern texts available to students and scholars. Not only does it boost that total, but it does so in a useful way: the texts are related by theme to each other, and in the critical editions that contributing editors provide, to the mainstream of the European intellectual tradition. In effect, the Other Voice project has helped to reshape the canon of early modern literature.

---

[2] There was an overlap between the Chicago and Toronto partnerships; the last Chicago volume came out in 2010, by which time the first Toronto volume had already appeared.

[3] Since January 2021, Iter Press is the sole publisher of the Other Voice Toronto Series.

[4] As of July 2022, that number had risen to 103.

[5] As of July 2022, that number rises to 163.

[6] As of July 2022, 150.

The Other Voice series also constitutes something like a data bank. Although the Other Voice series is not a born-digital production, but an assemblage of old-fashioned books, yet as its volumes accumulate, all related to a core theme and structured—despite their variety in genre, style, and purpose—according to a common template, it makes visible a phenomenon previously unseen. The construction of such a data bank was never, at the outset, the intention, but as the series has evolved over some twenty-five years, it has come to constitute a large trove of data that can be drawn on to illumine our cultural past.

Analysis

That trove of information invites analysis.[7] Some initial data about the Chicago series, the Toronto series, and, combining those two components, the entire Other Voice series are presented in the following discussion and in the five summary Figures provided. See Appendix 1 for related tables.

Languages

Titles in the Chicago series were translated from five European languages: Latin, the classical language that had long been the language of the learned and, more recently, of the humanist revival of ancient civilization; and modern French, German, Italian, and Spanish. These vernaculars were just achieving their modern form during the Renaissance and early modern centuries, absorbing dialectal variations and borrowing vocabulary and grammatical structures from Latin. As girls rarely received an education grounded in Latin grammar, which was standard for those boys who were

[7] Omitted from this analysis made in mid-2019 was any indication of the gender of authors or contributors. Overall figures as of November 2020 are as follows: the authors of texts published in the sixty volumes of the Chicago series include 63 females and 5 males (respectively, 93% and 7% of all 68 authors), while the contributing editors and translators include 63 females and 15 males (respectively, 81% and 19% of all 78 contributors); the authors of texts in the ninety volumes published or as of 2020 in the Toronto series include 93 females and 17 males (respectively, 85% and 15% of all 110 authors—a striking increase in the percentage of male authors over the Chicago number), while the contributing editors and translators include 114 females and 27 males (respectively, 81% and 19% of all 141 contributors). Altogether the Other Voice series, considering the 150 volumes published or in press presents the work of 156 female and 22 male authors (respectively 88% and 12% of all 178 authors), and 177 female and 42 male editors and translators (respectively 81% and 19% of all 219 contributors). These numbers exclude three volumes with collective and diverse authorship.

schooled, the maturation of the vernaculars opened new opportunities for women writers. Works published in the Chicago series were translated most often from French and Italian, those two languages together accounting for 73% of the list. A correspondence may be inferred between the prominence of those two languages in the series and the greater productivity of women speakers of those languages more generally.[8]

The range of languages broadens slightly in the Toronto series, which publishes titles in Latin (only one) and, again, French, German, Italian, and Spanish, but also in Polish (two), Russian (two), and English (sixteen).[9] The addition of the English category in 2011 with Elizabeth Hageman as editor greatly enriches the list, even as it departs from the original mission of translation that had been seen as appropriate for a non-specialist audience. The publication of four titles in Slavic languages is also significant, although the number is small, because the literary product of those nations during the early modern period is often overlooked. Even with this diversification, French and Italian titles predominate, as for the Chicago series, constituting together 58% of the Toronto series total.

For the 134 titles of the combined Other Voice list, French and Italian titles constitute 65% of the whole, again testifying to the great productivity of women writers of those languages, outdistancing English titles, constituting 12%,[10] and Spanish 10%, of the combined list. The other languages taken together—Latin, German, Polish, Russian—constitute 12% of the whole Other Voice list (see Figure 8.1).

The distribution of languages in Other Voice titles suggests also the geographical distribution of authors, complicated by the fact that Early Modern authors are associated not so much with nations as we understand them, but rather with regions (the Veneto and Tuscany for Italian authors, for instance), and even cities (notably Venice, Florence, and Rome for Italian authors; Paris and Lyon for French; and London for English).

---

[8] Of course, a measure of productivity (the rate of production) would require, for rigorous proof, the comparison of the number of works published in each language to the total population of women writing in each language—a precision that cannot be attained at this time.

[9] The Toronto list for future submissions includes titles in Dutch and Portuguese and one more in Russian. As of July 2022, Latin titles published or in press rise to three.

[10] The proportion of English titles understates the importance of that literature in early modern women's writing, as works in English were introduced only in 2011.

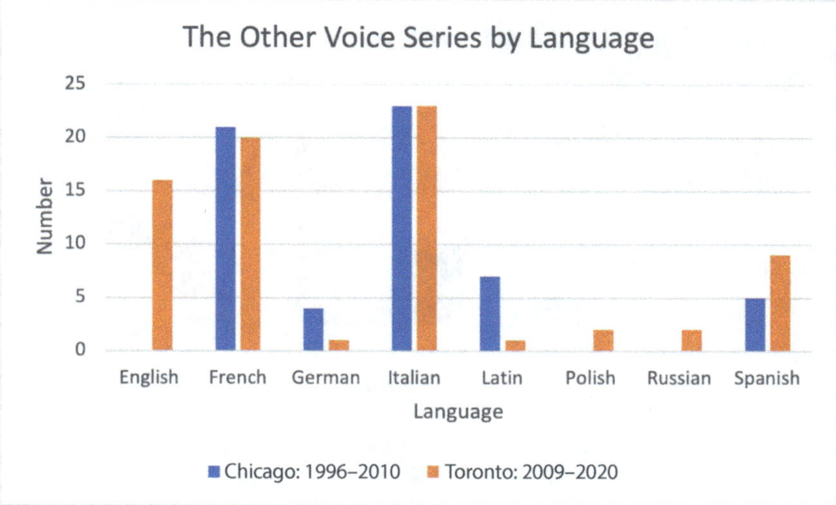

Figure 8.1: The Other Voice series by language (created by Kate Beers).

Distribution Over Time

The Other Voice series embraces the early modern period broadly conceived, ranging roughly from 1400 to 1800, but stretching back into the early Renaissance (or some might say the late Middle Ages) for one title, in Italian, and forward into the Enlightenment—and for one title, in Russian, a region where the "early modern" arrived late, into the early years of the nineteenth century. Overall, most titles date from the sixteenth and seventeenth centuries; works composed in those centuries constitute 82% of the Chicago titles, 77% of the Toronto titles, and 79% of the combined list. The comparable figures for the fifteenth century, the first century of Italian humanism, are 13% for the Chicago series, 9% for Toronto, and 11% for the combined list. The comparable figures for the eighteenth century, the culmination of the Early Modern era, are 5% for the Chicago series, 11% for Toronto, and 8% overall. More than the Chicago series, the Toronto series extends into the eighteenth century, in which despite the irruption of the Enlightenment, there is considerable continuity from earlier periods in the patterns of women's engagement with literary culture (see Figure 8.2).

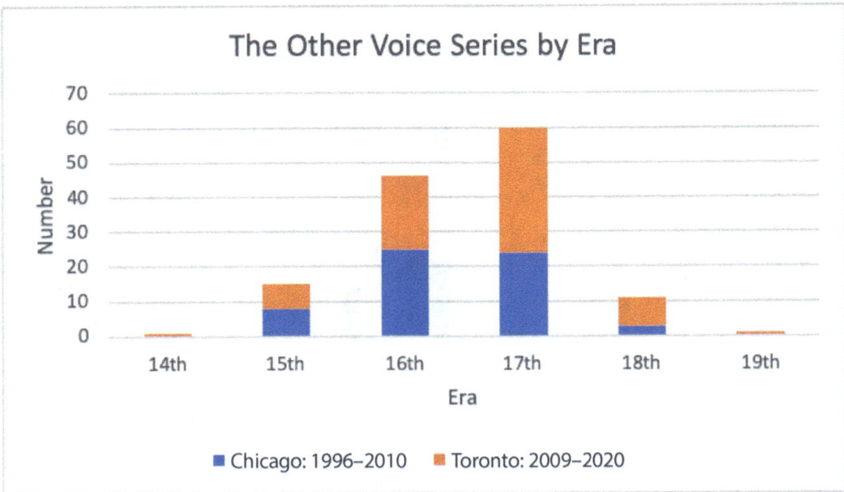

Figure 8.2. The Other Voice series by era (created by Kate Beers).

Genres

The genres represented by Other Voice titles cover the range of Renaissance and early modern literary production. They include such fictional genres as drama, epic, novel or romance, poetry, and story, as well as dialogue, letters, oration, and other various prose non-fiction forms such as treatise and essay. As some volumes contain works in more than one genre—for instance, a single volume may contain letters, orations, and sonnets—the total of the percentages for genres (as later for topics) exceeds 100%, complicating the analysis given here. Yet some clear patterns are evident. The category of prose non-fiction is the largest, with works in those genres appearing in 58% of the Chicago list, 47% of the Toronto list, and 52% of the combined list. Letters, not included in that catch-all category although they are also non-fictional prose works, are also prominent, appearing in 17% of the Chicago titles, 16% of the Toronto titles, and 16% of Other Voice titles overall, while the genres of dialogue and oration are more modestly represented. Of the fiction genres, the most prominent is poetry, represented in 20% of the Chicago titles, 27% of the Toronto titles, and 24% of the Other Voice series in total. Drama, represented in the Chicago series by only two titles, or 3% of that list, rises to 18% of the Toronto list, and 11% of the combined series (see Figure 8.3).

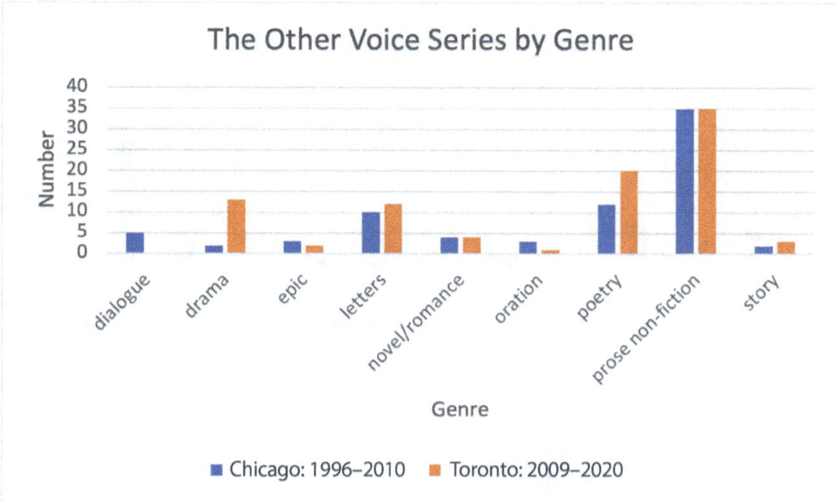

Figure 8.3. The Other Voice series by genre (created by Kate Beers).

The distribution of genres in Other Voice titles may serve to describe what observers might otherwise desire to know: the occupational distribution of authors—how many, that is, were humanists, or poets, or playwrights. An occupational distribution is not possible for women authors, who are the majority of all authors, as they had not received advanced, specialized educations, and held no professional positions. The relatively few male authors might be classified generally as humanist-educated professionals employed variously as secretaries, statesmen, physicians, high-ranking clerics, or courtiers.[11] These male occupations also reflect the social class distribution of both male authors and their more numerous female counterparts. Other Voice authors generally derive from the familiar upper strata of early modern society: professional or clerical elites, urban patriciate, landowning gentry, and courtier nobility.

Topics

The array of topics addressed in Other Voice titles is broad, and more suggestive than the range of genres of the particular interests of women as authors, and of male authors writing about women (see Figures 8.4 and 8.5). Here as with genres, analysis is complicated by the fact that many volumes in the series contain works on different topics, so that the percentages by which each topic is represented total a number greater than one hundred.

[11] For the gender breakdown of early modern authors and present-day editors and translators, see note 7.

Figure 8.4. The Other Voice series by topic (created by Kate Beers).

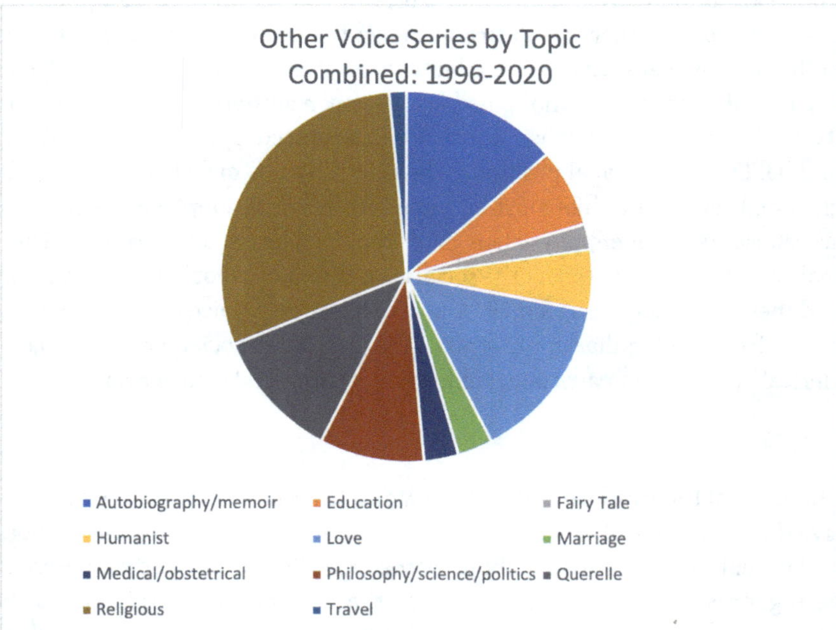

Figure 8.5. The Other Voice series by topic, combined (created by Kate Beers).

Works on religious topics predominate, including both devotional works and theological discussions and debates, presented in a variety of genres, including autobiography, dialogue, letter, and treatise. Works of largely religious content appear in 30% of the Chicago titles, 28% of the Toronto titles, and 29% in the Other Voice series overall.

Autobiographical works and life writings (diaries, memoirs, and family papers), often overlapping with the category of religious works, are also numerous, coming to, respectively, 7%, 19%, and 13% of the Chicago, Toronto, and combined lists. The topic of love is well-represented, especially in poetry and drama, encountered in 17% of the Chicago titles, 12% of the Toronto, and 14% of the combined list. Of the highly-represented topics, that of the *querelle* stands out. Gathered in the category of *querelle* are works (in a number of genres) in which is argued the moral and intellectual worthiness of women, or even the equality of the female to the male. Works dealing with *querelle* arguments appear in 15% of the Chicago list, 8% of the Toronto, and 11% overall.

Although they do not represent a large portion of the Other Voice product, some topics hold special interest. The fairy tale is a literary form particularly associated with women, who were perceived to be its main narrators. Although the Chicago series includes no volumes of fairy tales, the Toronto series includes three, and their presence constitutes an important contribution to the history of European literature. Works on medicine, and more particularly obstetrics or midwifery, constitute another notable though small category: one Chicago and three Toronto volumes are concerned with these topics, constituting 3% of the combined Other Voice series. Works discussing education constitute a notable 7% of the combined series, and those discussing philosophical, scientific, or political topics constitute another 9%. Finally, works in which women authors discuss their travels—lacking in the Chicago list and represented in the Toronto list by two titles, constituting a mere 1% overall of Other Voice titles published to date—are also of interest, as it is in this era that women are first seen traveling and commenting upon their experiences. Titles yet to be published will expand the weight of the topic of travel within the series total.

Chicago and Toronto: Continuities and Disjunctions

On the whole—and quite by accident, not by design, as the two lists developed in response to proposals submitted spontaneously by aspiring contributors—the patterns of the Toronto series roughly follow those of the Chicago series. As has been seen, French and Italian, and sixteenth- and seventeenth-century works, predominate in both. In both series, prose non-fiction titles are more numerous than those in other genres, while poetry and letters follow soon afterwards. And in both cases, in terms of topics, religious themes prevail, while texts concerned with love are also plentiful.

Some differences between the two series may also be noted, and arguably some trends. The language distribution of the Toronto texts is broader, made so primarily by the addition of an English-language stream edited by Elizabeth Hageman, but also by the appearance of four titles in Polish and Russian—a seemingly small variance, except that, apparently, very few texts by or about women exist in those languages during the early modern period, and fewer are familiar to Anglophone readers. The distribution of titles over time is also broader in the Toronto series, which includes one fourteenth- and one nineteenth-century work, while the Chicago series reaches only from the fifteenth to the eighteenth century; and the Toronto series, as well, has more than twice as many eighteenth-century works as the Chicago series. In addition, the Toronto series has published more drama and poetry than the Chicago series—respectively thirteen and twenty titles for Toronto to two and twelve for Chicago.

Matters of Substance

The foregoing description of the Other Voice series deals with the 134 component volumes as speechless entities that can be sorted and counted. Doing so yields a group portrait that displays in broad strokes the shape of the intellectual engagement of early modern women, whose activity was virtually invisible as recently as thirty or forty years ago. But it is important not only to consider that these works exist, but also to explore what it is they are saying. Considered below are some of the works exemplifying the key themes and messages conveyed in this collection of texts. [12]

The *querelle*

The Other Voice series includes many works, and several of the principal works, belonging to the *querelle* tradition. As is now well known, the Italian-born French author Christine de Pizan, writing around the turn of the fifteenth century, powerfully raised the issue of women's dignity and capacity both in her critique of misogynist texts such as the *Roman de la Rose* and in her adaptation of Boccaccio's *Famous Women* in her explosively original *Book of the City of Ladies*. Although the latter work has been available in English

[12] Full citations of Other Voice titles named in this discussion are given below under "Works Cited."

translation since the 1980s, the Other Voice has more recently published some of her other works: among them, her *Debate of the Romance of the Rose* (Chicago 2010), the *Mutability of Fortune* (Toronto 2017), and *Othea's Letter to Hector* (Toronto 2017).[13] In addition, the Other Voice has published works originally in Latin of all four of the most important early women humanists, all Italian—Isotta Nogarola, Laura Cereta, Cassandra Fedele, and Olympia Morata (Chicago 2004, 1997, 2000, 2003)—who vividly assert women's right to and capacity for intellectual parity with men. In addition, the series includes the polemical sixteenth-century defenses of women by the male humanists Henry Cornelius Agrippa and Symphorien Champier (Chicago 1996 and Toronto 2018), and three polemical texts by the Spanish male authors Pere Torrellas and Juan de Flores (Toronto 2013).

The Chicago series includes the proto-feminist works of monumental significance by the three Italian (and specifically Venetian) women authors from the early seventeenth century, Moderata Fonte (1997), Lucrezia Marinella (1999), and Arcangela Tarabotti (2004), and by their French contemporary, Marie de Gournay (2002). Included as well in the Chicago series are three feminist treatises composed in the 1670s by the French male philosopher François Poullain de la Barre (2002). Finally, works advocating the education of women, certainly pertinent to the *querelle* theme, appear in the Other Voice series, including the sixteenth-century treatise by the male humanist Juan Luis Vives (Chicago 2000) and, in the seventeenth century, works by the Dutch and English women authors Anna Maria van Schurman (Chicago 2000), Bathsua Makin (Chicago 1998), and Mary More (Toronto 2016).[14]

Religious Works

Thirty-nine, or nearly 30% of the combined Chicago and Toronto Other Voice series books are on religious subjects—so many that only a few exemplary titles are named here. They include devotional works such as Catharina Regina von Greiffenberg's *Meditations on the Incarnation, Passion, and Death of Jesus Christ* (Chicago 2009) or Cecilia del Nacimiento's *Journeys of a Mystic Soul in Poetry and Prose* (Toronto 2012); theological discussions such as Mary Astell's *The Christian Religion, as Professed by a Daughter of the Church of England* (Toronto 2013); works of witness, such as *Anna Trapnel's Report and Plea; or, a Narrative of Her Journey from London into Cornwall* (Toronto 2016); inquisitional

---

[13] Other works by Christine de Pizan, moreover, are in the pipeline for future publication.

[14] More's defense of women's education, included in the same volume with Makin's, is accompanied by the response to her argument by the male author Robert Whitehall.

proceedings, such as *The Inquisition of Francisca [de los Apóstoles]: A Sixteenth-Century Visionary on Trial* (Chicago 2005); convent chronicle, such as Giustina Niccolini's *Chronicle of Le Murate* (Toronto 2011); and others, including autobiographical texts such as those considered below.

Autobiography and Life Writings

The female-authored autobiographies of the fourteenth-century holy woman Margery Kempe and the sixteenth-century mystic and theologian Saint Teresa of Ávila were well-known before the 1990s. The Other Voice series has significantly expanded this legacy, publishing several woman-authored autobiographical works and memoirs from the early modern era. Those by religious women, include, from the seventeenth century, the Catholics Ana de San Bartolomé and Maria Vela y Cueto (Chicago 2008, Toronto 2016), both Spanish, and the Flemish Margaret Van Noort (Toronto 2015), who writes in Spanish, as well as, on the Protestant side, the Pietist Johanna Eleonora Petersen (Chicago 2005), and three French Huguenot memoirists (Toronto 2019). The series also includes important autobiographical texts by the English-born German princess Sophia of Hanover (Toronto 2013), the Polish poet Anna Stanisławska (Toronto 2016), both seventeenth-century, and the eighteenth-century French translator and essayist Marie-Geneviève-Charlotte Thiroux d'Arconville (Toronto 2018), as well as the extensive and diverse life writings in her *Book M* of the seventeenth-century English widow Katherine Austen (Toronto 2013). These do not include briefer autobiographical texts appearing among the collected works of other authors.

Letters

Letter-writing was a preferred literary activity of many early modern women, by which they could both build and sustain relationships with family members and others and also give expression, in an informal medium, to their opinions and perceptions. The Other Voice series publishes several important letter collections, of which perhaps the most important are three by Italian women of the fifteenth to sixteenth centuries: the Tuscan merchant's wife Margherita Datini (Toronto 2012); Alessandra Macinghi Strozzi, the wife, then widow, of an exiled Florentine magnate (Toronto 2016); and Isabella d'Este, daughter of the Duke of Ferrara and consort of the Marquis of Mantua, whose "selected letters" (Toronto 2017) number a scant 830, occupying a volume of not quite seven hundred pages. Other important letter collections, also in Italian, are those of the courtesans, Venetian and Roman, Veronica Franco and Tullia d'Aragona (Chicago 1998, Toronto 2014); the Neapolitan duchess Ippolita Maria Sforza (Toronto 2017); and the Venetian nun

Arcangela Tarabotti (Toronto 2012). Special note should be made, as well, of the correspondence between the princess of Bohemia and the French philosopher René Descartes (Chicago 2007); and that between the "two Sophies" (Sophia of Hanover and Queen Sophie Charlotte of Prussia) and the German philosopher Gottfried Wilhelm Leibniz (Toronto 2011). In addition, many letters are published as elements in the collected works of several other authors.

Drama

Several volumes in the Other Voice series contribute significantly to our understanding of women's participation in playwriting. As early modern develops from medieval and Renaissance sacred drama, it is important that the series publishes (in two separate editions) the sacred plays of the fifteenth-century Florentine writer Antonia Pulci (Chicago 1996; Toronto 2010). Soon, influenced by the development of humanist imitations of ancient theater, of the *commedia dell'arte*, and of opera, scripted plays in Italian appear. The Other Voice series has published plays by sixteenth-century authors Maddalena Campiglia (Chicago 2004), Barbara Torelli Benedetti (Toronto 2013), and Isabella Andreini (Toronto 2018); and seventeenth-century authors Valeria Miani and Margherita Costa (Toronto 2010, 2018). In other languages, the Other Voice has published a volume of seventeenth-century woman-authored plays in Spanish by Feliciana Enríquez de Guzmán and others (Toronto 2016); in French by Louise-Geneviève Gillot de Sainctonge (Toronto 2010) and a volume by Françoise Pascal and others (Toronto 2015); in English a volume of household drama by Mary Wroth and others (Toronto 2018), and dramas by the playwrights Delarivier Manley and Mary Pix depicting Islamic civilization (Toronto 2012); and in Polish by the eighteenth-century author Franciszka Urszula Radziwiłłowa (Toronto 2015). In addition, the Italian play by the seventeenth-century male author Giovan Battista Andreini, playwright son of playwright and actress Isabella Andreini, deals squarely with pro-woman themes (Toronto 2009).

Fairy Tales

Before women in any number wrote books, they told stories: to their children, to instruct them in the ways of the world; to each other, as they sat and labored at their spinning or embroidery; and to mixed-gender groups at night around the fire in the hours before sleep. Many of those stories were fairy tales, which began to be gathered and recorded from the sixteenth century. The Other Voice series has published two important fairy tale collections: the sixteenth-century collection by Gianfrancesco Straparola of tales told by female narrators, based on stories originally told by women (Toronto

2015); and, drawing on that trove, fairy tales composed by French women authors from the last years of the seventeenth century (*Enchanted Eloquence*, Toronto 2010), which in turn fed the modern fairy tale tradition.

Medicine and Midwifery

While physicians studied in universities the Greek medical tradition as conveyed by the then newly-translated works of Galen, medical services were actually delivered by healers of all sorts whose craft was often learned from other practitioners. The medical skill of particular relevance for women, of course, was midwifery, its tenets communicated orally until appearing in written form beginning in the fifteenth century—the very earliest of which, composed in the mid-fifteenth century for the midwives of Ferrara, will soon be published in the Other Voice series. Already published are the extensive obstetrical works of Louise Bourgeois, the early-seventeenth-century French midwife who delivered several royal infants (Toronto 2017); a volume containing five obstetrical texts by male physicians composed from 1581 to 1625 that were directed to midwives and to other male professionals (François Rousset et al., Toronto 2013); and the notebooks of Justine Siegemund, a practicing seventeenth-century German midwife (Chicago 2005). In addition, the series has published the unusual pro-woman medical text presumed to be by Oliva Sabuco, the sixteenth-century Spanish daughter of a physician (Toronto 2010).

Major Authors and Unique Titles

As the Other Voice series has developed, it has brought prominence, by publishing several of their works, to some exceptionally important women authors whose activity had gone largely unnoticed. Foremost among these is the fifteenth-century feminist Christine de Pizan, whose epochal *Book of the City of Ladies*, mentioned above, was published before the series launched. The Other Voice list now includes the three other volumes by Christine already named, and expects to publish four more in the future. Of works by the seventeenth-century nun and polemicist Arcangela Tarabotti, the series has published *Paternal Tyranny* (Chicago 2004); *Letters Familiar and Formal* (Toronto 2012); *Antisatire*, in response to Francesco Buoninsegni's *Satire* (Toronto 2019); and *Convent Paradise* (Toronto 2019); and anticipates publishing two more. By the sixteenth-century author Moderata Fonte, the series has published *The Worth of Women* (Chicago 1997) and *Floridoro* (Chicago 2006), and by her slightly junior contemporary Lucrezia Marinella, *The Nobility and Excellence of Women* (Chicago 1999); *Enrico; or, Byzantium Conquered* (Chicago 2009); *Exhortations to Women and to Others if They Please* (Toronto 2012); and *Love Enamored and Driven Mad* (Toronto 2019).

Furthermore, the series anticipates publishing a third work by Madeleine de Scudéry, having previously published her *Story of Sapho* (Chicago 2003) and her *Selected Letters, Orations, and Rhetorical Dialogues* (Chicago 2004); two more titles by the Italian poet Vittoria Colonna, having previously published her *Sonnets for Michelangelo* (Chicago 2005); a third title by Tullia d'Aragona, having previously published her *Dialogue on the Infinity of Love* (Chicago 1997) and *Poems and Letters* (Toronto 2014); and a second title by the Dutch thinker Anna Maria van Schurman, having previously published her *Whether a Christian Woman Should Be Educated* (Chicago 1998).

However meritorious as all of the Other Voice volumes may be, a few unique titles are particularly worthy of note. These include the two massive volumes already named of the letters of Isabella d'Este and the midwifery works of Louise Bourgeois (Toronto 2017, 2017). To these may be added Sarra Copia Sulam, *Jewish Poet and Intellectual in Seventeenth-Century Venice* (Chicago 2009); the *Selected Philosophical and Scientific Writings* of the eighteenth-century French thinker Émilie du Châtelet (Chicago 2009); and *Arcadia to Revolution*, selected writings of the eighteenth-century Italian Jacobin and journalist Eleonora Fonseca Pimentel (Toronto 2019). These titles elevate the profiles of a Jewish woman writer, a female scientist, and a female revolutionary.

The Toronto English Series

Although the original mission of the Other Voice series was to translate for an Anglophone audience works originally composed in foreign languages, since 2011 the Toronto Other Voice series has included English titles as well; sixteen have now been published or are in press.[15] Some of these have already been named. Among the English-language volumes are writings by a number of well-known women: Mary Astell, Anne Bradstreet (British-born, and transplanted to Massachusetts), Margaret Cavendish (and also her stepdaughters Jane Cavendish and Elizabeth Brackley), Margaret Fell, Lady Elizabeth Hoby, Anne Killigrew, and Mary Wroth, for example. Future publications will include, in addition, works by Anne Vaughan Lock and Margaret Roper.

[15] The addition of the English titles has impacted the statistical profile of the series in the distribution of languages, necessarily, but also of era: since the participation of women in literary culture came somewhat later to England than to the Continent, most of the English titles included are seventeenth-century, with few sixteenth-century titles and none earlier than 1500.

Among the English titles, notably, are those based on recently-discovered manuscripts created by writers such as Lady Hester Pulter, who in the 1640s and 1660s wrote poems, emblems, and a prose romance entitled *The Unfortunate Florinda* (Toronto 2014), and Katherine Austen, a London widow whose life writings include, as its editor says, "spiritual meditations, sermon notes, financial records, personal essays, and more than thirty occasional and religious lyric poems, including elegies and country house verse" (Toronto 2013, 2)—all woven together to create a lively image of Austen's own family and its place within "the business of the nation" from 1660 to 1682. The Devonshire Manuscript, an anthology of Tudor courtier verse written mostly by men but circulated and commented upon by women, principally Lady Margaret Douglas, edited in the Other Voice series by Elizabeth Heale (Toronto 2012), is enhanced by the ongoing electronic project of *A Social Edition of the Devonshire Manuscript* by Ray Siemens et al. (discussed in this volume), housed at itercommunity.org/—a resource that Heale was able to utilize as the foundation text for her edition, as acknowledged in her introduction. These related projects illustrate how print and electronic publishing may cooperatively bring early modern texts to life.

Other Voice Books

Other Voice books are beautiful! They are adorned with stunningly lovely covers. The Chicago books feature misty images of women's faces in soft monochromes. The Toronto books reproduce fine paintings, engravings, and manuscript illuminations depicting the authors or related themes. Beautiful on the outside, they are clearly presented within, employing a consistent style and standards across the series.

Production, Sales, and Distribution

Iter Press (an Iter Inc. enterprise) manages the production of Other Voice books. "Production" covers managing the series finances; acquiring Cataloging-in-Publication block from the Library of Congress; assessing cover and interior images and working with volume editors to ensure their high quality; tracking permissions to reproduce copyrighted materials, a process that includes providing support to volume editors (who acquire permissions); typesetting, including working with series and volume editors to resolve formatting issues and to ensure that the book is as free from error as possible; overseeing cover design, expertly handled by Information Technology Services, University of Toronto Library (a participating partner in Iter Inc.); designing marketing materials; coordinating printing; coordinating the distribution of review copies; and maintaining the Other Voice lists on the Iter and Other Voice web sites at itergateway.org/iter-press/Book and othervoiceineme.com/othervoice-toronto.html. The sale and distribution of Other Voice books is managed by the University of Chicago Press via their Chicago Distribution Center (CDC). Online orders may be placed via a CDC shopping cart on the Iter web sites itergateway.org/ or itergateway.org/iter-press/series/1. Telephone orders may be placed through CDC.

Other Voice books are displayed at conferences, including the annual meeting of the Renaissance Society of America; Sixteenth Century Society and Conference; Annual Symposium on Medieval and Renaissance Studies; Annual ACMRS Interdisciplinary Conference; International Congress on Medieval Studies; and the Annual Meeting of the Shakespeare Association of America.

Iter Press distributes the series in ebook format for institutions via IP authentication, and is working to expand ebook distribution to individuals via the CDC shopping cart on the Iter site.

Other Voice titles are regularly (and mostly positively) reviewed in a wide array of journals. Some of the journals that are known to have published reviews of Toronto titles are listed in Appendix 2.

Support, Subventions, and Awards

The publishers strive to keep production costs for each volume in the series to a minimum, but still rely on subventions from volume editors' institutions to ensure that the quality of books published remains high and that pricing does not put them beyond the reach of individual students and scholars.[16]

The series has enjoyed longstanding support from the Gladys Krieble Delmas Foundation, including a start-up grant awarded to Iter in 2008, and three grants (2015–2017) that supported the publication of nine titles lacking subventions, below:

- Charlotte Arbaleste Duplessis Mornay, Anne de Chaufepié, and Anne Marguerite Petit Du Noyer, *The Huguenot Experience of Persecution and Exile: Three Women's Stories* (2019)

[16] A subvention of $2,000 is requested for books up to 120,000 words; $3,000 for books between 120,000 and 160,000 words; and $4,000 for books over 160,000 words. Books by individuals whose institutions do not provide support for publication costs are published without prejudice, with Iter covering the expense from grants and private donations.

- Eleonora Fonseca Pimentel, *From Arcadia to Revolution: The Neapolitan Monitor and Other Writings* (2019)
- Mary Wroth, Jane Cavendish, and Elizabeth Brackley, *Women's Household Drama: Loves Victorie, A Pastorall, and The concealed Fansyes* (2018)
- Marguerite d'Auge, Renée Burlamacchi, and Jeanne du Laurens, *Sin and Salvation in Early Modern France: Three Women's Stories* (2017)
- Christine de Pizan, *The Book of the Mutability of Fortune* (2017)
- María Vela y Cueto, *Autobiography and Letters of a Spanish Nun* (2016)
- Alessandra Macinghi Strozzi, *Letters to Her Sons* (2016)
- Anna Stanisławska, *Orphan Girl* (2016)
- Jeanne d'Albret, *Letters from the Queen of Navarre with An Ample Declaration* (2016)

The series is also deeply grateful for the personal contributions of nine series/volume editors, which have helped to ensure that the series has been able to expand swiftly, and is testament to the view of the Other Voice as an esteemed series among the scholarly community it serves.

The Other Voice is proud to have received a total of thirty-three awards from the Society for the Study of Early Modern Women during the period 2002–19:

- Josephine Roberts Scholarly Edition: 2 Chicago and 8 Toronto; 1 honorable mention (Toronto)
- Teaching Edition: 4 Toronto
- Scholarly Edition in Translation: 3 Chicago and 3 Toronto; 5 honorable mentions (2 Chicago; 3 Toronto)
- Translation or Teaching Edition: 4 Chicago; 1 honorable mention (Chicago)
- Collaborative Project: 1 Chicago; 1 honorable mention (Chicago)

In addition, the series has been recognized by *Feminae: Medieval Women and Gender Index*, with ten Toronto titles chosen as Translation of the Month.

Conclusion

The Other Voice series has grown to remarkable and unanticipated dimensions, supported by energetic publishing and editorial personnel based in multiple cities (Chicago, New York, Toronto, and Washington, DC) in two nations, the United States and Canada, with contributors from three continents: North America, Europe, and Australia. It has transformed the landscape of early modern literature and thought.

Appendix 1

Data about the Other Voice Series. See also Figures 8.1–8.5. These data are current as of November 2020.

Era	**Chicago: 1996–2010**	**Toronto: 2009–2020**	**Combined**
14th	0	1	1
15th	8	7	15
16th	25	21	46
17th	24	36	60
18th	3	8	11
19th	0	1	1

Table 8.1: Era in the Other Voice series.

Language	**Chicago: 1996–2010**	**Toronto: 2009–2020**	**Combined**
English	0	16	16
French	21	20	41
German	4	1	5
Italian	23	23	46
Latin	0	1	8
Polish	7	2	2
Russian	0	2	2
Spanish	5	9	14

Table 8.2: Language in the Other Voice series.

Genre	Chicago: 1996–2010	Toronto: 2009–2020	Combined
dialogue	5	0	5
drama	2	13	15
epic	3	2	5
letters	10	12	22
novel/romance	4	4	8
oration	3	1	4
poetry	12	20	32
prose non-fiction	35	35	70
story	2	3	5

Table 8.3 Genre in the Other Voice series.

Topic	Chicago: 1996–2010	Toronto: 2009–2020	Combined
autobiography/memoir	4	14	18
education	7	2	9
fairy tale	0	3	3
humanist	5	2	7
love	10	9	19
marriage	1	3	4
medical/obstetrical	1	3	4
philosophy/science/politics	5	7	12
querelle	9	6	15
religious	18	21	39
travel	0	2	2

Table 8.4 Topic in the Other Voice series.

Appendix 2

Select list of journals reviewing Other Voice volumes.

Annali d'Italianistica
Arizona Journal of Hispanic Cultural Studies
Aspasia
Bibliothèque de l'École des chartes
Bulletin of the Comediantes
Cahiers du dix-septième
Caliope
The Catholic Historical Review
Choice
La corónica
Early Modern Women
Eighteenth-Century Fiction
Emotions: History, Culture, Society
Forum Italicum
French History
French Studies
Friends Journal
H-France Review
Italica
Journal of British Studies
Journal of Ecclesiastical History
Journal of the History of Philosophy
Letras Femeninas
Marvels and Tales
The Medieval Review
Medium Aevum
Modern Language Review
Papers on French Seventeenth-Century Literature
Parergon
The Polish Review
Quaderni d'Italianistica
Quaker Studies
Quaker Universalist Voice
Renaissance and Reformation / Renaissance et Réforme
Renaissance Quarterly
Revista de Escritoras Ibéricas
The Russian Review
The Sarmatian Review
Seventeenth-Century News
Sidney Journal
The Sixteenth Century Journal
Slavic and East European Journal
Social History of Medicine
Speculum
Studies in English Literature
Symposium
Tulsa Studies in Women's Literature
University of Toronto Quarterly
Women's History Review
Women in French Studies
Women's Writing

WORKS CITED

Selected Titles from the Chicago Series, Published by the University of Chicago Press

Agrippa, Henricus Cornelius. 1996. *Declamation on the Nobility and Preeminence of the Female Sex*. Edited and translated by Albert Rabil, Jr.

Ana de San Bartolomé. 2008. *Autobiography and Other Writings*. Edited and translated by Darcy Donahue.

Aragona, Tullia d'. 1997. *Dialogue on the Infinity of Love*. Edited and translated by Rinaldina Russell and Bruce Merry, with introduction and notes by Rinaldina Russell.

Campiglia, Maddalena. 2004. *Flori, a Pastoral Drama: A Bilingual Edition*. Edited by Virginia Cox and Lisa Sampson. Translated by Virginia Cox.

Cereta, Laura. 1997. *Collected Letters of a Renaissance Feminist*. Edited and translated by Diana Robin.

Christine de Pizan, et al. 2010. *Debate of the Romance of the Rose*. Edited and translated by David F. Hult.

Colonna, Vittoria. 2005. *Sonnets for Michelangelo: A Bilingual Edition*. Edited and translated by Abigail Brundin.

Du Châtelet, Emilie. 2009. *Selected Philosophical and Scientific Writings*. Edited by Judith P. Zinsser. Translated by Isabelle Bour and Judith P. Zinsser.

Elisabeth of Bohemia, Princess, and René Descartes. 2007. *The Correspondence between Princess Elisabeth of Bohemia and René Descartes*. Edited and translated by Lisa Shapiro.

Fedele, Cassandra. 2000. *Letters and Orations*. Edited and translated by Diana Robin.

Fonte, Moderata [Modesta Pozzo]. 1997. *The Worth of Women: Wherein is Clearly Revealed Their Nobility and Their Superiority to Men*. Edited and translated by Virginia Cox.

———. 2006. *Floridoro: A Chivalric Romance*. Edited with introduction by Valeria Finucci, with notes by Valeria Finucci and Julia Kisacky. Translated by Julia Kisacky.

Francisca de los Apóstoles. 2005. *The Inquisition of Francisca: A Sixteenth-Century Visionary on Trial*. Edited and translated by Gillian T. W. Ahlgren.

Franco, Veronica. 1998. *Poems and Selected Letters*. Edited and translated by Ann Rosalind Jones and Margaret F. Rosenthal.

Gournay, Marie le Jars de. 2002. *Apology for the Woman Writing and Other Works*. Edited and translated by Richard Hillman and Colette Quesnel.

Greiffenberg, Catharina Regina von. 2009. *Meditations on the Incarnation, Passion, and Death of Jesus Christ*. Edited and translated by Lynne Tatlock.

Marinella, Lucrezia. 1999. *The Nobility and Excellence of Women, and the Defects and Vices of Men*. Edited and translated by Anne Dunhill. Introduction by Letizia Panizza.

———. 2009. *Enrico; or, Byzantium Conquered: A Heroic Poem*. Edited and translated by Maria Galli Stampino.

Morata, Olympia. 2003. *The Complete Writings of an Italian Heretic*. Edited and translated by Holt N. Parker.

Nogarola, Isotta. 2004. *Complete Writings: Letterbook, Dialogue on Adam and Eve, Orations*. Edited and translated by Margaret L. King and Diana Robin.

Petersen, Johanna Eleonora. 2005. *The Life of Lady Johanna Eleonora Petersen, Written by Herself: Pietism and Women's Autobiography in Seventeenth-Century Germany*. Edited and translated by Barbara Becker-Cantarino.

Poullain de La Barre, François. 2002. *Three Cartesian Feminist Treatises*. Edited by Marcelle Maistre Welch. Translated by Vivien Bosley.

Pulci, Antonia. 1996. *Florentine Drama for Convent and Festival: Seven Sacred Plays*. Edited by James Wyatt Cook and Barbara Collier Cook. Translated with notes by James Wyatt Cook.

Schurman, Anna Maria van. 1998. *Whether a Christian Woman Should be Educated and Other Writings from Her Intellectual Circle*. Edited and translated by Joyce L. Irwin.

Scudéry, Madeleine de. 2003. *The Story of Sapho*. Edited and translated by Karen Newman.

———. 2004. *Selected Letters, Orations, and Rhetorical Dialogues.* Edited and translated by Jane Donawerth and Julie Strongson.

Siegemund, Justine. 2005. *The Court Midwife.* Edited and translated by Lynne Tatlock.

Sulam, Sarra Copia. 2009. *Jewish Poet and Intellectual in Seventeenth-Century Venice: The Works of Sarra Copia Sulam in Verse and Prose, along with Writings of Her Contemporaries in Her Praise, Condemnation, or Defense.* Edited and translated by Don Harrán.

Tarabotti, Arcangela. 2004. *Paternal Tyranny.* Edited and translated by Letizia Panizza.

Vives, Juan Luis. 2000. *The Education of a Christian Woman: A Sixteenth-Century Manual.* Edited and translated by Charles Fantazzi.

Selected Titles from the Toronto Series, Published by Iter Press of Iter Inc. (2009–14, in Collaboration with CRRS: The University of Toronto's Centre for Reformation and Renaissance Studies; 2015–20, in Collaboration with ACMRS: The Arizona Center for Medieval and Renaissance Studies)

Andreini, Giovan Battista. 2009. *Love in the Mirror: A Bilingual Edition.* Edited and translated by Jon R. Snyder. Vol. 2.

Andreini, Isabella. 2018. *Mirtilla, A Pastoral: A Bilingual Edition.* Edited by Valeria Finucci. Translated by Julia Kisacky. Vol. 62.

Aragona, Tullia d', and Others. 2014. *The Poems and Letters of Tullia d'Aragona and Others: A Bilingual Edition.* Edited and translated by Julia L. Hairston. Vol. 28.

Astell, Mary. 2013. *The Christian Religion, as Professed by a Daughter of the Church of England.* Edited by Jacqueline Broad. Vol. 24.

Austen, Katherine. 2013. Book M: *A London Widow's Life Writings.* Edited by Pamela S. Hammons. Vol. 26.

Bellefonds, Marie Gigault de, Marquise de Villars. 2020. *Letters from Spain: A Seventeenth-Century French Noblewoman at the Spanish Royal Court.* Edited and translated by Nathalie Hester. Vol. 80.

Bourgeois, Louise. 2017. *Midwife to the Queen of France: Diverse Observations.* Edited by Alison Klairmont Lingo. Translated by Stephanie O'Hara. Vol. 56.

Champier, Symphorien. 2018. *The Ship of Virtuous Ladies.* Edited and translated by Todd W. Reeser. Vol. 61.

Christine de Pizan. 2017. *The Book of the Mutability of Fortune.* Edited and translated by Geri L. Smith. Vol. 52.

———. 2017. *Othea's Letter to Hector.* Edited and translated by Renate Blumenfeld-Kosinski and Earl Jeffrey Richards. Vol. 57.

Costa, Margherita. 2018. *The Buffoons, A Ridiculous Comedy: A Bilingual Edition.* Edited and translated by Sara Díaz and Jessica Goethals. Vol. 63.

Datini, Margherita. 2012. *Letters to Francesco Datini.* Edited and translated by Carolyn James and Antonio Pagliaro. Vol. 16.

del Nacimiento, Cecilia. 2012. *Journeys of a Mystic Soul in Poetry and Prose.* Edited with introduction and prose translation by Kevin Donnelly. Poetry translation by Sandra Sider. Vol. 18.

d' Este, Isabella. 2017. *Selected Letters.* Edited and translated by Deanna Shemek. Vol. 54.

Douglas, Margaret, and Others. 2012. *The Devonshire Manuscript: A Women's Book of Courtly Poetry.* Edited and introduced by Elizabeth Heale. Vol. 19.

Duplessis-Mornay, Charlotte Arbaleste, Anne de Chaufepié, and Anne Marguerite Petit Du Noyer. 2019. *The Huguenot Experience of Persecution and Exile: Three Women's Stories.* Edited by Colette H. Winn. Translated by Lauren King and Colette H. Winn. Vol. 68.

Enchanted Eloquence: Fairy Tales by Seventeenth-Century French Women Writers. 2010. Edited and translated by Lewis C. Seifert and Domna C. Stanton. Vol. 9.

Enríquez de Guzmán, Feliciana, Ana Caro Mallén, and Sor Marcela de San Félix. 2016. *Women Playwrights of Early Modern Spain.* Edited by Nieves Romero-Díaz and Lisa Vollendorf. Translated and annotated by Harley Erdman. Vol. 49.

Erculiani, Camilla. 2020. Letters on Natural Philosophy: *The Scientific Correspondence of a Sixteenth-Century Pharmacist, with Related Texts.* Edited by Eleonora Carinci. Translated by Hannah Marcus. With a foreword by Paula Findlen. Vol. 77.

Fonseca Pimentel, Eleonora. 2019. *From Arcadia to Revolution: The Neapolitan Monitor and Other Writings.* Edited and translated by Verina R. Jones. Vol. 67.

Leibniz, Gottfried Wilhelm, Sophia, Electress of Hanover, and Queen Sophie Charlotte of Prussia. 2011. *Leibniz and the Two Sophies: The Philosophical Correspondence.* Edited and translated by Lloyd Strickland. Vol. 10.

Lock, Anne Vaughan. 2020. *Selected Poetry, Prose, and Translations, with Contextual Materials.* Edited by Susan M. Felch. Vol. 76.

Macinghi Strozzi, Alessandra. 2016. *Letters to Her Sons, 1447–1470.* Edited and translated by Judith Bryce. Vol. 46.

Makin, Bathsua, Mary More, and Robert Whitehall. 2016. *Educating English Daughters: Late Seventeenth-Century Debates.* Edited by Frances Teague and Margaret J. M. Ezell. Associate editor Jessica Walker. Vol. 44.

Manley, Delarivier, and Mary Pix. 2012. *English Women Staging Islam, 1696–1707.* Edited by Bernadette Andrea. Vol. 17.

Marinella, Lucrezia. 2012. *Exhortations to Women and to Others if They Please.* Edited and translated by Laura Benedetti. Vol. 15.

———. 2020. *Love Enamored and Driven Mad*, Edited and translated by Janet E. Gomez and Maria Galli Stampino. Vol. 72.

Miani, Valeria. 2010. *Celinda, a Tragedy: A Bilingual Edition.* Edited with an introduction by Valeria Finucci. Translated by Julia Kisacky. Annotated by Valeria Finucci and Julia Kisacky. Vol. 8.

Niccolini, Giustina. 2011. *The Chronicle of Le Murate.* Edited and translated by Saundra Weddle. Vol. 12.

Noort, Margaret van. 2015. *Spiritual Writings of Sister Margaret of the Mother of God. 1635–1643.* Edited by Cordula van Wyhe. Translated by Susan M. Smith. Vol. 39.

Pascal, Françoise, Marie-Catherine Desjardins, Antoinette Deshoulières, and Catherine Durand. 2015. *Challenges to Traditional Authority: Plays by French Women Authors, 1650–1700*. Edited and translated by Perry Gethner. Vol. 36.

Pilsztynowa, Regina Salomea. 2020. *My Life's Travels and Adventures: An Eighteenth-Century Oculist in the Ottoman Empire and the European Hinterland.* Edited and translated by Władysław Roczniak. Vol. 78.

Pulci, Antonia. 2010. *Saints' Lives and Bible Stories for the Stage: A Bilingual Edition*. Edited by Elissa B. Weaver. Translated by James Wyatt Cook. Vol. 7.

Pulter, Hester, Lady. 2014. *Poems, Emblems, and The Unfortunate Florinda.* Edited by Alice Eardley. Vol. 32.

Radziwiłłowa, Franciszka Urszula. 2015. *Selected Drama and Verse.* Edited by Patrick John Corness and Barbara Judkowiak, with an introduction by Barbara Judkowiak. Translated by Patrick John Corness. Translation editor Aldona Zwierzyńska-Coldicott. Vol. 37.

Rousset, François, Jean Liebault, Jacques Guillemeau, Jacques Duval, and Louis de Serres. 2013. *Pregnancy and Birth in Early Modern France: Treatises by Caring Physicians and Surgeons, 1581–1625*. Edited and translated by Valerie Worth-Stylianou. Vol. 23.

Sabuco de Nantes Barrera, Oliva. 2010. *The True Medicine.* Edited and translated by Gianna Pomata. Vol. 4.

Sainctonge, Louise-Geneviève Gillot de. 2010. *Dramatizing Dido, Circe, and Griselda.* Edited and translated by Janet Levarie Smarr. Vol. 5.

Sforza, Ippolita Maria. 2017. *Duchess and Hostage in Renaissance Naples: Letters and Orations.* Edited and translated by Diana Robin and Lynn Lara Westwater. Vol. 55.

Sophia, Electress of Hanover. 2013. *Memoirs, 1630–1680*. Edited and translated by Sean Ward. Vol. 25.

Stanisławska, Anna. 2016. *Orphan Girl: A Transaction, or an Account of the Entire Life of an Orphan Girl by Way of Plaintful Threnodies in the Year 1685; The Aesop Episode*. Verse translation, introduction, and commentary by Barry Keane. Foreword by Margaret L. King. Vol. 45.

Straparola, Giovan Francesco. 2015. *The Pleasant Nights.* Edited and translated by Suzanne Magnanini. Vol. 40.

Tarabotti, Arcangela. 2012. *Letters Familiar and Formal.* Edited and translated by Meredith K. Ray and Lynn Lara Westwater. Vol. 20.

———. 2020. *Antisatire: In Defense of Women, against Francesco Buoninsegni.* Edited and translated by Elissa Weaver. Vol. 70.

———. 2020. *Convent Paradise in Three Books with a Soliloquy to God.* Edited and translated by Meredith K. Ray and Lynn Lara Westwater. Vol. 73.

Thiroux d'Arconville, Marie-Geneviève-Charlotte. 2018. *Selected Philosophical, Scientific, and Autobiographical Writings.* Edited and translated by Julie Candler Hayes. Vol. 58.

Torelli Benedetti, Barbara. 2013. *Partenia, a Pastoral Play: A Bilingual Edition.* Edited and translated by Lisa Sampson and Barbara Burgess-Van Aken. Vol. 22.

Torrellas, Pere, and Juan de Flores. 2013. *Three Spanish Querelle Texts: Grisel and Mirabella, The Slander against Women, and The Defense of Ladies against Slanderers; A Bilingual Edition and Study.* Edited and translated by Emily C. Francomano. Vol. 21.

Trapnel, Anna. 2016. *Anna Trapnel's Report and Plea; or, a Narrative of Her Journey from London into Cornwall.* Edited by Hilary Hinds. Vol. 50.

Vela y Cueto, María. 2016. *Autobiography and Letters of a Spanish Nun.* Edited by Susan Laningham. Translated by Jane Tar. Vol. 51.

Wroth, Mary, Jane Cavendish, and Elizabeth Brackley. 2018. *Women's Household Drama:* Loves Victorie, A Pastorall, *and* The concealed Fansyes. Edited by Marta Straznicky and Sara Mueller. Vol. 66.

Digital Humanities' Shakespeare Problem[1]

Laura Estill
St. Francis Xavier University

Digital humanities has a Shakespeare problem; or, to frame it more broadly, a canon problem. Too many digital projects and sites focus on Shakespeare alone. Some sites highlight Shakespeare to the exclusion of other writers; other projects set their bounds at Shakespeare and "not Shakespeare." Digital humanities' Shakespeare problem both stems from and reifies Shakespeare's centrality to the canon of English literature. While this problem is, indeed, a digital humanities problem, it is also a problem in the arts and humanities more generally. Shakespeare is one of the few writers regularly featured in single-author undergraduate courses (alongside, perhaps, Chaucer, Milton, and Austen, albeit to a lesser extent). Shakespeare's works are so often produced on the twenty-first-century stage that American Theatre excludes Shakespeare from their annual list of top-produced American plays in order to "make more room on our list for everyone and everything else" (Tran 2018). Digital humanities has often been heralded as the solution to the canonicity problem, but it cannot bear this great burden alone.

This essay begins by demonstrating why we need to consider Shakespeare's position in the digital landscape, recognizing that Shakespeare's prominence in digital sources stems from his cultural prominence. I describe the Shakespeare/not Shakespeare divide in digital humanities projects and then turn to digital editions to demonstrate how Shakespeare's texts are treated differently from those of his contemporaries—and often isolated by virtue of being placed alone on their pedestal. In the final section, I explore the implications of Shakespeare's popularity among digital humanities projects, some of which exist solely because of Shakespeare's status. Shakespeare's centrality to the canon of digital humanities reflects his reputation in wider spheres such as education and the arts. No digital project will offer a complete, unmediated view of the past, or, indeed, the present. Ultimately, each digital humanities project presents an argument about the status of Shakespeare,

---

[1] This essay is reprinted with minor revisions from *Humanities* 8.1 (2019): 45; doi.org/10.3390/h8010045. I would like to thank Heidi Craig for her thoughtful feedback. Thanks also *Humanities* blind peer reviewers and guest editor, Stephen O'Neill, for their constructive suggestions.

ISBN 978-1-64959-063-3 (paper) ISBN 978-1-64959-064-0 (pdf) ISBN 978-1-64959-065-7 (epub)
New Technologies in Medieval and Renaissance Studies 11 (2025) 217–243

and we—as Shakespeareans, early modernists, digital humanists, humanists, and scholars—must determine what arguments we find persuasive and what arguments we want to make with the new projects we design and implement.

Although the definition of digital humanities (and perhaps even the definition of Shakespeare) is subject to disagreement, for this essay, I limit my scope to digital humanities resources for pedagogy and research. This excludes games such as *Richard III Attacks*! (P. 2015), online performances such as *Such Tweet Sorrow* (Silbert 2010), and social media hashtags like #ShakespeareSunday. Cultural studies often informs new media Shakespeare scholarship to show Shakespeare's continued prominence online (see O'Neill 2015 for an overview); consider recent issues of *Shakespeare Quarterly* (Rowe 2010) and *Borrowers and Lenders* (Calbi and O'Neill 2016) on this topic. Stephen O'Neill (2018), drawing on Douglas Lanier's notion of "Shakespearean rhizomatics" (Lanier 2014), equates "Our contemporary Shakespeares" to "digital Shakespeares," describing both as "fully rhizomatic in their extraordinary and seemingly endless flow of relations." Christy Desmet suggests that we need to encounter all digital Shakespeares (both digital humanities and new media) through the lens of Ian Bogost's "alien phenomenology" (Bogost 2012), considering "material objects and networks as models for posthuman relations" (Desmet 2017, 5). Although digital humanities and new media are often paired, for the purpose of this essay it is useful to differentiate the two: new media endeavors that participate in or create digital culture versus digital humanities projects that announce themselves as contributing to our general and scholarly knowledge. This essay focuses on digital humanities projects for two reasons: first, as one way of limiting the scope of the "seemingly endless flow of relations" in Digital Shakespeares, and second, because the majority of digital humanities projects exist primarily to educate rather than to entertain.

Digital humanities projects provide the resources we use to study and teach the early modern period: digital editions, bibliographies, digitizations, catalogs, and more. Often, digital humanities projects are expanded from earlier print resources: consider, for instance, the online English Short Title Catalogue (British Library 2006) and its print antecedents, the short-title catalogs by Pollard and Redgrave (1926) and Donald Goddard Wing (1945). Nondigital scholarly resources frequently skew towards Shakespeare; even the library catalogs we use to access archival resources are not neutral and emphasize Shakespeare above his contemporaries (Estill 2020). Many digital humanities resources replicate this Shakespeare-centric focus, and, as such, misrepresent the materials they provide or offer a skewed perspective on early modern literature, theatre, and culture. Biased sources can only lead to biased scholarship; and while some professors will be able to see the biases of the sites they visit, many students will not. This is particularly problematic because, as Christie Carson and Peter Kirwan explain, "Students are some of the key 'users' of digital Shakespeare" (Carson and Kirwan 2014a, 244).

It has been well-documented that major digital literary studies projects often focus on canonical authors. There is excellent work on the biases of digital humanities projects, particularly in relation to the status of women writers (see, for instance, Wernimont and Flanders 2010; Mandell 2015; Bergenmar and Leppänen 2017) and the canon of American literature (Earhart 2012; Price 2009), yet comparatively few scholars have critiqued how digital humanities overrepresents perhaps the most canonical figure in all of English literature: Shakespeare. "Shakespeare and Digital Humanities" has been and continues to be a fruitful area of research, with special issues of *Shakespeare* (Galey and Siemens 2008), the Shakespearean International Yearbook (Greatley-Hirsch and Craig 2014), *RiDE: Research in Drama Education* (Bell and Borsuk 2020), and the special issue of *Humanities* on "Shakespeare and Digital Humanities: New Perspectives and Future Directions" in which this essay was originally published (O'Neill 2019). The prevalence of digital humanities tools in Shakespeare teaching and research leads Carson and Kirwan to wonder, "are all Shakespeares digital now?" (Carson and Kirwan 2014a, 240). The questions less often asked are: When we focus on Shakespeare(s) in our digital projects, what is excluded by our Shakespeare-centrism? And how does that shape how we access and understand early modern drama? Digital Shakespeare studies often focuses on Shakespeare's place in the digital world, without questioning why he is given such primacy and the ramifications of his continued canonization.

A decade ago, Matthew Steggle (2008) showcased how digital projects were "developing a canon" of early modern literature. Building on the "interrelated cycles" that Gary Taylor (1993) identified as supporting Shakespeare's centrality to textual studies, Brett Greatley-Hirsch describes "the long shadows cast by the cultural, scholarly, and economic investments in Shakespeare" (Greatley-Hirsch 2011, 569), specifically as it pertains to digital editions of early modern plays. This essay furthers the work by Steggle, Greatley-Hirsch, and others by arguing that we must continually assess the landscape of digital projects available for teaching and researching the early modern period in order to understand and shape the future of the field.

As the argument goes, traditional anthologies and resources are constricted by page counts and other limited resources, unlike digital projects, which can be democratizing due to their lack of—or, more realistically, different—limitations. In that vein, Neil Fraistat, Steven E. Jones, and Carl Stahmer suggest that "one of the strengths of Web publishing is that it facilitates—even favors—the production of editions of texts and resources of so-called non-canonical authors and works" (1998, 2). Earhart, however, traces the familiar pattern of discovery then loss for noncanonical writers: their work is digitized, declared as recuperated, and then the site disappears (2015, especially chapter 3). Another way digital humanities has been announced to recover noncanonical writers is by projects that digitize on a large scale. Julia Flanders explains:

> It is now easier, in some contexts, to digitize an entire library collection than to pick through and choose what should be included and what should not: in other words, storage is cheaper than decision-making. The result is that the rare, the lesser known, the overlooked, the neglected, and the downright excluded are now likely to make their way into digital library collections, even if only by accident. (Flanders 2009)

Indeed, it is the decision-making where Shakespeare too often gets pulled artificially to the fore: sometimes even in the foundational decisions about project scope. The next section of the essay explores how single authors are represented in small-scale versus large-scale digital resources, thinking about them in terms of labor, funding, and project scope.

The Shakespeare/Not Shakespeare Divide in Digital Humanities Resources

There is a lopsidedness to early modern online resources: some, such as the English Short Title Catalog (ESTC; British Library 2006) and the Database of Early English Playbooks (DEEP; Lesser and Farmer 2007), deliver breadth of coverage that is, due to their large scope, necessarily shallow; others, such as The Shakespeare Quartos Archive (Bodleian Library 2009) or MIT's Global Shakespeares (Donaldson 2009), provide deep coverage of a much narrower topic. Both approaches are needed to support different avenues of early modern scholarship, but the latter, I contend, too often begins and ends with Shakespeare.

The logistical reasons for these very different kinds of projects (broad versus deep coverage) are readily apparent. The notion of "Shakespeare" offers a convenient scope and bounds for a given project. Many projects that include detailed metadata, extensive editorial annotation or encoding, expensive-to-create facsimiles, or streaming media center on the work of a single author. The Pulter Project (Knight and Wall 2018) is an example of a new project that focuses on a single author, and, indeed, a single manuscript, in order to offer a hypertext edition with multiple layers of editorial intervention, linked related texts, and comparative viewing options. The Digital Cavendish Project (Moore and Tootalian 2013) offers a range of ways to interact with Margaret Cavendish's life and texts: site visitors can explore Margaret Cavendish's social network, search the bibliography-in-progress of Cavendish scholarship, and make use of reference works such as a list of Cavendish's printers and booksellers and a spreadsheet locating all known copies of Cavendish's early publications. We can imagine extending these projects by adding another analysis section, another manuscript, or even another individual author. However, to extend these projects by any order of magnitude by, say, covering all seventeenth-century women writers or all previously unpublished manuscript poetry, would be to undertake significant amounts of labor and would require both time and money.

These single-author projects are the fruits of detailed scholarly attention; they are "boutique" digital projects. In their discussion of archival practices, Mark A. Greene and Dennis Meissner position "boutique digitization" at the far end of the continuum from "'Googlization' (ultra-mass digitization)" (2005, 196). Boutique projects require "extraordinary attention to the unique properties of each artifact" (Conway 2010, 76). While Greene, Meissner, and Conway focus on archival digitization projects, the continuum also applies to digital humanities projects, many of which include digitized elements alongside other interventions: transcriptions, editorial apparatus, bibliographic resources, and so forth. The Shakespeare Quartos Archive (Bodleian Library 2009) is an example of extraordinary attention to primary sources; the site's goal is to "reproduce at least one copy of every edition of William Shakespeare's plays printed in quarto before the theatres closed in 1642." Where possible, however, they include digitizations of as many copies of each Shakespeare quarto as possible. Their prototype offers thirty-two quartos of *Hamlet* (from Q1–Q5), carefully digitized and painstakingly encoded.[2]

With their attention to primary sources, the Shakespeare Quartos Archive project argues that scholars must pay attention to copy-specific details. The

---

[2] Just as digital humanities has a Shakespeare problem, Shakespeare studies has a *Hamlet* problem, although the prominence of *Hamlet* in Shakespeare studies, both digital and otherwise, is a topic for another essay. For evidence of *Hamlet*'s prominence, see Kliman et al. 2004 and Estill, Klyve, and Bridal 2015.

Shakespeare Quartos Archive text encoding highlights different marginalia in each copy, the binding, and even the library ownership stamps.[3] While the Shakespeare Quartos Archive can be used as an exemplar of a "boutique" project, it is not the labor of a single scholar. This project emerged from the collaboration of multiple major institutions, including, most notably, the Bodleian Library of the University of Oxford, the British Library, the University of Edinburgh Library, the Folger Shakespeare Library, the Huntington Library, and the National Library of Scotland. The project was made possible by major grant funding from the United States's National Endowment for the Humanities (NEH) and the United Kingdom's Joint Information Systems Committee (JISC).

The well-supported Shakespeare Quartos Archive raises another reason for author-centric approaches, namely, existing funding models. As Jamie "Skye" Bianco (2012) explains, "digital humanities is directly linked to the institutional funding that privileges canonical literary and historiographic objects and narratives" (see also Price 2009, 281). In her review, Desmet unpacks the project's "rationale for a focus on Shakespeare's quartos" (Desmet 2014, 143): the rarity and fragility of the material objects; their locations in libraries around the world; and the lack of Shakespearean manuscript texts. This rationale, while a compelling argument for why we need to digitize and encode all early modern play quartos, hardly touches on why Shakespeare is the focus of the project. We lack authorial manuscripts of many plays by many playwrights. The Shakespearean focus of the Shakespeare Quartos Archive is taken for granted.

It is hard to imagine the Ford Quartos Archive receiving much enthusiasm from funders, despite the fact that John Ford's plays are still edited, anthologized, taught, and performed today. There are many ongoing editorial projects focused on individual early modern playwrights, such as Oxford University Press's *The Complete Works of John Marston* (Butler and Steggle, forthcoming); yet to imagine digitizing and encoding all known early printings of Marston's work for a Marston Quartos Archives seems far-fetched, and the notion of turning to an even less canonical playwright—say, the Glapthorne Quartos Archive—hardly bears thinking about. Shakespeare sells. Shakespeare's name is itself a valuable commodity (Hodgdon 1998; McLuskie

[3] The Shakespeare Quartos Archive uses the Text Encoding Initiative (TEI) for their XML (eXtensible Markup Language), which includes elements such as <handNote>, <stamp>, and <fw> (form work, for running heads, as an example). For more on their detailed encoding, see Desmet 2014.

and Rumbold 2014; Olive 2015). Digital project funders and creators recognize its value as much as academic publishers who push for Shakespeare's name in book titles. As of 2020, the Shakespeare Quartos Archive is now archived, making funding and sustainability seem even more dire for non-Shakespearean projects (added during republication).

Martin Mueller points to tenure and promotion as part of the reason for the scholarly focus on major, canonical plays. He asks, "You can see why professional scholars stay away from minor plays, unless they explicitly deal with hot topics. A play may interest them, but how will an entry about it look on a c.v.?" (Mueller 2014). While there is a wealth of valuable scholarship on minor plays, as Mueller points out, "the annual number of publications about Shakespeare dwarfs—by at least an order of magnitude—the number of publications about his contemporaries" (2014). Before scholars can achieve tenure and promotion, they must first land that tenure-track job, which, in many cases, means demonstrating that they can teach the single-author undergraduate Shakespeare course(s). Just as work on noncanonical playwrights can be met with institutional skepticism, digital humanities publication has tended to be undervalued by tenure and promotion committees, prompting scholarly bodies such as the Modern Language Association (MLA) to publish interventions like "Guidelines for Authors of Digital Resources" and "Guidelines for Evaluating Work in Digital Humanities and Digital Media" (MLA Committee on Information Technology 2012a, 2012b). For scholars creating digital projects, both funding and institutional structures of tenure and promotion can offer disincentives to go beyond Shakespeare.

Shakespeare is so privileged in early modern digital humanities projects that some projects market themselves as a corrective. Mueller's now-defunct Shakespeare His Contemporaries (Mueller 2016) described itself as "a project devoted to the collaborative curation of non-Shakespearean plays from Shakespeare's world."[4] Despite offering a digital humanities project that recognizes and pushes back against Shakespeare's centrality to early modern drama studies, Shakespeare His Contemporaries's self-definition ("non-Shakespearean"), title (Shakespeare His Contemporaries), and scope

---

[4] Shakespeare His Contemporaries can be accessed on the Internet Archive's Wayback Machine (archive.org/web/) by inserting its former URL, shakespearehiscontemporaries.northwestern.edu/shc (site discontinued). The Shakespeare His Contemporaries XML—itself created by improving the encoding provided by the Early English Books Online Text Creation Partnership, or EEBO-TCP—is preserved in the Folger's Digital Anthology of Early Modern English Drama (Brown et al. 2016).

("Shakespeare's world") all gravitate around Shakespeare. This is hardly unique. Similarly, the "Beyond Shakespeare" project (a podcast and blog) has a Twitter bio announces their interest in "anything but the Bard," just as their handle, @BeyondShakes, and the project title evokes his name (Crighton 2013).

Andy Kesson, Lucy Munro, and Callan Davies's "Before Shakespeare" reveals valuable insights about mid-sixteenth century London theatres. In their article, "DH and Non-Shakespearean Theatre History," Davies and Kesson explain how the digital components of their project are an integral part of their outreach mission: "The digital presence of "Before Shakespeare" is centered around showcasing various media at once: archives, discussion, videos, images, performance, and song—from Soundcloud to YouTube—to increase the visibility of non-Shakespearean drama and diversify its availability and appeal beyond printed editions and text" (2018). Despite their non-Shakespearean focus, or, indeed, perhaps because of it, their project title, URL (beforeshakespeare.com), "About" description, and Twitter account similarly centralize Shakespeare in the literary canon, even while resisting this positioning. The "About" page explains, "Before Shakespeare is also the first project to take seriously the mid-century beginnings of those playhouses, seeing them as mid-Tudor and early Elizabethan phenomena rather than becoming distracted by the second generation of people working in the playhouses, the most famous of whom is William Shakespeare himself" (Kesson et al. 2016, "About"). Their Twitter avatar (@B4Shakes, as of January 2019) is a picture of Shakespeare himself, though with the word "before" covering his eyes and with his mouth silenced by a series of decorative fleurons. There hardly seems to be an elegant solution for digital projects designed to push attention away from Shakespeare. As the most recognizable literary figure from his day, it could be argued that a site designed to appeal to the general public would be remiss to avoid naming him: there is no need to turn him into he-who-must-not-be-named, giving the name of Shakespeare even more power. Furthermore, for a project aiming to reach "wider audiences within and beyond scholarship," name-dropping Shakespeare can be an effective way to attract people to their site and social media, which will then offer "a powerful advertisement for the force and fascination of currently 'non-canonical' plays" (Davies and Kesson, 2018).

Despite the potential for democratization or canon expansion, digital projects too often reify canon, even when they attempt to subvert it. Emma Smith describes how this effect is not limited to the digital: drawing on examples from scholarship, culture, and online, she shows how "attempts to decentre Shakespeare are thus often self-defeating." She continues, "Do we privilege Shakespeare above other writers? Self-evidently and self-fulfillingly so" (Smith 2017). Smith contends that "Shakespeare studies have begun to reflect on the conditions and consequences of their own cultural supremacy"; this article contributes to these ongoing reflections. Although Smith acknowledges the "cultural, theatrical and educational disadvantages of Shakespeare-centrism," she concludes by positioning Shakespeare as "the apex predator in a cultural ecosystem where he has no rivals, only prey," suggesting our focus on Shakespeare is somehow required for the metaphoric ecosystems of culture and scholarship (2017). Digital projects, however, have the potential to go beyond this status quo, by, for instance, positioning Shakespeare alongside his contemporaries or by highlighting the historical moments that led to Shakespeare's current position as cultural touchstone.

Digital Editions and the Privileging of Shakespeare's Text

When we turn to digital editions, those digital humanities stalwarts, we see the same "not Shakespeare" construction of projects as detailed above. For instance, Greatley-Hirsch's Digital Renaissance Editions was "inspired by the *Internet Shakespeare Editions*" (Greatley-Hirsch 2015, home page). That is to say, an online edition of Shakespeare's works inspired a site whose aim is to offer "electronic scholarly editions of early English drama and texts of related interest, from late medieval moralities and Tudor interludes, occasional entertainments and civic pageants, academic and closet drama, and the plays of the commercial London theaters, through to the drama of the Civil War and Interregnum" for all authors, except Shakespeare (Greatley-Hirsch 2015, home page). These sibling projects only reinforce the divide between Shakespeare and not-Shakespeare. Shakespeare's central position in the canon becomes exceptional; he no longer falls under the umbrella of "Renaissance" or "early English drama." By excluding Shakespeare, Digital Renaissance Editions follows the tradition of printed non-Shakespearean anthologies, such as Arthur F. Kinney's *Renaissance Drama* (1999) and David Bevington's *English Renaissance Drama* (2002).

With digital editions, however, this Shakespeare-not Shakespeare gulf can be bridged, for instance, with a federated search interface. It would be wonderful to see, in the future, a new way to access Digital Renaissance Editions, the Internet Shakespeare Editions (Jenstad 2018), and the Queen's Men Editions (Ostovich 2006), all of which are built on the same platform, where users can easily compare content from across all three sites, perhaps searching for keywords across plays from all three. There is, of course, a value to maintaining each site separately; each project makes an argument about how we need to approach early modern drama. The Internet Shakespeare Editions includes much non-Shakespearean content, such as the full text and facsimiles of the play *A Yorkshire Tragedy*; however, the non-Shakespearean content is provided as context for our understanding of Shakespeare. *A Yorkshire Tragedy* is included in the Internet Shakespeare Editions because of its status as "almost Shakespeare"; although now accepted as apocryphal, it was once attributed to Shakespeare and was published in the second imprint of the 1664 folio. Similarly, the Internet Shakespeare Editions includes an extract from Robert Greene's *Selimus* because Jessica Slights deemed Greene's play a valuable intertext for her edition of *Othello* (Slights 2017). *A Yorkshire Tragedy*, *Selimus*, and other non-Shakespearean works on the site are categorized as "resources" (the last option from the top menu) whereas Shakespeare's plays and poems are the "texts" the Internet Shakespeare Editions foregrounds (the first option from the top menu). The Internet Shakespeare Editions guides users to approach all non-Shakespearean content through the lens of Shakespeare, first and foremost. The argument of Digital Renaissance Editions emerges to counter this overreliance on Shakespeare, yet ends up making Shakespeare conspicuous in his absence. As a digital edition based on the plays performed by a single playing company, the Queen's Men Editions argues for the value of performance and the importance of repertory-based studies not defined by authorship (Ostovich 2006, "The QME brand").

As Scott McMillin and Sally-Beth MacLean (McMillin and MacLean 1998), Lucy Munro (2009), and others have demonstrated, repertory studies is a valuable field that could be bolstered with even more digital editions organized by theatre company or playing space. At this point, the ISE, DRE, and QME offer three sites, three goals, and three uneven slices of early modern drama. While "maintaining the integrity of [the] sites" and "eliminat[ing] confusion" about their roles and boundaries (Ostovich 2006) are important, there is still a place for a federated search that would allow users to approach the content on all three sites at once. Although this imagined federated search would, at this moment, be far from a universal view of early modern English drama, it could offer a more comprehensive overview than each site currently provides, connected for users only with the occasional hyperlink. Diane K. Jakacki's thoughtful description of the Internet Shakespeare Editions tagset, its relation to sibling sites, and the potential of linked open data insightfully considers the potential of "acts of editorial disruption" to "allow us to move forward toward infinity while maintaining editorial stability across digital projects" (Jakacki 2018, 158). As digital editions of early modern drama "move forward toward infinity," we must assess if we want Shakespeare to be the default number one.

The Folger Shakespeare Library has also published digital projects defined by the presence or lack of Shakespeare: Folger Digital Texts (Mowat et al. 2012) and the Digital Anthology of Early Modern English Drama Anthology (Brown et al. 2016). However, unlike the Internet Shakespeare Editions and their sister sites, the Folger sites provide edited texts without critical introductions or notes. Folger Digital Texts offers editions of Shakespeare; the Digital Anthology includes editions and bibliographic information about, as their homepage announces, "other plays from Shakespeare's time" (emphasis in the original). The Digital Anthology "Frequently Asked Questions" page anticipates that users will want to know "Where is Shakespeare? And how does this relate to him?" Their response runs, in full:

> William Shakespeare's plays are not part of EMED, for a simple reason: EMED was conceived as a way of showcasing all of the other playwrights writing in England's early modern era.
>
> By bringing together their plays, however, EMED recreates the theater world that made possible Shakespeare's career and influenced his work. Shakespeare knew many of the earlier plays as an actor or audience member. He also collaborated and competed with some of the playwrights. He directly influenced others. To read Shakespeare's works, we recommend another Folger resource: the Folger Digital Texts.
>
> Some of the plays in EMED have historically been attributed to Shakespeare, including *The London Prodigal, Sir John Oldcastle, and The Yorkshire Tragedy*. These are currently regarded as "Shakespeare Apocrypha" and are no longer attributed to Shakespeare. For an explanation of how The London Prodigal fits (or does not fit) into Shakespeare's corpus, see Peter Kirwan's article in Shakespeare Documented. (Hyperlinks removed from original.)

Even as they undertake important work on early modern drama beyond Shakespeare, the Digital Anthology repeatedly presents the non-Shakespearean plays at the center of their project as "other." They assert that their site is valuable because it adds to our knowledge of Shakespeare. Their anticipated users don't care about Sir John Suckling or even Christopher Marlowe. They highlight the value of their site's "almost Shakespeare" apocryphal content. The Digital Anthology links to two Folger projects focusing entirely on Shakespeare: the Folger Digital Texts and Shakespeare Documented, both examples of "deep" digital humanities projects with a focus on Shakespeare.

Even if we consider the Digital Anthology of Early Modern Drama and Folger Digital Texts as twinned projects, they are not identical, but fraternal twins. The interfaces for both sites are quite different; one of the most notable differences is that the Folger Digital Texts Shakespeare editions are presented in modern spelling, whereas the rest of the early modern drama corpus is not. This is because the Folger Digital Texts are based on the Folger's print series, edited by Paul Werstine and Barbara Mowat, which means they have a different level of editorial intervention. The Folger digital projects do not neatly fit into the "deep" and "broad" categories; rather, they exist to serve different audiences. A nonspecialist will have an easier time navigating Shakespeare's texts on Folger Digital Texts than the plays on the Digital Anthology of Early Modern English Drama. Conversely, the Digital Anthology appeals to scholars by offering extensive links to existing resources, such as DEEP and the ESTC, as well as the additional data about early performance and publication that offers easy comparison across the corpus. The artificial divide the Folger sites erect between Shakespeare and not Shakespeare, then, is only compounded when, for instance, a scholar wants to know plays first performed in 1599 and returns a list of eleven plays, which, based on the Digital Anthology's scope, excludes Shakespeare's *Julius Caesar*, *Henry V*, and *As You Like It*. (A similar search in DEEP will include all results, but with multiple entries for each play that has more than one pre-1660 publication.) This is to say, the Folger's Digital Anthology of Early Modern English Drama is a digital project both with breadth (including bibliographic data about 403 plays) and depth (offering full texts of twenty-nine plays), yet it is the project's very exclusion of Shakespeare that warps the search results to offer an unrepresentative view of early modern drama and instead presents results with a Shakespeare-sized hole at their center. Indeed, the work of other writers is also omitted with the Shakespearean: for instance, Fletcher's work in *Henry VIII* is cut out from the corpus simply because it is a collaboration with Shakespeare.

Even in digital editions ostensibly focused on non-Shakespearean early modern drama, Shakespeare's shadow looms. The Queen's Men Editions currently provides performance editions of nine plays from the Queen's Men repertory—and four of these nine plays (*Famous Victories of Henry V*, *King Leir*, *Troublesome Reign of King John*, and *True Tragedy of Richard III*) have Shakespearean counterparts. The repertory of the Queen's Men Company did not comprise 44 percent of plays directly related to Shakespeare (McMillin and

MacLean 1998, esp. appendix A); yet this digital project has begun by privileging those texts. The Folger's Digital Anthology of Early Modern English Drama similarly offers an edition of *The True Chronicle of King Leir*, as well as the apocrypha they highlight in their FAQ. Some of the same apocryphal plays (including *The London Prodigal*) appear in both the "resources" section of the Internet Shakespeare Edition and the Digital Anthology of Early Modern Drama. Just having proximity to Shakespeare means these works get more editorial attention than other plays.

Richard Brome Online (Cave 2010) remains remarkable in the history of open-access online editions of early modern drama.[5] Greatley-Hirsch notes, "Until the launch of Richard Brome Online in 2010, there were no electronic critical editions of non-Shakespearean Renaissance drama available" (Greatley-Hirsch 2011, 574). Today, it still stands alone in the landscape of digital humanities projects as the only non-Shakespearean author-based online edition. (The Cambridge Edition of the Works of Ben Jonson Online [Butler 2014], which expands and supplements their printed play editions, is paywalled.) Richard Brome Online argues for the value of considering the works of a single playwright as an oeuvre—an approach often taken to Shakespeare. Like repertory-based editions, there is the idea that if we could expand this model to every author or every repertory, we would have a complete representation of the plays of the period. The realities of early modern collaborative playwriting and anonymous works, however, will complicate future author-based online editions, although author-based editions will certainly have their place in digital humanities projects; I, for one, look forward to Christopher Marlowe Online or John Webster Online.

Let us take Webster's *The Duchess of Malfi* as an exemplar of the status of non-Shakespearean plays online. *The Duchess of Malfi* is not Shakespearean apocrypha, nor is it a source or adaptation of one of Shakespeare's plays. (Webster's play, however, was performed by the King's Men, Shakespeare's company.) Despite having only marginal Shakespearean ties, *The Duchess of Malfi* is of continued scholarly interest and has an ongoing performance history, including a 2018 Royal Shakespeare Company production directed by Maria Aberg (Aberg 2018). Although currently Shakespeare's plays are performed at much higher rates than those by his contemporaries, performance and scholarship about performance offer opportunities to effectively decenter Shakespeare. Even though *The Duchess of Malfi* is a relatively popular early modern play, it does not currently appear in any of the digital

[5] See Greatley-Hirsch (2010) for an insightful and extended review of this project.

editions discussed in this essay so far (The Internet Shakespeare Editions, Queen's Men Editions, Digital Renaissance Editions, Folger Digital Texts, Early Modern Anthology of Early Modern English Drama); it does, however, appear in both printed anthologies mentioned (Kinney 1999; Bevington 2002). In future expansions, it could fall into the scope of Digital Renaissance Editions and the Digital Anthology. Yet today, in 2019, it can only be found freely available online in out-of-copyright editions (on HathiTrust [Furlough 2008], GoogleBooks [Google 2004], and the Internet Archive [Kahle 1996]), in its Early English Books Online–Text Creation Partnership (EEBO-TCP 2009) transcription and derivatives, and in a single digital edition. The archived version on Renascence Editions (Moncrief-Spittle 2001) offers a transcription of William Hazlitt's 1857 edition; the 1910 Harvard Classics edition, edited by Charles W. Eliot, is available on Bartleby.com (1993), Project Gutenberg (Hart 1971), and the ebooks@Adelaide (Thomas 2015) sites—though not all of these sites are transparent about their sourcetexts. St John's College Digital Archive offers an unannotated, undated facsimile of a typewritten Duchess of Malfi text (King William Players 1947), with no clue as to its origins except that it is posted in the "Playbills and Programs" digital collection, many of which are "from productions by The King William Players, the St. John's student theater troupe" (St. John's College 1948).[6]

The only online scholarly edition of *The Duchess of Malfi* less than a hundred years old is Larry Avis Brown's 2010 edition (last updated 2018), which includes glosses, commentary on each scene, and photos from a 1998 production at Lipscomb University in Nashville (Brown 2010). Brown's useful edition, however, exists separately from most of the sphere of early modern English drama online: it is a boutique project that stands alone, without links to and from many scholarly resources. Brown links to The Internet Shakespeare Editions, noting that his edition won their "swan" award in 2003, yet in the ISE rebuild, all mentions of Brown's site (still findable in their site search) now result in "Page Not Found" errors. The usefulness of Brown's Duchess of Malfi edition, then, is hampered by its lack of findability. I admit I only stumbled upon this edition because it is linked from the Wikipedia page for *The Duchess of Malfi*. "Boutique" editions created by individual scholars, particularly when peer-reviewed, have the potential to democratize our access to early modern plays—but this access must include findability. As Jakacki notes, however, "the ambition of a network of linked sources has significant implications for the editorial processes of not one, but all of the

[6] The St. John's College Catalogue for 1947–48 reveals that the King William Players produced *The Duchess of Malfi* in their 1946–47 season.

resources involved" (Jakacki 2018, 165). Previously, *Early Modern Literary Studies* (Steggle 2004) and Renascence Editions (Bear 1994) made efforts to host boutique editions of early modern literature edited to varying degrees; however, these attempts seem to have been largely abandoned.

Shakespeare is separated from the other playwrights and poets of his day by our current scholarly digital editions. Greatley-Hirsch quantified the disproportionate number of digital editions of Shakespeare compared to his contemporaries (Greatley-Hirsch 2011); this analysis suggests that the disparity extends beyond the amount of Shakespearean texts online to the very ways the texts are made accessible. As Katherine Rowe (2014) argues, scholars need to assess if digital Shakespeare texts are "good enough" for the purposes we wish to apply them, including digital analysis.[7] Furthermore, I assert that we need to bring this awareness to our use of digital projects about early modern drama more generally: What questions do we bring to the projects? What are our goals as users?[8]

Proliferating Shakespeares

Shakespeare's cultural prominence accounts for many of the factors discussed thus far: funders' pro-Shakespeare predilections, appeals to general audiences, and the "non-Shakespeare" project backlash. Shakespeare's preeminence itself also leads to the development and shape of digital humanities projects themselves. Peter Donaldson's Global Shakespeares highlights Shakespeare's cross-cultural appeal and offers site visitors evidence of how Shakespeare's plays are adapted and performed around the world. The nature of the Global Shakespeares site (and similar sites such as Shakespeare in Taiwan or Shakespeare in Spain) is only possible because Shakespeare is a global commodity.[9] A Global Peeles site would have precious little content, because George Peele's works are not as frequently rewritten and staged. Global Shakespeares does not strive to be comprehensive; it is not a

---

[7] See also the discussion, cited by Rowe, on the open review for Andrew Murphy's "Shakespeare Goes Digital" (Murphy 2010) about how Shakespeareans use digital texts.

[8] See Fazel and Geddes 2017, particularly the chapter by Johnson (2017).

[9] For a thoughtful discussion of the strengths and weaknesses of the Global Shakespeares project, as well as a consideration of the opportunities for and threats to the project, see Henderson (2018). Henderson positions her in-depth analysis as "a case study that may assist others wrestling with the challenging, changing digital/Shakespeares studies landscape" (70). For additional reflections on Global Shakespeares, including by its editors, see Henderson's citations.

repository of full-length filmed productions, nor is it a record of all international Shakespeare productions. Rather, it is a gathering of curated videos, taken from a wealth of global Shakespeare materials; it is the very wealth of materials that makes the project possible.

Other examples abound of digital projects that exist precisely because of Shakespeare's cultural prominence. The four hundredth anniversary of Shakespeare's death in 2016 led to the reimagining or launch of multiple new digital projects, many of which are devoted to Shakespeare's legacy. Shakespeare & The Players (Rusche and Shaw 2016), for instance, is a collection of nearly one thousand postcards of Shakespearean performances from 1880 to 1914. The Victorian Illustrated Shakespeare Archive (Goodman 2016) offers a repository of illustrations of Shakespeare's works by four Victorian illustrators. Performance Shakespeare 2016 (Massai and Bennett 2016) captured a database of those productions that were performed in honor of the quadricentennial anniversary. Exploring Shakespeare's ongoing and changing cultural impact is an important part of Shakespeare studies, which naturally lends itself to the creation of resources that, in turn, highlight Shakespeare's prominence.

It is not then surprising that Shakespeare is overrepresented in scholarship about the early modern period. Shakespeare's prominence in digital humanities now contributes to this cycle: scholars write about Shakespeare because they can research him in innovative ways (easily comparing, for instance, early printed texts on the Shakespeare Quartos Archive, or watching a production on the Global Shakespeares site); the interest in Shakespeare, in turn, generates more Shakespeare-centric sites, often specifically designed for teaching and research. The World Shakespeare Bibliography Online (Estill 2019) serves as a record of this research and as another element of the self-reinforcing cycle of Shakespeare publication. The World Shakespeare Bibliography is a database of performances of and publications about Shakespeare, which ultimately shapes how and what we research.[10] The boundaries of the World Shakespeare Bibliography (it includes only works that focus on Shakespeare) means that scholars using the WSB will not be able to find related work about early modern literature or the professional Elizabethan stage more broadly, unless that scholarship includes a sustained focus on Shakespeare. Users of any other author-focused bibliography, such as the Marlowe Bibliography Online (McInnis and Allan 2019) or the Margaret

[10] For a history of the World Shakespeare Bibliography and its move online, see Estill 2014.

Cavendish Bibliography Initiative (Siegfried 2019), will face similar limitations; however, the sheer scope of the World Shakespeare Bibliography (currently over 126,000 records) can lead scholars to forget about the world of scholarship beyond its scope, whereas the limits of smaller, boutique bibliographies are more readily apparent.

The bibliography with breadth to complement the World Shakespeare Bibliography's depth is the MLA International Bibliography ([1922] 2018). The World Shakespeare Bibliography, of course, covers much material outside the scope of the MLAIB, such as professional productions, podcasts, digital projects, and reviews. The World Shakespeare Bibliography's depth of scope leads to multiple benefits, including having descriptive annotations and cross-referencing between items (for instance, a journal article about film adaptations of *Hamlet* would be cross-referenced to entries for each post-1960 film discussed, which in turn would have an annotation describing the cast as well as a list of reviews and other scholarly works that had discussed the film). Yet, even where their scopes are the same, the Shakespeare-centric focus of the World Shakespeare Bibliography means that there are items in the WSB that should appear in the MLAIB but simply aren't included. Books offer the most striking disparity: only 14 percent of the books published after 1960, annotated in the World Shakespeare Bibliography, are indexed in the MLA International Bibliography.[11] Despite being the MLA *International* Bibliography (emphasis added), it is too often the global, non-English contributions that are among the thousands of overlooked texts. As such, perhaps counterintuitively, it is the World Shakespeare Bibliography's specificity of focus that leads to its greater inclusivity of global materials.

The digital projects that reflect Shakespeare's cultural prominence, in turn, reinforce his position in our scholarship by opening new avenues for research, often focused entirely on Shakespeare and his legacy. Indeed, digital humanities' Shakespeare problem extends beyond the framing and focus of existing and in-progress digital projects (what we study) by affecting the kinds of research we can undertake (how we study). For instance, Shakespeare, and the consideration of what is Shakespearean or not, has been central to stylometry, an area of study that now uses primarily digital

[11] This figure was based on searches undertaken in January 2019. Choosing "book collection" and "book monograph" as document types in the World Shakespeare Bibliography yielded 28,706 entries, compared to 4,416 results in the MLA International Bibliography, limited from 1960 to 2019 and by document type "book," "translation," and "edition," searching with the keyword "Shakespeare."

methodologies. Shakespeare has long been the testing ground and often bellwether for new approaches to both literary criticism and textual studies (Parvini 2012; Machan 2000); new digital humanities approaches are no exception, and often turn to Shakespeare as a first case study. The cycle that reinforces Shakespeare's centrality continues into the digital: online projects about Shakespeare beget new research questions that are, in turn, focused on Shakespeare. The boundaries of Shakespeare-centric projects affect the very questions we can bring to our research and teaching and the new questions we are conditioned to develop.

Conclusions

If we could imagine an early modern digital project with both depth and breadth that positions Shakespeare in his changing historical contexts, the rise of bardolatry over time would mean reflecting Shakespeare's rising cultural prominence over the past centuries. A synchronic project might choose to focus only on Shakespeare's lifetime or only on the heyday of Elizabethan and/or Jacobean professional theatre, yet such a digital project would not capture Shakespeare's legacy. Even if we could conceptualize (let alone realize) the most idealized, unbiased digital project, we would certainly not be able to navigate or query it without bringing in our conditioned, canonical biases.

Too frequently, we protest that we are "Shakespeareans" or "early modernists" first and digital scholars second;[12] yet, in order to be effective scholars, we must train ourselves and future generations about digital research methods, including how to determine scope and functionality. To make the most of the valuable early modern digital projects we have, scholars must understand what questions these resources can effectively answer. As John Lavagnino (2014) has observed, today, all humanists undertake research with digital tools, whether they consider themselves digital humanists or not. In both building and using tools about the early modern period, we need to create and reference transparent and detailed project descriptions and guidelines. The future of early modern studies will be shaped by the digital tools that will change the way we research. The potential of linked open data

[12] See, for instance, the proud claim in the introduction to Shakespeare and the Digital World that "this is a collection that does not come out of the vanguard of digital humanities specialists, but from the trial-and-error approaches of committed Shakespearean professionals working within an evolving field" (Carson and Kirwan 2014b, 3–4). This claim suggests that a scholar cannot be both a digital humanities specialist and a Shakespearean professional.

or other digital advances, however, will not be realized if scholars do not critically analyze each digital project as we would a monograph, an edition, a performance, or a bibliography. This essay's critical engagement of digital projects both individually and in their online ecosystem demonstrates that digital humanities has a Shakespeare problem. As these projects evolve and depreciate and as new projects are built, we will have to continue our assessments. How we choose to respond to these early modern digital resources and how we design our future projects will, in turn, shape how we understand the literary canon.

WORKS CITED

Aberg, Maria, dir. 2018. *The Duchess of Malfi*. Stratford-upon-Avon: Royal Shakespeare Company.

Bartleby.com: Great Books Online. 1993. Accessed 20 November 2018. bartleby.com/hc/.

Bear, Risa Stephanie. 1994. "Renascence Editions." Archived 2018. Accessed 28 February 2019. scholarsbank.uoregon.edu/xmlui/handle/1794/507.

Bell, Henry, and Amy Borsuk, eds. 2020. "Teaching Shakespeare: Digital Processes." Special issue, *Research in Drama Education: The Journal of Applied Theatre and Performance* 25 (1): doi.org/10.1080/13569783.2019.1704241.

Bergenmar, Jenny, and Katarina Leppänen. 2017. "Gender and Vernaculars in Digital Humanities and World Literature." *NORA: Nordic Journal of Feminist and Gender Research* 25: 232–46. doi.org/10.1080/08038740.2017.1378256.

Bevington, David. 2002. *English Renaissance Drama: A Norton Anthology*. New York: Norton.

Bianco, Jamie "Skye." 2012. "This Digital Humanities Which Is Not One." In *Debates in the Digital Humanities*, edited by Matthew K. Gold. Minneapolis: University of Minnesota Press. dhdebates.gc.cuny.edu/debates/text/9.

Bodleian Library. 2009. "Shakespeare Quartos Archive." Accessed 18 December 2018. quartos.org (site discontinued).

Bogost, Ian. 2012. *Alien Phenomenology: Or, What It's Like to Be a Thing.* Minneapolis: University of Minnesota Press.

British Library. 2006. "English Short Title Catalogue." Accessed 18 December 2018. estc.bl.uk.

Brown, Larry Avis, ed. 2010. *The Duchess of Malfi: The Complete Texts with Notes and Commentary.* Accessed 27 January 2019. larryavisbrown.com/duchess-of-malfi/.

Brown, Meaghan, Michael Poston, and Elizabeth Williamson, eds. 2016. *A Digital Anthology of Early Modern English Drama.* Folger Shakespeare Library. Accessed 27 January 2019. emed.folger.edu.

Butler, Martin, ed. 2014. *The Cambridge Edition of the Works of Ben Jonson Online.* Cambridge: Cambridge University Press. Accessed 29 January 2019. universitypublishingonline.org/cambridge/benjonson/.

Butler, Martin, and Matthew Steggle. Forthcoming. *The Complete Works of John Marston.* Oxford: Oxford University Press. Accessed 15 January 2019. johnmarston.leeds.ac.uk.

Calbi, Maurizio, and Stephen O'Neill. 2016. "Shakespeare and Social Media." Special issue, *Borrowers and Lenders: The Journal of Shakespeare and Appropriation* 10. Accessed 25 January 2019. openjournals.libs.uga.edu/borrowers/issue/view/223.

Carson, Christie, and Peter Kirwan. 2014a. "Conclusion: Digital Dreaming." In *Shakespeare and the Digital World*, edited by Christie Carson and Peter Kirwan, 238–57. Cambridge: Cambridge University Press.

———. 2014b. "*Shakespeare and the Digital World*: Introduction." In *Shakespeare and the Digital World*, edited by Christie Carson and Peter Kirwan, 1–7. Cambridge: Cambridge University Press.

Cave, Richard, ed. 2010. "Richard Brome Online." Accessed 28 January 2019. dhi.ac.uk/brome.

Conway, Paul. 2010. "Preservation in the Age of Google: Digitization, Digital Preservation, and Dilemmas." *Library Quarterly* 80: 61–79. doi.org/10.1086/648463.

Crighton, Robert. 2013. "Beyond Shakespeare." Accessed 27 January 2019. beyondshakespeare.blogspot.com.

Davies, Callan, and Andy Kesson. 2018. "Digital Humanities and Non-Shakespearean Theatre History." *Shakespeare Newsletter.*

Desmet, Christy. 2014. "The Shakespeare Quartos Archive." *Shakespearean International Yearbook*, 14: 143–54.

———. 2017. "Alien Shakespeares 2.0." In *Shakespeare après Shakespeare/ Shakespeare after Shakespeare,* edited by Anne-Valérie Dulac and Laetitia Sansonetti. Société Française Shakespeare. journals.openedition.org/ shakespeare/3877.

Donaldson, Peter S. 2009. "Global Shakespeares: Video and Performance Archive." Accessed 25 January 2019. globalshakespeares.mit.edu/ about/.

Earhart, Amy. 2012. "Can Information Be Unfettered? Race and the New Digital Humanities Canon." In *Debates in the Digital Humanities*, edited by Matthew K. Gold. Minneapolis: University of Minnesota Press. dhdebates.gc.cuny.edu/debates/text/16.

———. 2015. *Traces of the Old, Uses of the New: The Emergence of Digital Literary Studies.* Ann Arbor: University of Michigan Press.

Early English Books Online-Text Creation Partnership (EEBO-TCP). 2009. Accessed 25 January 2019. quod.lib.umich.edu/e/eebogroup/.

Estill, Laura. 2014. "Digital Bibliography and Global Shakespeare." *Scholarly and Research Communication*, 5 (4): 13 pp. Accessed 27 January 2019. doi. org/10.22230/src.2014v5n4a187.

———, ed. 2019. "World Shakespeare Bibliography." Created by Sidney Thomas, 1950, moved online by James L. Harner in 2011. Current editor Heidi Craig. Accessed 27 January 2019. worldshakesbib.org.

———. 2020. "Shakespearean Extracts and the Misrepresentation of the Archive." In *Rethinking Theatrical Documents in Shakespeare's England*, edited by Tiffany Stern, 175–92. London: Bloomsbury. dx.doi.org/ 10.5040/9781350051379.ch-009.

Estill, Laura, Dominic Klyve, and Kate Bridal. 2015. "'Spare your arithmetic, never count the turns': A Statistical Analysis of Writing about Shakespeare, 1960–2010." *Shakespeare Quarterly*, 66: 1–28. jstor.org/ stable/24778623.

Fazel, Valerie M., and Louise Geddes. 2017. *The Shakespeare User: Critical and Creative Appropriations in a Networked Culture*. Cham: Palgrave Macmillan.

Flanders, Julia. 2009. "The Productive Unease of 21st-Century Digital Scholarship." *Digital Humanities Quarterly* 3. digitalhumanities.org/dhq/vol/3/3/000055/000055.html.

Fraistat, Neil, Steven E. Jones, and Carl Stahmer. 1998. "The Canon, the Web, and the Digitization of Romanticism." *Romanticism on the Net*, 10. doi.org/10.7202/005801ar.

Furlough, Michael. 2008. "HathiTrust Digital Library." Accessed 27 January 2019. hathitrust.org.

Galey, Alan, and Ray Siemens, eds. 2008. "Reinventing Shakespeare in the Digital Humanities." Special issue, *Shakespeare* 4: 201–07.

Goodman, John Michael. 2016. "Victorian Illustrated Shakespeare Archive." Accessed 20 November 2018. shakespeareillustration.org.

Google. 2004. "GoogleBooks." Accessed 27 January 2019. books.google.com.

Greatley-Hirsch, Brett. 2010. "Bringing Richard Brome Online." *Early Theatre*, 13: 137–53. jstor.org/stable/43499553.

———. 2011. "The Kingdom Has Been Digitized: Electronic Editions of Renaissance Drama and the Long Shadows of Shakespeare and Print." *Literature Compass* 8: 568–91. doi.org/10.1111/j.1741-4113.2011.00830.x.

———, ed. 2015. "Digital Renaissance Editions." Accessed 27 January 2019. digitalrenaissance.uvic.ca.

Greatley-Hirsch, Brett, and Hugh Craig. 2014. "Digital Shakespeares." Special section, *Shakespearean International Yearbook* 14.

Greene, Mark A., and Dennis Meissner. 2005. "More Product, Less Process: Revamping Traditional Archival Processing." *The American Archivist* 68: 208–63. doi.org/10.17723/aarc.68.2.c741823776k65863.

Hart, Michael. 1971. "Project Gutenberg." Accessed 27 January 2019. gutenberg.org.

Henderson, Diana. 2018. "This Distracted Globe, This Brave New World: Learning from the MIT Global Shakespeares' Twenty-First Century." In

Broadcast Your Shakespeare: Continuity and Change Across Media, edited by Stephen O'Neill, 67–86. London: Bloomsbury Arden Shakespeare.

Hodgdon, Barbara. 1998. *The Shakespeare Trade: Performances and Appropriations.* Philadelphia: University of Pennsylvania Press.

Jakacki, Diane K. 2018. "Internet Shakespeare Editions and the Infinite Editorial Others: Support Critical Tagsets for Linked Data." In *Shakespeare's Language in Digital Media: Old Words, New Tools,* edited by Janelle Jenstad, Mark Kaethler and Jennifer Roberts-Smith, 157–71. London and New York: Routledge.

Jenstad, Janelle, ed. 2018. "Internet Shakespeare Editions." Created by Michael Best, 1996. Accessed 17 January 2019. internetshakespeare.uvic.ca.

Johnson, Eric. 2017. "Opening Shakespeare from the Margins." In *The Shakespeare User: Critical and Creative Appropriations in a Networked Culture*, edited by Valerie M. Fazel and Louise Geddes, 187–206. Cham: Palgrave Macmillan.

Kahle, Brewster. 1996. "The Internet Archive." Accessed 27 January 2019. archive.org.

Kesson, Andy, Lucy Munro, and Callan Davies. 2016. "Before Shakespeare." Accessed 20 January 2019. beforeshakespeare.com.

King William Players. 1947. "The Duchess of Malfi. St. John's College Digital Archives." Accessed 9 January 2019. digitalarchives.sjc.edu/items/show/1261.

Kinney, Arthur F. 1999. *Renaissance Drama: Anthology of Plays and Entertainments.* Malden: Blackwell.

Kliman, Bernice W., Frank Nicholas Clary, Hardin Aasand, Eric Rasmussen, Laury Magnus, and Marvin Hunt, eds. 2004. "HamletWorks." Accessed 10 December 2018. hamletworks.org.

Knight, Leah, and Wendy Wall. 2018. "The Pulter Project." Accessed 7 January 2019. pulterproject.northwestern.edu/.

Lanier, Douglas. 2014. "Shakespearean Rhizomatics: Adaptation, Ethics, Value." In *Shakespeare and the Ethics of Appropriation*, edited by Alexa Huang [now Joubin] and Elizabeth Rivlin, 21–40. New York: Palgrave.

Lavagnino, John. 2014. "Shakespeare in the Digital Humanities." In *Shakespeare and the Digital World*, edited by Christie Carson and Peter Kirwan, 238–57. Cambridge: Cambridge University Press.

Lesser, Zachary, and Alan Farmer. 2007. "Database of Early English Playbooks." Accessed 2 December 2018. deep.sas.upenn.edu.

Machan, Tim William. 2000. "'I Endowed Thy Purposes': Shakespeare, Editing, and Middle English Literature." *Text*, 13: 9–25.

Mandell, Laura. 2015. "Gendering Digital Literary History: What Counts for Digital Humanities." In *A New Companion to Digital Humanities*, edited by Susan Schreibman, Raymond G. Siemens, and John Unsworth, 511–23. Malden: Wiley-Blackwell.

Massai, Sonia, and Susan Bennett, eds. 2016. "Performance Shakespeare 2016." Accessed 28 February 2019. performanceshakespeare2016.org.

McInnis, David, and Gayle Allan. 2019. "The Marlowe Bibliography Online." *Marlowe Society of America* Release 2017.1. Accessed 20 January 2019. marlowesocietyofamerica.org/mbo/.

McLuskie, Kate, and Kate Rumbold. 2014. *Cultural Value in Twenty-First Century England: The Case of Shakespeare*. Manchester: University of Manchester Press.

McMillin, Scott, and Sally-Beth MacLean. 1998. *The Queen's Men and Their Plays*. Cambridge: Cambridge University Press.

MLA Committee on Information Technology. 2012a. "Guidelines for Authors of Digital Resources." Accessed 15 November 2018. mla.org/About-Us/Governance/Committees/Committee-Listings/Professional-Issues/Committee-on-Information-Technology/Guidelines-for-Authors-of-Digital-Resources.

———. 2012b. "Guidelines for Evaluating Work in Digital Humanities and Digital Media." Accessed 15 November 2018. mla.org/About-Us/Governance/Committees/Committee-Listings/Professional-Issues/Committee-on-Information-Technology/Guidelines-for-Evaluating-Work-in-Digital-Humanities-and-Digital-Media.

MLA International Bibliography. 2018. Available online by subscription. First Published 1922. Accessed 27 January 2019. mla.org/Publications/

MLA-International-Bibliography/About-the-MLA-International-Bibliography.

Moncrief-Spittle, Malcolm, trans. 2001. "The Duchess of Malfi." By John Webster. Edited by William Hazlitt. *Renascence Editions*. Accessed 27 January 2019. scholarsbank.uoregon.edu/xmlui/handle/1794/776.

Moore, Shawn, and Jacob Tootalian, dirs. 2013. "The Digital Cavendish Project." Accessed 15 January 2019. digitalcavendish.org.

Mowat, Barbara, Paul Werstine, Michael Poston, and Rebecca Niles, eds. 2012. "Folger Digital Texts" [now "The Folger Shakespeare"]. *Folger Shakespeare Library*. Accessed 19 December 2018. folgerdigitaltexts.org.

Mueller, Martin. 2014. "Shakespeare His Contemporaries: Collaborative Curation and Exploration of Early Modern Drama in a Digital Environment." *Digital Humanities Quarterly*, 8. digitalhumanities.org/dhq/vol/8/3/000183/000183.html.

———. 2016. "Shakespeare His Contemporaries." Now Defunct. Accessed archive 23 January 2019. web.archive.org/web/*/shakespearehiscontemporaries.northwestern.edu/shc/home.html.

Munro, Lucy. 2009. *Children of the Queen's Revels: A Jacobean Theatre Repertory*. Cambridge: Cambridge University Press.

Murphy, Andrew. 2010. "Shakespeare Goes Digital: Three Open Internet Editions." *Shakespeare Quarterly* 61: 401–14.

Olive, Sarah. 2015. *Shakespeare Valued: Education Policy and Pedagogy 1989–2009*. Bristol and Chicago: Intellect.

O'Neill, Stephen. 2015. "Shakespeare and Social Media." *Literature Compass* 12: 274–85.

———. 2018. "Shakespeare's Digital Flow: Humans, Technologies and the Possibilities of Intercultural Exchange." *Shakespeare Studies* 46: 120–33.

———, ed. 2019. "Shakespeare and Digital Humanities: New Perspectives and Future Directions." Special issue, *Humanities* 8(1). mdpi.com/journal/humanities/special_issues/Shakespeare#published.

Ostovich, Helen, ed. 2006. "The Queen's Men Editions." Accessed 27 January 2019. qme.internetshakespeare.uvic.ca.

P., Cildas. 2015. "Richard III Attacks! Playfool.net"; Thomas Jolly, La Piccola Familia. Accessed 20 November 2018. lapiccolafamilia.fr/richard-iii-attacks/.

Parvini, Neema. 2012. *Shakespeare and Contemporary Theory: New Historicism and Cultural Materialism*. New York: Bloomsbury.

Pollard, Alfred W., and Gilbert Richard Redgrave. 1926. *A Short-Title Catalogue of Books Printed in England, Scotland & Ireland, and of English Books Printed Abroad, 1475–1640*. London: Bibliographical Society.

Price, Kenneth M. 2009. "Digital Scholarship, Economics, and the American Literary Canon." *Literature Compass* 6: 274–90. doi.org/10.1111/j.1741-4113.2009.00622.x.

Rowe, Katherine, ed. 2010. "Shakespeare and New Media." Special issue, *Shakespeare Quarterly* 61. doi.org/10.1093/sq/60.2.127.

———. 2014. "Living with Digital Incunables, or a 'Good-Enough' Shakespeare Text." In *Shakespeare and the Digital World*, edited by Christie Carson and Peter Kirwan, 144–59. Cambridge: Cambridge University Press.

Rusche, Harry, and Justin Shaw. 2016. "Shakespeare & The Players." Accessed 20 November 2018. shakespeare.emory.edu/.

Siegfried, Brandie. 2019. "Margaret Cavendish Bibliography Initiative." *Digital Cavendish Project.* Accessed 10 December 2018. digitalcavendish.org/resources/margaret-cavendish-bibliography-initiative/.

Silbert, Roxana, dir. 2010. *Such Tweet Sorrow.* Story grid by Beth Marlow and Tim Wright. Stratford-upon-Avon and Sheffield: Royal Shakespeare Company and Mudlark Production Company.

Slights, Jessica, ed. 2017. *Othello*. Internet Shakespeare Editions. Accessed 27 January 2019. internetshakespeare.uvic.ca/Library/Texts/Oth/.

Smith, Emma. 2017. "Shakespeare: The Apex Predator." *TLS: Times Literary Supplement*. 4 May 2017. the-tls.co.uk/articles/public/shakespeare-apex-predator/.

Steggle, Matthew, ed. 2004. *Early Modern Literary Studies.* Hosted Resources. Accessed 28 January 2019. extra.shu.ac.uk/emls/iemls/resources.html.

———. 2008. "'Knowledge Will Be Multiplied': Digital Literary Studies and Early Modern Literature." In *A Companion to Digital Literary Studies*, edited by Ray Siemens and Susan Schriebman, 82-105. Malden: Blackwell. Accessed 2 December 2021. digitalhumanities.org/companionDLS/.

St. John's College in Annapolis. 1948. "St John's College Catalogue 1947–1948." *St. John's College Digital Archives.* Accessed 9 January 2019. digitalarchives.sjc.edu/items/show/181.

Taylor, Gary. 1993. "The Renaissance and the End of Editing." In *Palimpsest: Editorial Theory in the Humanities,* edited by George Bornstein and Ralph G. Williams, 121–49. Ann Arbor: U of Michigan P. 121–49.

Thomas, Steve. 2015. "Ebooks@Adelaide." Accessed 27 January 2019. ebooks.adelaide.edu.au.

Tran, Diep. 2018. "The Top 10* Most Produced Plays of the 2018–2019 Season." *American Theatre.* 20 September 2018. americantheatre.org/2018/09/20/the-top-10-most-produced-plays-of-the-2018-19-season/.

Wernimont, Jacqueline, and Julia Flanders. 2010. "Feminism in the Age of Digital Archives: The Women Writer's Project." *Tulsa Studies in Women's Language and Literature* 29: 425–35. jstor.org/stable/41337287.

Wing, Donald. 1945. *A Short-Title Catalogue of Books Printed in England, Scotland & Ireland, and of English Books Printed Abroad, 1641-1700.* New York: Columbia University Press.

Data That Last: Reflections on Sustainability in Digital Humanities Projects[1]

Marieke M. A. Hendriksen
Royal Netherlands Academy of Arts and Sciences (KNAW)

In 2013, Ikea launched an app that allows customers to digitally place furniture in their own living room (Dishman 2013). Yet in 2015, they launched a video advertising campaign entitled "Experience the power of a bookbook" in which its paper catalog was presented as if it was the latest Apple gadget. Although the ad was dripping with irony and Ikea announced in 2019 that it would stop producing and distributing over two hundred million copies of its annual catalog, it was relatable exactly because the underlying truth is undeniable: books are an incredibly successful and sustainable information technology. A recurring issue in historical research projects with a digital humanities component is the lack of sustainability of their outcomes, with many valuable datasets, software, and digital editions disappearing or withering away after the project ends. As Eschenfelder et al. (2016) point out,

[1] The research for this essay was funded by the European Research Council under the European Union's Horizon 2020 Research and Innovation Programme (Grant Agreement No. 648718), an Utrecht University Digital Humanities Grant, a Renaissance Society of America travel grant for the Digital Humanities Summer Institute 2018, and NWO Big Data/Digital Humanities grant no. 314–99–301.

Many thanks to the ARTECHNE and Art DATIS project teams and their collaborators for their ongoing support: Sven Dupré, Jenny Boulboullé, Thijs Hagendijk, Mariana Pinto, Jill Briggeman, Roland van Blokland, Jurjen Munk, Deborah van den Herik, Maartje Stols-Witlox, Martijn van der Klis, Alex Hebing, José de Kruijf, Anita Hopmans, Reinier van 't Zelfde, Erik Samson, Evangelos Kanoulas, Vera Provatorova, Svitlana Vakulenko, Anna Carlgren, and Suzanne Bul. Thanks to Richard Freedman for discussing DH sustainability issues with me over coffee in Chicago and Philadelphia. I would also like to thank Meaghan Brown, formerly of the Folger Library, for inviting me to the Folger Miranda workshop in September 2018, and Ray Siemens for inviting me to present my work on the RSA New Technologies in Medieval and Renaissance Studies panels in 2017 and 2019, as these events helped me to develop the arguments in this essay. Laura Estill and the anonymous reviewers I thank for their help in finalizing the text.

ISBN 978-1-64959-063-3 (paper) ISBN 978-1-64959-064-0 (pdf) ISBN 978-1-64959-065-7 (epub)
New Technologies in Medieval and Renaissance Studies 11 (2025) 245–258

sustainability is a multifaced concept, which can encompass facets such as technology, management, relationships, revenue, assessment, disaster planning, policy, and more. In this chapter, I focus on the institutional, infrastructural, and pedagogic conditions necessary to ensure continued storage and accessibility.

Often the need to deposit relevant materials in repositories and take further measures to ensure the continued accessibility of research data, especially within smaller projects, is an afterthought, if it is thought of at all. This essay argues that one of the first questions within every DH project should be: how are we going to store our data and project outcomes in a sustainable manner? Two Dutch research projects with a strong DH component in which the author is personally involved, ARTECHNE and Art DATIS, are used as a starting point to explore possible answers to that question, and will discuss the institutional, pedagogical, and infrastructural changes that we will need to make in order to create data that last as long as books—if that is possible at all.

Case Studies: ARTECHNE and Art DATIS

This essay uses two research projects with a strong DH component, one finished and one ongoing, as case studies to analyze the challenges researchers face in the sustainable preservation of research data. The first case is the European Research Council-funded project ARTECHNE: technique in the arts 1500–1950, directed by Sven Dupré at Utrecht University and the University of Amsterdam between 2015 and 2020. Within the ARTECHNE project, an online database of art technological sources was developed (Hendriksen 2020). This database contains very heterogenous data: fully searchable texts in six languages from the period 1500 to 1900, images, records on historical people, geo tags, and historical and current names of artistic materials and techniques. The contents are linked to The Getty Research Institute's Getty Vocabularies, and the database also contains documentation on reconstructions of historical artistic techniques created within the project, including lab records, photos, and videos. To make things even more complicated, this database was built on a dataset of historical recipes for pigments and dyes coming out of a previous project. A dataset containing historical recipes for painting grounds, created by one of the project members for a previous project, was also integrated within the ARTECHNE database. All in all, at least twelve different people were involved in the creation of the database and dataset at some point: scientific programmers, information managers, researchers, and data entry assistants.

Within the ARTECHNE research project the database served two main purposes: it created a place to store, share, and retrieve research data, and a tool to discover connections between and patterns within the abundance of materials a project with a core team of five fulltime researchers inevitably accumulates over the course of four years. To ensure that the data would remain usable for external parties and after the project as well, the team committed to the International Council of Museums' (ICOM) International Committee for Documentation's Conceptual Reference Model (CIDOC-CRM)-based ontology and to linking to the Getty Vocabularies; the database was also indexed using Apache Solr, allowing for export of data from the application to .csv-format, and was given stable URIs. The database thus adhered to the 5-star open data plan formulated by Tim Berners-Lee in 2006 (5stardata.info/en/), which should make it possible to link it to more open data, enriching our own data. From the start, the team kept two things in mind: first, that this database and dataset could be useful for other researchers; second, that if it had to remain accessible after the project's end, a better solution than the depositing of the dataset and code in an open-access online repository (as the requirements of the funding body stipulated) was needed.

Although most funding bodies now do require a data management plan to be submitted with applications, the requirements for these plans tend to be rather minimal. In 2014, when this project was granted, the European Research Council asked no more than that the project data be deposited in an open-access online repository. For this purpose, we primarily used Zenodo (zenodo.org). Zenodo is a general-purpose open-access repository developed under the European OpenAIRE program and operated by CERN. It allows researchers to deposit data sets, research software, reports, and any other research related digital artefacts. For each submission, a persistent Digital Object Identifier (DOI) is minted, which makes the stored items easily citable. Other options included DANS (Data Archiving and Networked Services), a similar repository run by the Royal Netherlands Academy of Arts and Sciences, or GitHub, a web-based hosting service which is aimed more at version control for open source code. In addition, many university and research libraries now host digital repositories too.

The upside of repositories like Zenodo and DANS is the fact that they are hosted and managed by large research support organizations with a long history, based in politically stable countries, making the likelihood that they will suddenly collapse or disappear highly unlikely. The downside, however, is that there is no great sense of urgency or attention for user friendliness and workable interfaces. For example, when the ARTECHNE team checked for the most recent version of DANS guidelines in the winter of 2018 in order to plan the depositing of data, a rather obscure data format for relational databases was recommended. It would involve considerable time and effort to convert the project data to that format, and some of the valuable relational tables in it would be lost in the process. Upon contacting DANS to check whether this was indeed the best choice, the airy response was "O no, actually your current data format is much more sustainable, so just use that. We haven't updated that web page in a while."[2]

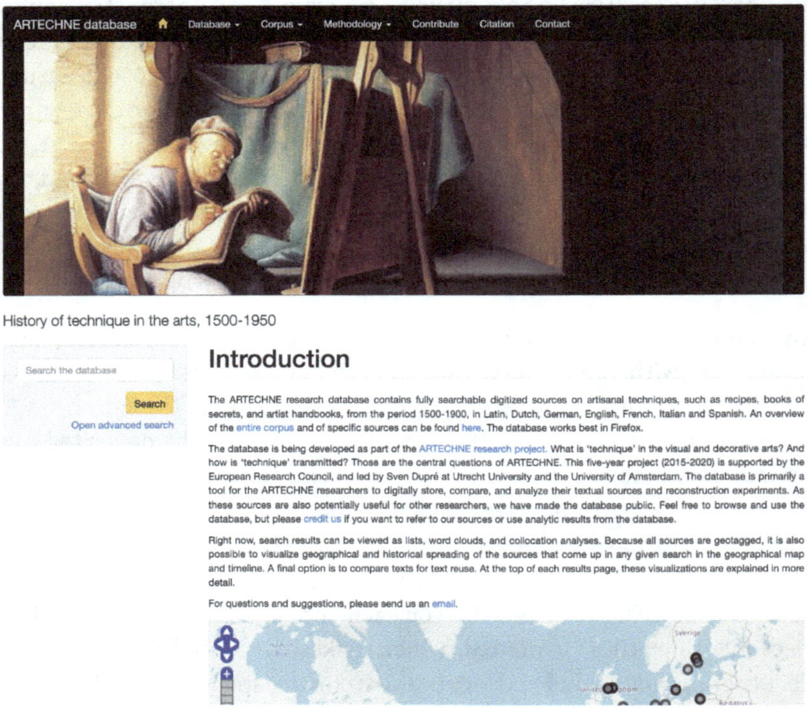

Figure 10.1. The ARTECHNE database homepage.

[2] Phone conversation with DANS helpdesk, 22 February 2019.

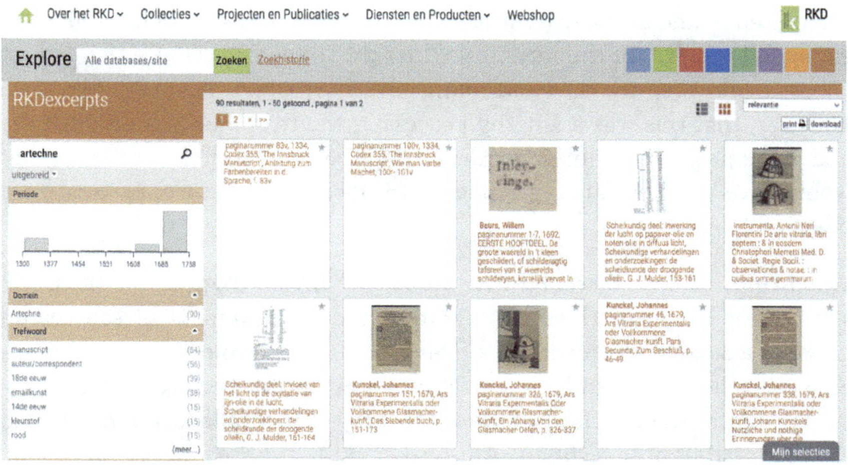

Figure 10.2. First batch of ARTECHNE records as published on RKD Explore.

Conversely, when ARTECHNE researchers tried to figure out whether either of these large repositories contained data sets from previous projects that could be useful for their project, they had a hard time finding and accessing stored data. These difficulties are typical for the depositing and retrieval of historical and art historical research data sets, not just in DANS but in other open-access repositories as well. This is problematic on two levels. First, it discourages individual researchers and research teams from retrieving data for reuse, and from depositing their own data for reuse. Second, even if researchers do persist, the lack of user-friendliness of these repositories means that this aspect of their research will be much more time-consuming than necessary, wasting precious time and resources.

Exploring these repositories at the start of the project made clear that even though depositing the research data there met the formal criteria for data management, another solution should be sought in order to grant sustainable access to the data after the project ended. Hence, the team approached the RKD (Rijksdienst voor Kunsthistorische Documentatie; the Netherlands Institute for Art History). Fully funded by the Dutch Ministry of Education, this institute is currently in the process of digitizing its own extensive collections and making them accessible online through a user-friendly web interface called RKD Explore. Fortunately, the collections and research managers at RKD understood the predicament and the value of the data, and an agreement was reached that ensured that the largest part of the dataset was integrated in and accessible through RKD Explore after the ARTECHNE project ended in 2020. In the meantime, Utrecht University, where the project is based, will keep the database online on its servers. It should be stressed, however, that this was a lengthy process. If the team had waited until the end of the project to think about depositing their research data in a way that would have kept the data accessible for the foreseeable future, it would have been too late.

This brings us to the second case study. Art DATIS (Digital Art Technical sources for the Netherlands: Integration and improvement of sources on glass for a Sustainable future) is a five-year research project (2018–23) funded within the Netherlands Organization for Scientific Research's (NWO) Big Data / Digital Humanities program. The project is a collaboration between the Universities of Utrecht and Amsterdam, RKD, the Free Glass Foundation, and the Dutch heritage digitization company Picturae.

The production of free glass saw significant technological innovations in the twentieth century. Dutch glass artist Sybren Valkema's (1916–96) study of historical sources and his practical work contributed crucially to these innovations. The project explores what role historical sources on the changing production of glass in Europe between 1500 and 1996 play in his work, and how he used these sources to innovate technology and education. Valkema's digitized archives provide a unique, indispensable resource in answering these questions, but for optimal analysis they need to be extended, enriched, and linked to open data. Sources containing historical recipes and techniques for glass production, as well as images and object documentation, are currently digitized by museums and research institutions around the world.

As two key Dutch players in these digitization processes, the creators of RKD Explore and the ARTECHNE database proposed to link important historical sources and the Valkema archives to existing big data in the field of (technical) art history, thus enriching and contributing to big data and smart culture. The project aims to develop new digital methods to efficiently link the enormous amount of newly digitized art technical sources on glass production, such as object documentation, technical texts, images, and research data, and to integrate and enrich existing databases containing different kinds of data on the history of artistic glass production. The first step in the process is to develop existing thesauri in the field. Next, tools for automated annotation and a portal to access these enriched, linked, open, multimedial (textual, visual, and geographical) data will be developed.

Within Art DATIS, parts of the data generated in ARTECHNE are combined with newly digitized archives on the historical production of and education in artistic glass objects, and linked to data provided by glass museums, such as the Corning Museum of Glass in upstate New York and the Glass Museum Henntrich in Düsseldorf. A team of data scientists and art historians develops analytical tools to write the history of artistic glass production and education in Europe and the US from the eighteenth to the twentieth century; the team involves researchers from six countries based at two different Dutch universities, the RKD, a foundation managing the archives and collections of a leading glass artist, glass museums in the Netherlands, Germany, and the US, and a commercial business. An incredibly complex project, its data management and storage had to be thoroughly thought through before the project had even started. The project began in September 2018, and despite our thorough preparation, the conversation about what is stored where and how is ongoing.

Changes Needed

Which lessons can we draw from the data management issues in these two projects? Which changes do we need to make as a field in order to create and maintain research data in a sustainable manner? One of the most important lessons appears to be that while the guidelines and industry standards—of which there are many—focus on the description and structuring of data, there are as yet no truly golden standards for sustainable data storage and retrieval. Most famous is probably Tim Berners-Lee's 2006 5-star deployment scheme for Linked Open Data. For digitized images there is IIIF, the International Image Interoperability Framework (iiif.io), which defines application programming interfaces that provide a standardized method of describing and delivering online images. CIDOC-CRM meanwhile provides definitions and a formal structure for describing the implicit and explicit concepts and relationships used in cultural heritage documentation and is a useful starting point for anyone developing a database ontology.

Of course, following such standards greatly improves the chances of data being reused, and there are formats that are more likely to remain accessible than others, but even if we use those, there is a significant chance that at some point at least some of these data will have to be transformed into different formats again in order to keep them accessible (Smithies et al. 2019). Software and interfaces will continue to change, making it unpredictable whether the format that works perfectly fine for most users now will still do so in ten years. This is where a shared responsibility comes in: individual researchers and research project teams have a responsibility to take an active approach when it comes to storing and retrieving data, while institutions need to take responsibility for developing sustainable, current, and user-friendly standards, repositories, and interfaces. Humanities educators meanwhile need to train themselves and others in the storage, retrieval, use, and analysis of historical data sets in order for digital methods to become a serious part of historical methodology. This means that three interlinked domains need our attention in the near future: pedagogy and research practices, institutions, and infrastructure.

Pedagogy and Research Practices

This also means that we, as researchers and teachers, need to think critically about pedagogy, as well as about roles in humanities research and the skills and knowledge they require. To use an analogy: in order to use books for our research and publish the outcome in print, no one demands that we learn typesetting, bookbinding, printing, professional photography, library cataloging, or online publishing, although admittedly it can be very useful for humanities researchers to have some basic knowledge about these skills and techniques. However, we do think it is reasonable for historians and art historians to learn how to access and search library collections and archives, to learn foreign languages and paleography. So rather than expect humanities scholars to become data scientists, just as we do not expect them to become professional librarians, publishers, or printers, we should determine a minimum digital skill set. This is of course difficult, as digital tools and methods are continuously changing. Yet it should be possible to establish some foundational knowledge and skills for humanities researchers, and attempts to do so are indeed made (Rousseau 2020). Possible subjects to cover in foundational courses include, but are not limited to, the basic principles of coding, the nature of data processing, databases, software, and user interfaces, while raising awareness of the fact that digital data, like analogue, are not neutral.

In all likelihood, this rethinking of roles and skill sets will result in new professions, both within research projects and libraries. Some of these are already emerging, in the form of data curators and librarians, and what Alison Langmead et al. (2018) call data stewards: the people "responsible for ensuring that the essential character of the historical evidence is not lost throughout the process of converting primary source material into computable information, and also that this data will be suitable for the technological processes that it will undergo." Moreover, as has been demonstrated by, for example, Burkert (2017), the disappearance of the output of digital projects tells us how vital it is that the meaning of digital and computational humanities work is articulated within existing intellectual and disciplinary traditions. So although our research practices do change because of digital methods, as is also shown by Kyle Dase in this volume, we need to make sure that we connect them to existing methods and output formats in order for them to be effective and sustainable. One way of doing so might be the creation of material texts from digital archives (Alexander 2020), or to bring traditional practices such as peer review to the world of digital resources, as Randa El Khatib argues in her chapter this book.

Institutions

Institutions, from the European Research Council and national libraries to universities and the smallest independent research libraries, should also become more aware of and communicate more clearly their role as data curators and potential data management partners (e.g., Cox 2016). Given their power in the field of data curation, they have a responsibility in making research datasets available to new generations of researchers. Of course, some institutions do this very well already, but it appears the humanities would benefit greatly from more collaboration in this respect. For example, Dutch research libraries almost without exception rely on the Online Computer Library Center's (OCLC) WorldCat, the largest online public access catalog (OPAC) in the world, to disclose their collections to users. In theory, deposited datasets with a Digital Object Identifier can be found through WorldCat, yet for the average user this proves extremely difficult. WorldCat's standard interface has designated tabs to search for books, DVDs, CDs, and articles, and users can refine their results into (for example) printed works and manuscripts, but data sets are not a distinct category in WorldCat.

Yet data sets behave differently and thus should be described differently than physical archives, even when they are digitized physical archives (Brown 2009, Escobar Varela 2016, Kassell 2021). Not doing so potentially contributes to data becoming obsolete. Data sets deposited in DANS for example, can be found through WorldCat when their exact title is entered into the search field, yet appear as "books" rather than data sets. Although this manner of describing the data sets in the catalog has probably been done with the best intentions, it is confusing at best and off-putting for users at worst. The Dutch Royal Library meanwhile stores a copy of everything published in the Netherlands—books and journals, either in print or digital, but not data sets. If we want data sets to become a go-to source, like books and articles for humanities researchers, these kinds of obstacles have to be resolved, something which can only be achieved through collaboration and structural investments.

Infrastructure

Together, researchers and institutions are responsible for creating a sustainable infrastructure to provide access to deposited data. This might be the biggest challenge listed here, but also one that will be hugely beneficial to the humanities if successfully addressed. In the domain of infrastructure, we face two major challenges: overall sustainability and the quality of interfaces. Overall sustainability of data infrastructure is a challenge because so many digital humanities initiatives depend on one-off grants and temporary rather than structural funding.

Think, for example, of the Irish Digital Humanities Observatory (DHO), a knowledge resource providing outreach and education on a broad range of digital humanities topics between 2008 and 2013. The DHO provided data management, curation, and long-term access to—and greater exploitation of—digital resources in the creation of new models, methodologies, and paradigms. An economic downturn meant that no new funding could be obtained, and the DHO had to cease its activities. In this case, key players signalled this in time (Gourley and Viterbo 2010). They managed to ensure that the raw data of projects such as DHO: Discovery, a gateway to Irish digital collections and resources, information, and knowledge, remained available online for the foreseeable future. This is just one case that demonstrates the danger of applying a neoliberalist market model to research funding.

Yet the DHO example also makes something else strikingly clear, namely the importance of investing in and maintaining user-friendly interfaces. Although the DHO: Discovery data can be downloaded as a .csv file, in reality very few users will be able to understand how to access and interpret this. Many large grants are used to develop fundamental infrastructure, such as the European Digital Research Infrastructure for the Arts and Humanities (DARIAH) and the Dutch Common Lab Research Infrastructure for the Arts and Humanities (CLARIAH). Although it is understandable that technical challenges at the backend receive a lot of attention, the importance of user-friendly interfaces should not be underestimated. After all, access technologies shape users' understanding and interpretation of historical information

(Heyliger, McLoone, and Thomas 2016). Johanna Drucker's (2013) concept of performative materiality, based on the conviction that a system should be understood by what it does, not only by how it is structured, could provide useful guidance here, as can Matthew Kirschenbaum's (2007) argument that interface cannot be decoupled from either functionality or aesthetics.

Over the past decade, various initiatives have been developed to improve data sustainability. One example is the Socio-Technical Sustainability Roadmap (STSR), a module-based workshop intended to help DH teams sustain their web-based, user-facing, digital humanities projects over time. As part of this, a National Endowment for the Humanities ODH Institute for Advanced Topics in the Digital Humanities took place at five locations scattered across the United States in the winter of 2018–19, designed to help professionals create sustainability plans and address preservation concerns at any point in the life of a digital humanities project (but it is also possible to use the modules on the website). Such DIY approaches are definitely helpful, and it is good to realize that with a little planning and support, many valuable DH data sets can be sustainably preserved for future use. Or, as Christine Madsen of Athenaeum 21 (A21), an international digital strategy and innovation consultancy, argued in a 2018 presentation: rather than creating new repositories for data from DH projects, sustainability requires continuous, granular access. These conclusions were based on extensive interviews with DH project leads, followed by technical and functional analyses for more than thirty DH projects at Oxford University. This, in effect, is exactly what we have done with the ARTECHNE database. The complete data and code are available from two OA online repositories, and the data will still be discoverable and usable at a granular level via the RKD website.

Conclusion

The analysis of challenges faced by medium-sized research projects with a digital output component and a desire to make their digital data sustainably available to future generations of researchers shows that fundamental changes on the pedagogic, professional, institutional, and infrastructural levels need to be made. In pedagogy and research practices, we need to critically reflect on which knowledge and skills are essential and which are optional, and adjust or design our curricula accordingly. Meanwhile, institutions will have to become more aware and vocal about their role as data stewards. Finally, for infrastructure to be sustainably developed and maintained, we will need long-term financial commitment from governments and funding bodies. In the meantime, do not underestimate the power of a book.

WORKS CITED

Alexander, Gia. 2020. "Mining Digital Humanities Archives to Produce Accessible Material Editions of Scholarly Texts." *IDEAH* 1 (1). doi.org/10.21428/f1f23564.4e680428.

Art DATIS project website. Accessed 16 October 2019. artdatis.nl.

ARTECHNE Database. Accessed 16 October 2019. ARTECHNE.hum.uu.nl/home.

ARTECHNE Dataset. Accessed 16 October 2019. doi.org/10.17026/dans-x6b-2749 or doi.org/10.5281/zenodo.3460551.

Athenaeum21 UK. "A Proposed Service Model for a Sustainable Digital Humanities Technology Infrastructure." Last modified 30 October 2018. athenaeum21.com/news/a-proposed-service-model-for-a-sustainable-digital-humanities-technology-infrastructure.

Brown, Susan, Patricia Clements, Isobel Grundy, Stan Ruecker, Jeffery Antoniuk, and Sharon Balazs. 2009. "Published Yet Never Done: The Tension between Projection and Completion in Digital Humanities Research." *Digital Humanities Quarterly* 3 (2). digitalhumanities.org/dhq/vol/3/2/000040/000040.html.

Burkert, Mattie. 2017. "Recovering the *London Stage Information Bank*: Lessons from an Early Humanities Computing Project." *Digital Humanities Quarterly* 11 (3). digitalhumanities.org/dhq/vol/11/3/000321/000321.html.

CLARIAH Dutch Common Lab Research Infrastructure for the Arts and Humanities website. Accessed 16 September 2020. clariah.nl.

Cox, John. 2016. "Communicating New Library Roles to Enable Digital Scholarship: A Review Article." *New Review of Academic Librarianship* 22 (2–3): 132–47. doi.org/10.1080/13614533.2016.1181665.

DANS (Data Archiving and Networked Services) website. Accessed 16 October 2019. dans.knaw.nl/en.

DARIAH European Digital Research Infrastructure for the Arts and Humanities website. Accessed 16 September 2020. dariah.eu.

Dishman, Lydia. 2013. "Beyond Paper: IKEA's New Catalog Places Furniture Right in Your Room." *Forbes*. Accessed 16 October 2019. forbes.com/sites/lydiadishman/2013/08/05/beyond-paper-ikeas-new-catalog-places-furniture-right-in-your-room/?sh=5c94ce075bad.

Drucker, Johanna. 2013. "Performative Materiality." *Digital Humanities Quarterly* 7 (1). digitalhumanities.org/dhq/vol/7/1/000143/000143.html.

Eschenfelder, Kirsten, Kalpana Shankar, Rachel Williams, Allison Lanham, Dorothea Salo, and Mei Zhang. 2016. "What Are We Talking About When We Talk About Sustainability of Digital Archives, Repositories and Libraries?" *Proceedings of the Association for Information Science and Technology* 53 (1).

Escobar Varela, Miguel. 2016. "The Archive as Repertoire: Transience and Sustainability in Digital Archives." *Digital Humanities Quarterly* 10 (4). digitalhumanities.org/dhq/vol/10/4/000269/000269.html.

Getty Research Institute. n.d. "Getty Vocabularies." Accessed 16 October 2019. getty.edu/research/tools/vocabularies/.

Gourley, Donald, and Paolo Battino Viterbo. 2010. "A Sustainable Repository Infrastructure for Digital Humanities: The DHO Experience." In *Digital Heritage: Third International Conference, EuroMed 2010 Lemessos, Cyprus, November 8–13, 2010 Proceedings*, edited by Marinos Ioannides, Dieter Fellner, Andreas Georgopoulos, and Diofantos G. Hadjimitsis, 473–81. Berlin: Springer.

Hendriksen, Marieke M.A. 2020. "Building the ARTECHNE Database: How to Develop a Multi-Purpose Database for an Interdisciplinary Project." *IDEAH* 1 (1): 1–13. doi.org/10.21428/f1f23564.e6779c76.

Heyliger, Sean, Juli McLoone, and Nikki Lynn Thomas. 2016. "Moving Toward 'Mega-choice': The Evolution of Access Technologies in Special Collections." *RBM: A Journal of Rare Books, Manuscripts, and Cultural Heritage* 17 (1): 17–31.

IKEA. 2015. "Experience the power of a bookbook™." Accessed 16 October 2019. youtube.com/watch?v=MOXQo7nURs0.

International Council of Museums, International Committee for Documentation (ICOM CIDOC). "The CIDOC Conceptual Reference

Model (CRM) Version 7." Accessed 16 September 2020. cidoc-crm.org/Version/version-7.0.

Kassell, Lauren. 2021. "Inscribed, Coded, Archived: Digitising Early Modern Medical Casebooks." *Journal for the History of Knowledge* 2 (1), p. 4. DOI: http://doi.org/10.5334/jhk.31.

Kirschenbaum, Matthew G. 2007. "'So the Colors Cover the Wires': Interface, Aesthetics, and Usability." In *A Companion to Digital Humanities*, edited by Susan Schreibman, Ray Siemens, and John Unsworth. doi.org/10.1002/9780470999875.ch34.

Langmead, Alison, Tracey Berg-Fulton, Thomas Lombardi, David Newbery, and Christopher Nygren. 2018. "A Role-Based Model for Successful Collaboration in Digital Art History." *Journal for Digital Art History* 3. doi.org/10.11588/dah.2018.3.34297.

Madsen, Christine. 2018. "Are Digital Humanities Projects Sustainable? A Proposed Service Model for a DH Infrastructure." 10 December 2018. slideshare.net/mccarthymadsen/are-digital-humanities-projects-sustainable-a-proposed-service-model-for-a-dh-infrastructure.

NEH Institute for Advanced Topics in the Digital Humanities. "Sustaining DH." Accessed 16 October 2019. sites.haa.pitt.edu/sustainabilityinstitute/.

Rousseau, Paulina. 2020. "Technical Skills Acquisition in a Graduate Public History Course - Planning for Success." *IDEAH* 1 (1). doi.org/10.21428/f1f23564.4c598089.

Royal Irish Academy. "DHO: Discovery." Accessed 16 October 2019. ria.ie/dho-discovery.

Smithies, James, Carina Westling, Anna-Maria Sichani, Pam Mellen, and Arianna Ciula. 2019. "Managing 100 Digital Humanities Projects: Digital Scholarship & Archiving in King's Digital Lab." *Digital Humanities Quarterly* 13 (1): digitalhumanities.org/dhq/vol/13/1/000411/000411.html.

Socio-Technical Sustainability Roadmap. n.d. "Welcome and getting started." Accessed 16 October 2019. sites.haa.pitt.edu/sustainabilityroadmap/getting-started/.

The Way We Read Now: Criticism in the Age of EEBO[1]

Michael Ullyot
University of Calgary

Introduction: Exemplary Criticism

In his foundational book on reader-response theory, Stanley Fish describes the function of interpretive communities (1980). They serve to validate knowledge, he writes; they dispute readings of texts in order to determine whether or not they are valid and plausible—not by some empirical or theoretical yardstick, but by the measure of credibility. Fish's interpretive communities inform later assertions from digital humanists like Matthew Jockers (2013) and Stephen Ramsay (2011), assertions that their research data never ought to foreclose discourse. Their findings serve to inform disputations and conversations, not to solve old conundrums to prove or disprove critical claims.

Literary criticism is a rhetorical discipline, fueled by contestation and conversation. That's why after four centuries, Fish writes, we still haven't been able to "solve the puzzle" of Shakespeare's sonnets: because our goal is not to address them as they were, to "solve" them reductively and definitively, but to address them as they exist in our minds, as they are here and now (1980, 353). The worst fate to befall a text is for it to be unread, neglected and ignored; like a paper that provokes no argument, delivered to an empty room, its life is exhausted before it begins.

For me to describe literary criticism as rhetorical is hardly revolutionary; there needs no digital humanist, my lord, to tell us this. Critics make arguments to sway audiences, and that depends on our credibility. Among Aristotle's three branches (deliberative, judicial, and epideictic), the second, judicial or forensic, best describes criticism (Lanham 1991, 164–66). It aims to influence audience judgments about past objects of study, to convince

[1] Previously delivered as the Plumer Lecture in Early Modern English Literature, St. Anne's College, University of Oxford; and to the Renaissance Graduate Seminar, University of Cambridge (2019). Thanks to Tania Demetriou, Hester Lees-Jeffries, Lorna Hutson, and Robert Stagg.

ISBN 978-1-64959-063-3 (paper) ISBN 978-1-64959-064-0 (pdf) ISBN 978-1-64959-065-7 (epub)
New Technologies in Medieval and Renaissance Studies 11 (2025) 259–273

you through artificial proofs (Aristotle's term, again) of logos, ethos, and pathos. Pathos or mood is perhaps the least prominent. Logos or rational logic we can simply assume. So this paper will focus on the critic's ethos of resourceful trustworthiness: that is, our credibility in choosing just the right amount and kind of textual evidence (evidence that Aristotle calls "inartificial") to make our readings plausible in interpretive communities like this one. Criticism is rhetoric whose credibility depends on an ethos of resourceful trustworthiness. The *Oxford English Dictionary* defines resourcefulness as "practical ingenuity," but I mean our literal ability to use resources, namely textual evidence.

Critical interpretations offer a proxy for the text, an argumentative reading of filtered evidence. (Certainly the readiest way to undermine interpretations is to misread evidence or ignore contrary evidence.) Another way of saying this is that critics make maps of the territory, maps that are necessarily smaller than that territory—not, as in the Borgesian allegory, coextensive with the territory. To be smaller, our interpretive maps rely on two things: summative paraphrases of texts, and exemplary quotations from texts.

By "exemplary" I mean a resonant particular instance, one particular that stands both for others and for the general truth. If that sounds contradictory, it is: Irene Harvey describes Derrida and de Man deconstructing exemplarity's contradictions, the example's insistence on being unexceptional and general, and yet particular enough to be intelligible (2002, 2). I quote a particular passage, rather than another, because it says what I want it to say, and it does for my argument what I want it to do. And I implicitly ask (or really, I insist) that you trust me, the judicious critic, to choose evidence that resonates beyond itself: both with my argument, and with the surrounding evidence I've necessarily excluded.[2]

I'm belabouring these assumptions to introduce my argument, here, that they are not the only way to do criticism in our time. I believe in the enduring value of linear close-readings, of starting at the beginning of one text and reading to the end, and then doing the same with the next, gathering exemplary evidence as we go. But their dominance of our discipline is loosening, as human readers collaborate with machines. New methods of algorithmic criticism, in the broad category of text analysis, complement close with distant readings, or micro- with macroanalysis.

[2] For an extended argument about exemplary criticism and new historicism, see the conclusion to Ullyot 2022.

In this essay I'll describe some of them, and their insights, but will focus on their implications for the discipline of Renaissance English literary criticism. For this I'll draw on two projects I've been involved in: the search for rhetorical figures (of repetition and variation, from anadiplosis to gradatio), and the construction of a quantitative model of the English sonnet. I'll conclude that one of the ways critics ought to mitigate against the problems of exemplarity is through increasingly nuanced search algorithms that reassure readers that we really *are* being resourceful; that our choice of evidence isn't limited by our "linear reading and the powerful directionality of human attention" (Hope and Witmore 2010, 359) but augmented by pattern-matching machines. It is what the machines do best: tell us what passages resemble the passages we have read, and what's complementary and worth close-reading next. We should collapse binaries like close and distant reading, humans and machines, knowledge and information, books and data—and do literary criticism that preserves a central role for linear readings of exemplary passages.[3] What should change is our selection procedures, to make the passages truly exemplary.

Why Text Analysis Is in the Wilderness

That is not happening sufficiently often. Algorithmic text analyses are largely divorced from evidence-gathering in our discipline. I think there are at least two reasons for this. One is methodological, as machines flatten the nuances of our texts by turning them into quantifiable metrics. Machines are very good at doing certain things very quickly, but they need that certainty—like reliable, quantifiable metadata at the word level (e.g., part-of-speech tags). Criticism is not empirical; a list of adverbs in *The Faerie Queene* is not criticism, but only potential raw material for criticism. This flattening is changing, as machines are capable of ever more nuanced search algorithms, as I'll address in a moment.

Another reason text analysis remains at the margins is that its insights can seem either blindingly obvious or unsettlingly alien. Before I give you some examples of the latter, it's worth asking why quantifiable reaffirmation of the seemingly "obvious" is an invalid argument. In few other disciplines would confirmation be treated with suspicion; it's not the case in climate science, for instance, and psychology has a notorious problem with the reproducibility of key experiments. But both of my chosen examples are notably

[3] I agree with Anupam Basu that Martin Mueller's term "scalable reading" is preferable to "distant reading," because it emphasizes continuities with close reading (Basu 2018, 112–13); see also Visualizing English Print, n.d.

empirical disciplines. Literary critics value novelty and departure above all else, perhaps reflexively. Our purpose can be both rhetorical *and* empirical understandings of our objects of study. Let me offer you some examples, before I argue that testing our critical orthodoxies is also a positive trend for our discipline.

A project that has made significant progress with the contents of early printed books is EarlyPrint, a collaboration between Martin Mueller at Northwestern and Joseph Loewenstein and Anupam Basu et al. at Washington University in St. Louis. It offers both a "library" for correcting transcriptions of those books, and a "lab" for visualization and text-analysis tools, including an n-gram browser to explore these "fundamental building blocks of many large scale computational and corpus-linguistic approaches to language" (EarlyPrint, n.d.). EarlyPrint's Basu is the foremost expert on early print's orthographic variation, a tractable problem for computation that he has tracked through time (Basu 2016). On a more local scale, scholars like Mattie Burkert have vectorized their principal components of more than one hundred plays from 1690 to 1699, showing how the "productive estrangement" offered by "quantitative analysis reveal[s] the inherited categories and narratives that we bring, sometimes unawares, to our materials of study" (Burkert 2016, 56); this includes our unwitting categories and gendered assumptions about plays by "female wits" like Delarivier Manley, Catherine Trotter, and Mary Pix at the close of the seventeenth century (Burkert 2016, 56). Focusing on more canonical texts, Jonathan Hope and Michael Witmore (2010) have rendered Shakespeare's plays in 101-dimensional space and conclude that *Othello*'s sentences are more characteristic of comedy than of tragedy.

Those last two sentences might convey why machine-augmented research hasn't upended Renaissance drama. Word vectors, principal components, and 101-dimensional space are unfamiliar text features for archival literary critics, more accustomed to deciphering Elizabethan secretary marginalia on half-sheet impositions. Critics are humans who read texts, not computational linguists who analyze word vectors; and we are rhetoricians who exchange arguments, not statisticians who publish datasets.

Hope and Witmore do an exemplary job presenting their quantitative research through qualitative arguments, but few of us are reshelving *Othello* next to *Twelfth Night*. Most simply admire Hope and Witmore's contribution to our knowledge about *Othello*'s language without reorienting what we already know about *Othello*'s genre. The features that make it a tragedy are discernible at the human rather than the algorithmic scale—features like the outcome of its story or the quality of its characters, not the statistical proximity of its fine-grained linguistic model to those in another genre altogether. Certain heuristic orthodoxies undergird our discipline—for instance, that Shakespeare writes tragedies, and *Othello* is one of them. Such certainties are based on past perceptions and judgments, and reinforced by our own perceptions and judgments. It is difficult to imagine an algorithm unsettling them. We have never needed algorithms before to identify a play's genre, so why start now?

That is a loaded question. Are we so invested in our preconceptions about matters of genre that we have confirmation bias about them? One way to find out is to imagine our preconceptions away. Start from a blank slate, and consider how our knowledge about genre has accumulated over time—not simply who asserted it and when, from Heminges and Condell to A. C. Bradley, but what kinds of assumptions they made to assert those orthodoxies we now accept. The plain fact is that they read as humans read, from the start to the end of a text, in *Othello*'s case from happiness to horror.

Another way to examine our preconceptions is to imagine a different set of them. The technology historian Steven Johnson asks us to imagine an alternate set of historical circumstances, to make us recognize that our generic hierarchies are contingent rather than fixed. Johnson describes our standard valuation of novels above interactive video games, and asks whether that hierarchy wouldn't be inverted if video games were invented four centuries ago, and books arrived just a few decades ago. Would we not bemoan the passivity and isolation of reading in favour of the interactivity of gameplay? Johnson imagines our objections: "Why would anyone want to embark on an adventure utterly choreographed by another person?" (2006, 5).

Similarly, if Hope and Witmore's algorithms had preceded all our generic categorizations of *Othello* due to its narrative shape, its *hamartia*, and other Aristotelian qualities that make it tragic—if algorithms had preceded Aristotle, more succinctly—would we not be reading plays with the assistance of a computer program, rather than a classical theory? Ramsay (2011) has described the text-analysis app as a formalization of interpretive theory: count this, because it is valuable. Yet there is knowledge about texts that can be counted, that only computers can reveal, because we humans can't recognize certain features. As Witmore writes, "something that is arguably true now about a collection of texts can only be known in the future" (2011). And Lisa Samuels and Jerome McGann have argued in a seminal essay, "Deformance and Interpretation" (1999), for the benefits of disrupting linear readings. Both linear readings and human heuristics are being complemented, not displaced, by machine processes that do things differently: both more distantly (corpus analysis), and more granularly (stylometry, deformance).

Canonical authors seem inescapable. But we can imagine escaping them. Try another thought experiment using the sort of "veil of ignorance" that John Rawls advocates in *A Theory of Justice* (1971). Imagine that we are inventing the discipline of literary criticism. From the table of your memory wipe away all trivial fond record: all the canons of authors and texts, all the critical taxonomies and literary-historical orthodoxies, including every periodization.[4] (For me, this necessitates that I forget the *Norton Anthology of English Literature*'s table of contents, my first guide to the discipline's major authors, stages, schools, and influences.) Imagine that instead of all our editions and anthologies, all our *Cambridge Companions* and *Oxford Handbooks*, we had only texts—about which we knew just a few things: dates, authors, nationalities, genders. Our first task would be to grasp this domain, to understand its totality. We would begin to sort, and we would face a choice of which metadata to begin with: dates, authors, nationalities, or genders?

In this scenario, literary criticism would borrow more, I suspect, from computational linguistics. But where it would differ is in our valuing of particularities. Literary critics follow "a hermeneutic of concentration, of inwardness—looking at the object rather than always seeing the outward-leading network" (Parker 2013, 52). Jan Parker offers a cautionary lesson about digital methods to humanists, who address the singularity of our objects of study: "Our hermeneutic is one of deriving interpretative narratives, often plural, avowedly partial, from singular, particular events. With digital data [. . .] there is, rather, a sense of dizzying plurality, seemingly stretching almost to infinity" (2013, 56). Caroline Levine writes that humanists value the "local, resistant, exceptional, nuanced, situated, concrete, embodied, and historically specific" (2017, 633)—albeit at the expense of "designing generalizable political models for the common good" (2017, 636).

How did this come to be? Defences of particularization over generalization are valid and principled, but some (at least) are post-hoc rationalizations making a virtue of cognitive necessity. Humans can read just one thing at a time, or hold a certain amount of evidence in our heads, and therefore we ought to. We sort and filter because we must, to make sense of things; but our sense-making is also anthropomorphic. We forget the law of the instrument, when the instrument is our own cognition. Our limitations shape and limit

[4] Ted Underwood (2013) disrupts periodization and proposes an alternate future for literary history.

our understanding, our methods, and our heuristics, but we should be able to think beyond ourselves. We can de-anthropomorphize humanities disciplines without dehumanizing them—by using tools to extend our cognition, as we do with the codex or the dictionary or even our eyeglasses.

The Universal Digital Library

It's about time this essay got more concrete. My subtitle refers to "the Age of EEBO," but so far I've only described the projects that use this text corpus.[5] What is EEBO, and what are its implications for our critical methods? Early English Books Online (EEBO) is the biggest corpus of early printed texts that English Renaissance critics have to work with; it's as close as we get to a universal digital library.[6] EEBO contains between 70,000 and 146,000 texts, depending on how you count them; I say "texts" to include variant copies, individual issues of the Thomason Tracts periodicals, and so on. EEBO began by transferring UMI microfilms into digital images, and offering them on a subscription platform. The march of digitization didn't change our discipline: that's merely the transfer from analog to digital media; that's just an evolving technology, of *access*. The real change has been in the revolutionary technology, of *address*: that is, the consequences of converting human-readable texts to machine-readable data.

That was EEBO's next step: the Text Creation Partnership (TCP). The TCP transcribed some sixty thousand of EEBO's texts, which is (again, depending on your count) about 85 percent of the unique books or 41 percent of the variants.[7] Whether it will get to 100 percent is unclear; the TCP appears to have ended in 2015. But its completion is less important than data curation, or text fixing. Martin Mueller once estimated that 93 percent of the transcriptions in the TCP are correct, letter for letter; but that's still one in ten words that contains an illegible character, which is problematic in different ways: distracting for human readers, and noisy data for machine readers.[8]

[5] For a more detailed and comprehensive list, see Barth et al. n.d. and Kelling n.d.

[6] Caveat: whereas EEBO-TCP is the largest corpus of texts transcribed directly and exclusively from those early printed texts, there are other substantial corpora of English Renaissance literature—including those in the HathiTrust Digital Library, which has texts from the Google Books and Internet Archive projects. Those texts are from editions printed much later, and are accordingly more mediated.

[7] For detailed documentation, see ProQuest LibGuides, "Early English Books Online (EEBO) on the Proquest Platform" and connected support articles.

[8] As mentioned, the EarlyPrint "Library" site is the locus of Mueller's heroic ongoing data-curation project. For details on error rates see Mueller n.d.

Distant Reading Early Modernity (DREaM) is a now-defunct project that also did highly impactful work to regularize spellings and text-level metadata of a TCP sub-corpus of forty-four thousand files, the necessary first step to processing (Milner, Wittek, and Sinclair 2017).

In my own research I've worked with the Folger Shakespeare Library's Digital Anthology of Early Modern English Drama to find instances of rhetorical figures or schemes, particularly the low-hanging fruit of word repetitions and variations: anadiplosis ("featured like him, like him with friends possessed") and gradatio, which is anadiplosis in sequence ("pleasure might cause her read, reading might make her know, | Knowledge might pity win, and pity grace obtain"). Again, those are just two pieces of exemplary evidence. When my collaborator Adam J. Bradley and I set an algorithm loose on a large corpus, we found many thousands of other instances. But one of our curious conclusions from a vast collection of gathered gradatios was that the most interesting specimens were variations on the form, ones like Sidney's that alter the root word (lemma) of the repetition (*e.g. know > knowledge*). Unsurprisingly, human critics (like me and Bradley) are more interested in exceptions than in rules.[9] Another potential area of research in this realm is to move past pattern-matching to pattern-detecting. If you think of figural taxonomies like George Puttenham's or Richard Lanham's as the equivalent of a natural-history museum, their drawers full of pinned specimens, it's fairly straightforward to build algorithms that match those patterns in the wild. But naturalists do more than that; they go into the rainforest to gather unrecognized specimens. To find those in the EEBO-TCP corpus requires a quite different detection system.

What Machine Learning Can Do for Literary Critics

That brings me to my concluding section, which is more about what we literary critics might do with future technologies to augment our evidence-gathering, to make more categorical arguments, while still focusing on luminous details. The prospect of machine learning for text processing is the technique I'm gesturing toward.[10] In essence, as I understand it, this is a search that approaches the human capacity for verbal nuances and connotations.

Consider the rainforest of figures that I mentioned: critics recognize rhetorical schemes when we see them, even when they resemble nothing like those we've seen before. Similarly, we recognize metaphors even when they

---

[9] For details, see Ullyot and Bradley 2017 and 2018.

[10] I address this topic at more length in Ullyot 2017.

lack the verbal cues of a simile (i.e., "like" or "as"). Machine learning is the process of making the ineffable differences between schemes and ordinary language, or metaphors and ordinary language, something that a computer can quantify and apply to novel instances. It operates by evidence rather than by rules; it gives the machine many pictures of cats, say, then many pictures of kangaroos, and tasks the machine to figure out which of a third set of unidentified pictures are which animal. (A comparatively difficult task for such a machine is then to look at the billion words in the EEBO-TCP corpus and identify every cat metaphor.) Its decision process is sometimes called a "black box" due to its opaque complexity, but this is akin to calling the pre-medieval world "the dark ages": the darkness is in our perceptual limits, not in the thing itself.

In other words, we can now expand the arbitrary limitations of human attention and retention by augmenting our evidence-gathering. And in the future, critics will have tools that machine learning is already making possible. The reason I can blithely forecast such possibilities is because the progress of machine learning is geometric; and because we can already see in AI projects like Deep Mind that natural-language processing is a domain in which machines are making strides. Google Translate may make elementary errors, which we eagerly point to, to reassure ourselves that human translations are still better. And they are, and they will be. The idiomatic example that Gideon Lewis-Kraus gives is translating "minister of agriculture" in a foreign language as "priest of farming" in English; clearly wrong, but those kinds of errors are diminishing over time (2016). Not because engineers and linguists are fixing them, one by one—that's called supervised learning and it's highly inefficient—but because the machines are comparing human translations like Hansard records from Canada's House of Commons, seeing how such idioms ought to be translated. They're doing that learning in an unsupervised way, and that's what makes it so powerful, because it is cumulative.

Before I conclude this argument, let me offer one more example of the kinds of problems Renaissance literary critics can address with machine learning. It's a problem that Bradley and I propose to undertake in our next project: to build a quantifiable model of the English sonnet, capable of gathering every instance of this poetic type in a master corpus, and analyzing their linguistic features.[11] Why would we want to do that? We intuit that the sonnet is more

[11] This project, Modelling the Sonnet, is more prospective than actual at the time of publication; its feasibility depends on grant applications. For preliminary speculations see Ullyot 2021.

than a mere form; that its generic qualities of arguments, subjects/topics, tones, moods, and forms of address are implicated in its form. Its division of octave from sestet lends itself to a volta from problem to resolution. Yet both form and genre are functions of its poetic diction: some words are chosen to suit its rhyme, meter, and length; others to suit its rhetoric or narrative.

Any well versed (as it were) human reader can look at an unclassified poem and readily identify it as a sonnet, more or less. The way you determine if a poem is "more" or "less" sonnet-like is to consider how its qualities compare to the sonnet-like qualities you have in your head. Our project quantifies those qualities, for two reasons: because the reader's idea of sonnets is constituted by those they have read and distilled into heuristics; and any rules thus codified are only applicable to other poems on which humans do close readings. This is, and has long been, a wholly adequate methodology for building knowledge incrementally and collaboratively about all manner of poems. But its inherent limits of arbitrary rules particularly applied, of knowledge acquired and shared through exemplary evidence and "the somewhat serendipitous noting of interesting features" (Hockey 2000, 66), are no longer necessary constraints to interpretation.

The benefits of our quantifiable model of the sonnet will be manifold: a vastly expanded canon of sonnets, beyond the most anthologized specimens; a categorical definition of sonnets that exactly specifies the degree to which it is formal or generic; a sense of its historical development through time and across periods, authors, and anglophone poetic cultures; and a knowledge of sonnet subgenres and just how they depart from each other. In sum: an empirical grasp of one poetic type that accounts for its multivariate complexity—not a flattening of differences, but a set of metrics to measure differences.

Conclusion: A Manifesto for Augmented Criticism

In conclusion, let me give you two reasons why nothing I've proposed in this essay is wildly revolutionary: or rather, why everything I've proposed is continuous with the way literary critics have long practiced our discipline. Stephen Ramsay's subtitle for *Reading Machines* (2011) is "Toward an Algorithmic Criticism." But criticism is already algorithmic. That is, it follows set procedures to convert inputs into outputs, primary texts into interpretive readings. There are multiple different procedures, as many as there are critical theories that prescribe methodologies of reading, of filtering and comparing and sifting and organizing. And there are the habits of a lifetime of training, of watching how others do it, of paper-giving and article-writing.

Critics practice these algorithms unconsciously, until a theorist comes along to induce some self-consciousness. We begin at the beginning, the first line of a text; and as we proceed onward we gather impressions and form quandaries and so on. We make comparative, linear readings; and then we gather them into expositions for our interpretive community. But we know, and must acknowledge, that our evidence is exemplary. That is a sign of our own cognitive limits, and time and attention.

Today we're able to surpass those limits, so we should. We need to acknowledge the gap between an ethos of resourcefulness and actual, real resourcefulness: that is, "more-like-this" searches so that we are actually trustworthy in our choices, from the actual best available evidence. We'll still make discursive arguments, but on a more empirical, thorough, machine-sourced foundation. There will still be, and always will be, a measure of exemplary selection and judgment: just with a diminished sense of arbitrariness, of happenstance, of narrow applicability.

What are the implications of a "more-like-this" algorithm for critical evidence-gathering? To answer that, consider an analogy of how it could work. Google has a tool called Smart Compose that predicts what you are trying to say in a sentence: How are you going to end a sentence, based on what you've said in it so far? The evidence is basic enough: feed a very powerful machine with a vast number of sentences, and it will get very good at figuring out the semantic and linguistic possibilities that emerge from the first half of a sentence. Every word you use in the first half circumscribes the words that typically, at least, would complete the second half. So it is not difficult to conceive of a Smart Compose for textual evidence. Each quotation you take from a set of texts has something in common, or you wouldn't have chosen it. At the very least, each one is a building-block of a synthetic argument you intend to make, based on your evidence's complementarity and contrasts.

Another reason that augmenting our criticism with machines isn't revolutionary is that we've seen this expansion of evidence before. There are continuities between the digital humanities in our time and cultural materialism and new historicism in the 1980s. (This ignores earlier expansions of the canon, but those two critical methods embraced and accelerated this tendency.) Evidence for their arguments about social energies deliberately surpassed the canons of received reading-lists. It left the cathedral of literary and dramatic culture for the bazaar of letters, wills, broadsheets, inventories, pamphlets, and other historical emphemera that jostled for attention alongside translations, tragedies, epithalamia, and romances. Picking and choosing evidence from that unruly crowd, literary critics transferred methods from literature, interpreting the rhetoric and poetics of archival documents alongside literary texts.[12] In place of the old formal and generic distinctions, the important criteria of selection were resonance and contemporaneity.

But those critical methods still cited exemplary evidence; they still resorted to the rhetoric of uncanny surprise at how well their archival fragments resonated with the canonical texts that were their teleological objects of study (see Ullyot 2011). They still ignored contradictory or unwelcome evidence that would complicate their arguments. And that's because ultimately all exemplary evidence suffers from what I call the problem of metonymy. It implicitly claims that its chosen parts represent other, missing parts; that its texts account for missing texts. But no matter how resourceful and thorough it seems, it is missing the textual evidence that would complicate and might contradict it. An augmented criticism, using machines to find more evidence, does not solve the problem of metonymy. But it does begin to address it, by addressing the current limitations of exemplary criticism.

WORKS CITED

Barth, Emily, et al. n.d. "Distant Reading for Close Analysis: Projects Building on EEBO-TCP." EarlyPrint. Accessed 9 November 2019. earlyprint.org/posts/eebo-tcp-projects.html.

Basu, Anupam. 2016. "'Ill Shapen Sounds, and False Orthography': A Computational Approach to Early English Orthographic Variation." In *Early Modern Studies After the Digital Turn*, edited by Laura Estill, Diane K. Jakacki and Michael Ullyot, 167–200. Toronto: Iter Press.

———. 2018. "Form and Computation: A Case Study." In *Digital Milton*, edited by David Currell and Islam Issa, 111–28. Basingstoke: Palgrave Macmillan.

Burkert, Mattie. 2016. "Plotting the "Female Wits" Controversy: Gender, Genre, and Printed Plays, 1690–1699." In *Early Modern Studies after the Digital Turn*, edited by Laura Estill, Diane K. Jakacki, and Michael Ullyot, 35–59. Toronto: Iter Press.

[12] See Paul Voss and Marta Werner 1999, and the essays in the same issue of *Studies in the Literary Imagination*, including Cyndia Susan Clegg 1999. See also, more recently, Sonja Laden 2004.

Clegg, Cyndia Susan. 1999. "Archival Poetics and the Politics of Literature: Essex and Hayward Revisited." *Studies in the Literary Imagination* 32 (1999): 115–32.

EarlyPrint. n.d. "Earlyprint Lab." Accessed 9 November 2019. earlyprint.org/lab/.

Fish, Stanley Eugene. 1980. *Is There a Text in this Class?: The Authority of Interpretive Communities.* Cambridge, MA: Harvard University Press.

Harvey, Irene E. 2002. *Labyrinths of Exemplarity: At the Limits of Deconstruction.* Albany, NY: State University of New York Press.

Hockey, Susan. 2000. *Electronic Texts in the Humanities.* Oxford: Oxford University Press.

Hope, Jonathan, and Michael Witmore. 2010. "The Hundredth Psalm to the Tune of "Green Sleeves": Digital Approaches to Shakespeare's Language of Genre." *Shakespeare Quarterly* 61 (3): 357–90.

Jockers, Matthew L. 2013. *Macroanalysis: Digital Methods and Literary History.* Urbana: University of Illinois Press.

Johnson, Steven. 2006. *Everything Bad is Good for You.* New York: Penguin.

Kelling, Meredith. n.d. "The Uses of EEBO-TCP." *EarlyPrint.* Accessed 9 November 2019. earlyprint.org/posts/eebo-tcp-uses.html.

Laden, Sonja. 2004. "Recuperating the Archive: Anecdotal Evidence and Questions of 'Historical Realism.'" *Poetics Today* 25 (1): 1–28.

Lanham, Richard. 1991. *A Handlist of Rhetorical Terms.* Berkeley: University of California Press.

Levine, Caroline. 2017. "Model Thinking: Generalization, Political Form, and the Common Good." *New Literary History* 48 (4): 633–53.

Lewis-Kraus, Gideon. 2016. "The Great A. I. Awakening." *New York Times Magazine*, 14 December 2016.

Milner, Matthew, Stephen Wittek, and Stéfan Sinclair. 2017. "Introducing DREaM (Distant Reading Early Modernity)." *Digital Humanities Quarterly* 11 (4): n.p.

Mueller, Martin. n.d. "Curation and Quality Assurance." Accessed 8 March 2021. earlyprint.org/posts/curation-and-quality-assurance.html.

Oxford English Dictionary Online. 2021. "resourcefulness, n." Oxford University Press. Accessed 14 September 2021. oed.com.

Parker, Jan. 2013. "Speaking Out in a Digital World: Humanities Values, Humanities Processes." In *Humanities in the Twenty-First Century: Beyond Utility and Markets*, edited by Eleonora Belfiore and Anna Upchurch, 44–62. New York: Palgrave Macmillan.

ProQuest LibGuides. n.d. "Early English Books Online (EEBO) on the Proquest Platform." Accessed 8 March 2021. proquest.libguides.com/eebopqp.

Ramsay, Stephen. 2011. *Reading Machines: Toward an Algorithmic Criticism*. Urbana: University of Illinois Press.

Rawls, John. 1971. *A Theory of Justice*. Cambridge, MA: Belknap Press of Harvard University Press.

Samuels, Lisa, and Jerome McGann. 1999. "Deformance and Interpretation." *New Literary History* 30 (1): 25–56.

Ullyot, Michael. 2011. "The Rhetoric of Anecdotes in New Historicism." *Clio: A Journal of Literature, History, and the Philosophy of History* 40 (3): 307–29.

———. 2017. "What Can Machine Learning Do for Literary Critics?" Accessed 8 March 2021. ullyot.ucalgaryblogs.ca/2017/04/10/what-can-machine-learning-do-for-literary-critics/.

———. 2021. "Fieldwork in the Sonnet: Milton, Donne, and Critical Orthodoxy." *Renaissance and Reformation / Renaissance et Réforme* 44(3): 25–43.

———. 2022. *The Rhetoric of Exemplarity in Early Modern England*. Oxford: Oxford University Press.

Ullyot, Michael, and Adam J. Bradley. 2017. "Past Texts, Present Tools, and Future Critics: Toward Rhetorical Schematics." In *Shakespeare's Language in Digital Media: Old Words, New Tools*, edited by Janelle Jenstad, Jennifer Roberts-Smith, and Mark Kaethler, 144–56. New York: Routledge.

———. 2018. "Machines and Humans, Schemes and Tropes." *Early Modern Literary Studies* 20 (2): n.p.

Underwood, Ted. 2013. *Why Literary Periods Mattered: Historical Contrast and the Prestige of English Studies*. Stanford: Stanford University Press.

Visualizing English Print. n.d. "Scalable Scholarship." Accessed 9 November 2019. graphics.cs.wisc.edu/WP/vep/scalable-scholarship/.

Voss, Paul, and Marta Werner. 1999. "Towards a Poetics of the Archive." *Studies in the Literary Imagination* 32 (1): i–viii.

Witmore, Michael. 2011."The Ancestral Text," *Wine Dark Sea*. Accessed 8 March 2021. winedarksea.org/?p=979.

Contributors

Alyssa Arbuckle is the Associate Director of the Electronic Textual Cultures Lab at the University of Victoria, where she is Operational Lead for the Implementing New Knowledge Environments Partnership and a co-facilitator of its Connection cluster, as well as a Co-Director of the Digital Humanities Summer Institute with her colleagues Ray Siemens and Randa El Khatib. Alyssa holds an Interdisciplinary PhD from the University of Victoria; her dissertation focused on open social scholarship and its implementation. Alyssa's work has appeared in *Digital Studies*, *Digital Humanities Quarterly*, *KULA: Knowledge Creation, Dissemination, and Preservation Studies*, and *Scholarly and Research Communication*, among other venues, and she has co-edited print and online book collections titled *Social Knowledge Creation in the Humanities* and *Feminist War Games?: Mechanisms of War, Feminist Values, and Interventional Games.*

William R. Bowen has published on speculative musical thought, Renaissance platonism, book history, and digital technologies. His contributions to digital humanities include being the founding director of Iter Inc., list owner and past editor of *FICINO*, and founding co-editor of New Technologies in Medieval and Renaissance Studies and the *Early Modern Digital Review*. He is currently editor of *Renaissance and Reformation / Renaissance et Réforme* and editor-in-chief of Iter Press. After serving as director of the Centre for Reformation and Renaissance Studies (Victoria University), chair of the Department of Humanities (University of Toronto Scarborough), and chair of the Department of Arts, Culture and Media (UTSC), he retired in 2019 and received the Canadian Society for Renaissance Studies Lifetime Achievement Award/Société canadienne d'études de la Renaissance Prix pour l'ensemble de la carrière.

Constance Crompton (orcid.org/0000-0001-6611-3663) is an Assistant Professor in the Department of Communication at the University of Ottawa and Canada Research Chair in Digital Humanities. She directs the University of Ottawa's Labo de données en sciences humaines/The Humanities Data Lab (humanitiesdata.ca), and is a member of the Lesbian and Gay Liberation in Canada, Linked Infrastructure for Networked Cultural Scholarship, and Implementing New Knowledge Environments Partnership research teams. She serves as VP English of the Canadian Society for Digital Humanities / Société canadienne des humanités numériques and an associate director of the Digital Humanities Summer Institute.

Kyle Dase is a SSHRC Postdoctoral Fellow in the Department of English and Electronic Textual Cultures Lab at the University of Victoria. His primary research interests include the literature of late medieval and early Renaissance England, Neo-Latin studies, digital humanities and network visualization, and textual editing, and his dissertation, "Friendship and Sociability in the Verse Letters of John Donne," reassesses and reframes the literary significance of John Donne's verse letters through an investigation of their classical models, material culture, and manuscript contexts. Kyle has contributed to a number of digital humanities projects, including *The Canterbury Tales Project* and *The Social Network of Early Modern Collectors of Curiosities*, and he is part of the editorial team for the *Journal of the Northern Renaissance*, a member of the Radical Open Access Collective. Kyle's work can be found in *Digital Studies*, *Digital Medievalist*, and *Intersectionality in the Digital Humanities*, among other places.

Randa El Khatib (randaelkhatib.com) is the Assistant Director (Open Knowledge Initiatives) of the Electronic Textual Cultures Lab (ETCL), where she leads the Open Knowledge Program and engages in other open scholarship activities. She is also the Associate Director of the Digital Humanities Summer Institute (DHSI). El Khatib is currently a doctoral candidate in English at the University of Victoria specializing in digital humanities and early modern studies. She is the co-founder and managing editor of *Early Modern Digital Review*, a journal that reviews digital projects that study the early modern period. To date, her research has appeared in *Digital Humanities Quarterly*, *Digital Scholarship in the Humanities*, and *Digital Studies / Le champ numérique*, among other venues.

Laura Estill (orcid.org/0000-0003-0904-3325) is a Tier 2 Canada Research Chair in Digital Humanities and Associate Professor of English at St. Francis Xavier University in Nova Scotia, Canada. Her monograph (*Dramatic Extracts in Seventeenth-Century English Manuscripts: Watching, Reading, Changing Plays*, 2015) and co-edited collections (*Early Modern Studies after the Digital Turn*, 2016 and *Early British Drama in Manuscript*, 2019) speak to her interest in how we understand the early modern period from manuscripts to digital. Her most recent articles and chapters have appeared in *The Seventeenth Century*, *Humanities*, *Doing More Digital Humanities*, *Shakespeare's Theatrical Documents*, and *The Arden Research Handbook of Shakespeare and Textual Studies*. She is co-editor of *DEx: A Database of Dramatic Extracts.*

Elizabeth Grumbach is the Assistant Director of the Institute for Humanities Research at Arizona State University, where she is also the Program Lead for the Digital Humanities Initiative. She is an affiliated researcher at ASU's Lincoln Center for Applied Ethics, an organization committed to exploring co-creative and participatory strategies for ethical technological innovation. Elizabeth serves on the Board of Directors for Digital Frontiers, a non-profit organization that brings together the makers and users of digital resources for the humanities. Her current research and scholarly goals include investigating critical methodologies for sharing cultural data, digital public humanities, and the formation of feminist, anti-racist digital commons and cooperatives that actively engage with questions of labor and social justice. Her work has been published in scholarly publications such as *Digital Humanities Quarterly, Scholarly Research and Communication, Digital Scholarship in the Humanities*, and the *Journal on Computing and Cultural Heritage*.

Marieke M.A. Hendriksen is senior researcher in the history of knowledge at the Humanities Cluster of the Royal Netherlands Academy of Arts and Sciences. Before she came to Amsterdam in 2019, she held positions in the Netherlands, Germany, the UK, and the USA. Her research focuses on materiality and sensory experience in early modern knowledge production, in particular taste in eighteenth-century chemistry and medicine. Hendriksen combines traditional approaches with Digital Humanities and performative methods. She has published a wide range of scholarly and popular work, and is the recipient of numerous fellowships and research awards.

Anne James teaches English at the University of Regina, Canada. She is a principal investigator on the GEMMS (Gateway to Early Modern Manuscript Sermons) project, a bibliographic database of early modern sermons and sermons notes in manuscript. Her current research focuses on the roles of early modern sermons in developing dissenting religious communities and in celebrating political occasions. She is the author of *Poets, Players, and Preachers: Remembering the Gunpowder Plot in Seventeenth Century England* and a contributing commentary editor to the Oxford University Press edition of John Donne's prose letters (forthcoming).

Margaret L. King, author of 16 books and some 70 articles, book chapters, and reviews, is editor of the text series The Other Voice in Early Modern Europe and editor-in-chief of Oxford Bibliographies: Renaissance and Reformation, and works in the fields of the Italian Renaissance; the classical tradition; the social and cultural history of early modern Europe; women and learning 1300–1800; and the history of childhood from antiquity to the present. Professor emerita of history at Brooklyn College and the Graduate

Center, City University of New York, she is the recipient of the Paul Oskar Kristeller Lifetime Achievement Award (Renaissance Society of America, 2018) and the Lifetime Achievement Award of the Society for the Study of Early Modern Women and Gender (2016).

Luis Meneses is a Professor in the Department of Computer Science at Vancouver Island University. He is a Fulbright scholar, and a Mitacs Elevate Postdoctoral Fellow. He has served on the board of the TEI Consortium and on the IEEE Technical Committee on Digital Libraries. His research interests include digital humanities, digital libraries, information retrieval, and human-computer interaction. His research focuses on the development of tools that facilitate and preserve open multidisciplinary scholarship.

Daniel Powell is a Publishing Systems Analyst at the Legislative Assembly of British Columbia. He was previously a Marie Skłowdowska-Curie Fellow in the Digital Scholarly Editions Initial Training (DiXiT) Network at the Department of Digital Humanities at King's College London and affiliated with the Electronic Textual Cultures Lab at the University of Victoria. His academic work has appeared in *Digital Studies / Le champ numérique*, *Renaissance and Reformation / Renaissance et Reforme*, *Scholarly and Research Communication*, and *Religion and Literature*, as well as in volumes published by the Modern Language Association, NeDiMAH, and the International Journal of Learning and Media. His current role focuses on developing and maintaining infrastructure and systems for the digital publication of Parliamentary publications in British Columbia, as well as leading large digitization and publication projects with the Legislative Library of British Columbia.

Jeanne Shami is Professor Emeritus at the University of Regina where she taught for 35 years. Her interest in sermons, particularly the sermons of John Donne, spans over four decades. In 1992, she identified a hitherto unknown manuscript of Donne's 1622 Gunpowder sermon, corrected in his hand, at the British Library. Although she has published most extensively on Donne's place in early Stuart religious culture, she has also written on women as preachers, patrons, and transmitters of sermons, on building a community of sermons scholars, and more generally on the place of the sermon in early modern religious and political culture. She co-edited *The Oxford Handbook of John Donne*, was Commentary Editor for the Verse Letters of the *Variorum Edition of the Poetry of John Donne*, and is currently serving as contributing editor to the Oxford Donne *Letters*. Her current research (*GEMMS*: *Gateway to Early Modern Manuscript Sermons*) is a SSHRC-funded bibliographic database of manuscript sermons and sermon notes, a collaborative project with co-investigators Anne James and Brent Nelson and an international research team. GEMMS is Jeanne's ticket to the world's manuscript sermon archives.

Maggie Shirley is grateful to live in unceded snʕaýčkstx (Sinixt) territory, (West Kootenays) where she works as Curator at the Kootenay Gallery of Art in Castlegar, BC. Shirley has curated a number of solo and group exhibitions including *Building the World We Want* and *The Hidden Hero Project.* Shirley is currently co-curating *Overburden: Geology, Extraction and Metamorphosis in a Chaotic Age* (overburden.ca) with artist and independent curator, Genevieve Roberston.

Ray Siemens (web.uvic.ca/~siemens/) is Distinguished Professor in the Faculty of Humanities at the University of Victoria, Canada, in English and Computer Science, and past Canada Research Chair in Humanities Computing; in 2019, he was also Leverhulme Visiting Professor at U Loughborough and, 2019–22, Global Innovation Chair in Digital Humanities in the Centre for 21st Century Humanities at U Newcastle. He is founding editor of the electronic scholarly journal *Early Modern Literary Studies*, and his publications include, among others, Blackwell's *Companion to Digital Humanities* (2004, 2015 with Schreibman and Unsworth), Blackwell's *Companion to Digital Literary Studies* (2007, with Schreibman), *A Social Edition of the Devonshire MS* (2012, 2015; MRTS/Iter & Wikibooks, with Crompton *et al.*), *Literary Studies in the Digital Age* (2014; MLA, with Price), *Doing Digital Humanities* (2017; Routledge, with Crompton and Lane), and *The Lyrics of the Henry VIII MS* (2018; RETS). He directs the Implementing New Knowledge Environments project, the Digital Humanities Summer Institute, and the Electronic Textual Cultures Lab, recently serving as a member of governing council for the Social Science and Humanities Research Council of Canada, as Vice President / Director of the Canadian Federation of the Humanities and Social Sciences (for Research Dissemination), Chair of the MLA Committee on Scholarly Editions, and Chair of the international Alliance of Digital Humanities Organizations.

Michael Ullyot (orcid.org/0000-0002-2781-8545) is an Associate Professor of English at the University of Calgary, specializing in early modern literature and the digital humanities. His book, *The Rhetoric of Exemplarity in Early Modern England*, was published by Oxford University Press in 2022. He also researches how computers augment human expertise, including a quantitative model of English-language sonnets.

NEW TECHNOLOGIES IN MEDIEVAL AND RENAISSANCE STUDIES

SERIES TITLES

New Technologies and Renaissance Studies
Edited by William R. Bowen and Raymond G. Siemens
Volume 1, 2008

Electronic Publishing: Politics and Pragmatics
Edited by Gabriel Egan
Volume 2, 2010

Digitizing Medieval and Early Modern Material Culture
Edited by Brent Nelson and Melissa Terras
Volume 3, 2012

New Technologies and Renaissance Studies II
Edited by Tassie Gniady, Kris McAbee, and Jessica Murphy
Volume 4, 2014

A Social Edition of the Devonshire Manuscript (BL MS Add 17,492)
Edited by Raymond Siemens, Karin Armstrong, Constance Crompton, and The Devonshire MS Editorial Group
Volume 5, 2015

Early Modern Studies after the Digital Turn
Edited by Laura Estill, Diane K. Jakacki, and Michael Ullyot
Volume 6, 2016

Social Knowledge Creation in the Humanities: Volume 1
Edited by Alyssa Arbuckle, Aaron Mauro, and Daniel Powell
Volume 7, 2017

Social Knowledge Creation in the Humanities: Volume 2
Edited by Aaron Mauro
Volume 8, 2022

New Technologies and Renaissance Studies III
Edited by Matthew Evan Davis and Colin Wilder
Volume 9, 2022

Digital Pedagogy in Early Modern Studies: Method and Praxis
Edited by Andie Silva and Scott Schofield
Volume 10, 2023